MAKING ASSESSMENT WORK FOR EVERYONE

How to Build on Student Strengths

Patricia Kusimo — Appalachia Regional Educational Laboratory

Melissa G. Ritter — Northwest Regional Educational Laboratory

Kathleen Busick — Pacific Resources for Education and Learning

Chris Ferguson — Southwest Educational Development Laboratory

Elise Trumbull
Guillermo Solano-Flores — WestEd

Assessment Laboratory Network Project
of the Regional Educational Laboratories

Regional Educational Laboratories

Appalachia Regional
Educational Laboratory
Charleston, West Virginia

The LAB at Brown (LAB)
Providence, Rhode Island

Laboratory for
Student Success (LSS)
Philadelphia, Pennsylvania

Mid-continent Research for
Education and Learning (McREL)
Aurora, Colorado

North Central Regional
Educational Laboratory (NCREL)
Oak Brook, Illinois

Northwest Regional Educational
Laboratory (NWREL)
Portland, Oregon

Pacific Resources for Education
and Learning (PREL)
Honolulu, Hawaii

The Regional Educational
Laboratory at SERVE
Greensboro, North Carolina

Southwest Educational
Development Laboratory (SEDL)
Austin, Texas

WestEd
San Francisco, California

This publication was funded wholly or in part by the U.S. Department of Education, Office of Educational Research and Improvement, under contract number RJ96006901. The content of this publication does not necessarily reflect the views of any individual laboratory, the Department of Education, or any other agency of the U.S. government.

To order additional copies of *Making Assessment Work for Everyone* please contact:

Tom Ross, Information Resource Center
WestEd
730 Harrison Street
San Francisco, CA 94107-1242
email: tross@wested.org
phone: (415) 615-3144, fax: (415) 512-2024.

Table of Contents

The Assessment Laboratory Network Project (LNP) of the Regional Educational Laboratories

The REL Assessment LNP is dedicated to improving student learning on a national scale by providing access to resources, technical assistance, and professional development in the area of classroom assessment. *Making Assessment Work for Everyone* results from a collaborative effort of seven of the regional educational laboratories that make up the Language, Culture, and Diversity work strand of the REL Assessment LNP. In some cases, core Assessment LNP staff contributed to the development of this publication; in other cases, REL staff with particular expertise in language, culture, and diversity issues in assessment contributed their efforts to this publication.

Other products and publications developed by the REL Assessment LNP include:

- *Improving Classroom Assessment: A Toolkit for Professional Developers, Toolkit98* — 1,200+ power-packed pages including text, 37 training activities with instructions, teacher-friendly readings about classroom assessment issues, and sample assessments representing a variety of design options to be used to promote discussion.

- The Assessment LNP Web site at www.wested.org/acwt/ which houses information about existing and upcoming Assessment LNP products and events.

- The *Promising Practices in Assessment Database (PPAD)* accessible through the Assessment LNP Web site — a searchable, online database containing a variety of high quality, assessment-focused materials developed by the 10 regional educational laboratories.

New products in process include a training module to help teachers and districts to better use assessment data to enhance classroom practice and a database/Web site of assessment software packages.

Making Assessment Work for Everyone

For further information about any of these products or services, please contact your Assessment LNP core work group representative.

Jane Hange
AEL
P.O. Box 1348
Charleston, WV 25301
hangej@ael.org
(304) 347-0476
(800) 624-9120
(304) 347-0486 (fax)

Eileen F. Ferrance
The LAB at
Brown University
222 Richmond Street
Suite 300
Providence, RI
02903-4226
Eileen_ferrance@brown.edu
(401) 274-9548 Ext. 228
(401) 421-7650 (fax)

Jeong-Ran Kim
LSS — Temple University
9th Floor, Ritter Annex
(004-00)
Philadelphia, PA 19122
jkim3@vm.temple.edu
(215) 204-3006
(215) 204-5130 (fax)

Arlene Mitchell
McREL
2550 So. Parker Road
Suite 500
Aurora, CO 80014
amitchell@mcrel.org
(303) 337-0990
(303) 752-6388 (fax)

NCREL
1900 Spring Road,
Suite 300
Oak Brook, IL
60523-1480
(630) 571-4700
(800) 356-2735
(630) 571-4716 (fax)

Melissa Ritter
NWREL
101 S.W. Main Street
Suite 500
Portland, OR 97204-3297
ritterm@nwrel.org
(503) 275-9562
(503) 275-0450 (fax)

Donald L. Burger
PREL
1099 Alakea Street
Suite 2500
Honolulu, HI 96813
Burgerd@prel.org
(808) 441-1300
(808) 441-1385 (fax)

Monica Mann
PREL
1099 Alakea Street
Suite 2500
Honolulu, HI 96813
Mannm@prel.hawaii.edu
(808) 441-1300
(808) 441-1385 (fax)

Nancy McMunn
SERVE
P.O. Box 5367
Greensboro, NC 27435
nmcmunn@SERVE.org
(910) 334-3211
(800) 755-3277
(910) 334-3268 (fax)

Chris Ferguson
SEDL
211 East Seventh Street
Austin, TX 78701-3281
cferguso@sedl.org
(512) 476-6861 Ext. 281
(512) 476-2286 (fax)

Mahna Schwager
Coordinator
WestEd
730 Harrison Street
San Francisco, CA
94107-1242
mschwag@wested.org
(415) 615-3201
(415) 615-3200 (fax)

Sharon Horn
OERI
555 New Jersey Ave. NW
Washington, DC 20208
Sharon_Horn@ed.gov
(202) 219-2203

Acknowledgments

With thanks to participating regional educational laboratory leaders for their support, encouragement, and resources. Many other individuals also contributed time and ideas during the production of *Making Assessment Work for Everyone.*

Thanks to Mahna Schwager, Fredrika Baer and Jerome Shaw of WestEd; Suzie Boss and Kathy Petersen of NWREL; David van Broekhuizen of PREL; and Gerald D. Swick (associated with AEL) for their work on copyediting, production, formatting, and layout.

Thanks to those authors allowing us to reprint their articles for Section VII: *Rethinking Schools*, David Sadker, and Debra Viadero.

Special thanks to those individuals whose review of *Making Assessment Work for Everyone* provided insights, thoughtful suggestions, and external perspectives essential to the quality of our work: Judy Arter, Training Director, Assessment Training Institute, Portland, Oregon; Ruth Sutton, Consultant, Salford, England; Wendy Feerer, Valencia Elementary, Los Lunas, New Mexico; and Amada Pérez, Mar Vista Elementary School, Oxnard, California.

Introduction

We must change from a model that *picks*
winners to one that will *create* winners.

Harold Hodgkinson, *Michigan and
Its Educational System,* 1989

Making Assessment Work for Everyone: How to Build on Student Strengths is intended to provide teachers with research information and practical ideas for modifying assessments to make them more effective. Throughout the document, examples demonstrate how to make the process equitable and beneficial for students and teachers alike.

For many, the term "diversity" initially evokes the thought of people different from themselves. So it's not surprising that many classroom teachers, the majority still European American, may tend to equate diversity with ethnic minorities. Yet in reality, of course, the term simply refers to the variance within any group — a variance to which all members contribute. In the classroom, that includes those who have traditionally been considered a part of the "norm" or "mainstream."

Diversity encompasses differences in culture, language, ethnicity, gender, social class, age, physical attributes, learning styles, religion, locale, nationality, sexual orientation, and more. This publication is based on the recognition that such overlapping and interconnected sociocultural factors contribute greatly to students' identity as learners and to their overall educational experience. If we, as teachers, are to be effective across the broad range of students we encounter, we must know how to accurately and equitably assess the learning that goes on in our classrooms. To do so, we must understand the base of experience and culture that students bring with them to the classroom, as well as how sociocultural factors play out in assessment. This publication specifically focuses on those aspects of diversity associated with culture and language, with some attention to gender and ethnicity.

In a perfect world, we would know each individual learner's strengths and needs and be able to tailor all learning experiences and assessments to fit their unique circumstances. In reality, we must help all students meet common standards for excellence while recognizing that their paths to success may vary significantly, especially for those students whose language or culture is different from our own. The challenge throughout this document is to think about how to maintain high standards and expectations for all learners while building on the uniqueness each learner brings to the classroom environment.

Making Assessment Work for Everyone is intended to help educators:

- Understand the essential characteristics of good assessment

- Uncover the strengths and cultural perspectives of diverse learners

- Create or select classroom assessments that meet high standards *as well as* support and reveal the learning of every child

- Increase awareness of potential sources of bias and inequity in assessments

- Use strategies to improve inequitable assessments

DID YOU KNOW?

The following facts have been compiled from information available through the National Center for Education Statistics.

- In 1995, 33 percent of all students were ethnic minorities and, by the year 2020, this figure will rise to 46 percent.

- In 2008, 41 percent of all students will be minorities; however, only 5 percent of teachers will be minorities.

- Forty-two percent of all public schools have no minority teachers. By 2008, 2.7 million new teachers will be needed.

- More than 700,000 teachers will be needed in inner-city urban and rural areas where language and cultural dissonance between staff and students may be greatest.

- Forty-three percent of U.S. school districts enroll students with native languages other than English. More than 80 different languages are spoken within the Los Angeles School District alone.

- In 1996-97, there were 3.5 million English language learners enrolled in K-12 schools across the United States.

- Between 1990 and 1997, the percentage of English language learners in schools grew at least 50 percent in 35 states and by over 200 percent in 12 of those states.

- In California, New Mexico, and Arizona, more than 20 percent of students begin school without proficiency in English, and in 18 other states, between 5 and 15 percent of students begin school without that proficiency.

The following fact comes from the work of Richard Valencia (1991):

- In 1988, researchers found that only 5 percent of future teachers in California take any course in multicultural education.

Our Guiding Principles

As we encounter more students whose culture and language differ from our own, we will need to expand the ways we assess their knowledge and skills. The information and guidance offered in this publication for doing so is grounded in the following research-based realities and in our understanding of what these realities imply for school and, more specifically, for classroom practice:

1. Culture is inherent in every aspect of schooling; *therefore,* we need to be aware of the cultural values underlying our schooling practices and how they may result in confusion or conflict for some students.

2. Diversity should be seen as a benefit and as additive; *therefore,* the strengths in all cultures should be acknowledged and built on in the classroom.

3. Language, the primary vehicle for thought and learning, is inherent in virtually all assessment; *therefore,* it is important to understand how the forms and uses of language in assessment coincide or conflict with the forms and uses students have learned in their own homes and communities.

4. All learners are born curious and can acquire new knowledge, skills, and patterns of behavior; *therefore,* when students are not achieving, our educational practices need to change.

5. No single method of assessment is capable of showing achievement on a full range of learning objectives; *therefore,* multiple assessments must be used to provide adequate opportunities for learners to demonstrate achievement.

6. Assessment experiences should be part of a positive learning process; *therefore,* assessment tasks should not erode students' sense of self-worth.

7. All learners deserve opportunities for authentic assessment of their learning and honest feedback; *therefore,* assessments should make sense to students, and their performance should be reported and interpreted in terms they can understand.

8. Assessment is a high stakes activity. Assessment outcomes often determine who is allowed to enroll in courses or receive job, college, or scholarship opportunities; *therefore,* we are ethically bound to ensure that it is fair and valid.

9. The most important purpose of assessment is to improve teaching and learning; *therefore,* assessments that do not contribute to these processes should be questioned.

Organization and Contents

Making Assessment Work for Everyone contains eight sections; each provides information, suggestions, and opportunities to try out key ideas. In addition, there are activities to use with students and reflective exercises. Brief vignettes bring to life the challenges of equitable assessment and enable readers to look over the shoulders of educators who have developed strategies and tips for success. This book is intended to be helpful both to individual readers and for use as part of a professional development program. Activities for this latter purpose are included with facilitator notes in Section VII.

Section I: Seeing Our Students' Cultures with "New Eyes"

The first two sections provide a framework for thinking about equitable assessment. Section I provides an overview of research on issues of cultural diversity, particularly as those issues relate to assessment. There are insights into cultural patterns that open up opportunities for creating instructional activities and assessments that encourage and reveal — rather than limit and mask — learning.

Section II: Recognizing All Students' Language Abilities

Section II continues to build a framework for understanding high quality assessment for all students. Like culture, the linguistic background of students has a profound effect on their interactions with school. We, as educators, must be aware of the linguistic strengths and ways of communicating that our students bring to the classroom.

Section III: Defining Good Assessment

Section III focuses on the criteria for ensuring high quality assessment for all students. Five keys to quality are described with detailed explanations, examples, and classroom strategies.

Section IV: Using Students' Cultural and Linguistic Strengths to Build Good Assessments

Sections IV and V are "how to" oriented. Section IV describes how to consider the five keys and students' cultural and linguistic strengths in designing and interpreting assessments. There are examples from a variety of schools and cultures as well as practical steps for individual settings.

Section V: Repairing and Improving Externally Developed Assessments

When the starting point is an existing assessment, Section V helps educators evaluate its quality, identify pitfalls for diverse students, and provide specific ideas for getting around the barriers.

Section VI: Readings to Deepen Our Learning

This section includes four excellent articles for learning more about the impact of language, culture, and gender on assessment: "Embracing Ebonics and Teaching Standard English" by *Rethinking Schools; Gender Equity: Still Knocking at the Class* by David Sadker; *Alternative Assessment: Issues in Language, Culture, and Equity* by Elise Trumbull Estrin; and *Culture Clash* by Debra Viadero.

Section VII: Professional Development Activities for Teachers

This section includes nine training activities to use with teachers (and others) to explore the issues of culture, language, and gender in assessment.

Section VIII: Resources and More Information

The final section of *Making Assessment Work for Everyone* includes bibliographic information and identifies print and electronic references for educators interested in each of the following areas: general resources on assessment, ethnicity and assessment, culture and assessment, language and assessment, and gender and assessment.

To help readers quickly identify various types of information, the following icons are used throughout the book:

KEY 1

What?

Clear &
Appropriate
Learning Targets

KEYS TO GOOD ASSESSMENT

The standards of high quality assessment

VIGNETTES

Examples from the classroom

THINGS TO CONSIDER

Reflective comments to accompany the vignettes

DID YOU KNOW?

Interesting statistics and research findings

THINGS TO TRY

Short activities to develop deeper understanding

The Glue That Holds Sections Together

Throughout this book, the emphasis is on classroom assessment for a vitally important reason. It is from the everyday interactions we have with our students about their work — its quality, its areas for renewed effort, its progress toward learning goals we've set together — that our students gain or lose their sense of academic worth.

On the basis of their ongoing assessment experiences, young people draw conclusions about their own abilities. They decide that...

"I can learn"	OR	*"I can't"*
"I have a future"	OR	*"I don't"*
"I have value"	OR	*"I don't"*

The authors hope that this publication will bring about awareness that, by using appropriate assessments, teachers can help all students come to believe in themselves and their ability to learn and succeed.

SECTION I

Seeing Our Students' Cultures With "New Eyes"

The real voyage of discovery consists not in seeking new landscapes, but in having new eyes.

Marcel Proust, *A Remembrance of Things Past*, 1913–1927

If assessment is to serve all students equally well, we must begin to understand diversity in new ways. To that end, this section provides some insight into how some of the ingredients of diversity must be considered to ensure assessment equity. We propose a sociocultural approach to assessment, which takes into account individual student differences based on culture, language, gender, and other aspects of students' lives and identities. In this sociocultural approach, we believe, lies the best possibility for ensuring valid assessment outcomes.

The section focuses on culture and, to a much lesser extent, gender as sources of important difference. Of course, as the Introduction suggests, there are numerous other social and individual factors that could be addressed. Ethnicity is also an important part of a student's identity, but it is often differences in cultural values rather than ethnicity that cause conflicts with the dominant culture. In fact, students from many ethnic backgrounds experience similar *culture*-based conflicts in school. Given the space limitations in this document, the authors believe that an emphasis on culture is more productive for understanding where schooling goes wrong for many students.

Race is another extremely important factor in students' experience in schools and in society at large. In the sections on language and on avoiding bias in assessment, race is implicitly — if not explicitly — part of the conversation. While race has not been used here as a broad rubric for understanding how assessment can be made more equitable, the authors certainly recognize race as an element of diversity that affects how students are perceived, students' sense of belonging, and students' motivation. Race and ethnicity are not equivalent. Haitians and African Americans, for example, are both Black but belong to groups with different histories, geographical backgrounds, and languages. Nevertheless, they may share some underlying cultural values that influence how they experience schooling.

With regard to gender, at times it seems that one could characterize male and female differences as cultural differences. However, gender differences themselves look different, depending on what culture one is observing. Boys and girls in any culture are socialized to behave in particular ways and take on different roles. Much of the gender research related to schooling that we are able to cite is based on studies of mainstream U.S. students. One of the things teachers need to learn about their students from various cultures is the kinds of expectations those cultures hold for boys versus girls. In this short publication, gender differences are not dealt with to the degree that they deserve. However, some examples from gender research are offered that can help us understand how the classroom may operate differently for boys and girls. The authors hope readers will take these examples as points of entry to the topic and continue to build their knowledge in this area beyond what is offered here.

We begin our exploration with a short classroom vignette that exemplifies the challenge teachers face on a daily basis in trying to understand the state of student learning:

VIGNETTE: HERMANA'S STORY

Ms. Day is reading her first-graders a story that, over the years, has captured the imagination of her students, Maurice Sendak's Where the Wild Things Are. *It's easy to tell that most of the class is eagerly involved. She can almost feel Sam's interest as he wiggles, frowns, and smiles along with the story. But one student, Hermana, sits quietly, eyes down.*

The young girl has recently moved to the United States from Palau, an island republic in the Pacific. Because Hermana is new to the classroom (and the country) and is rather quiet, Ms. Day has been trying to get a sense of how much classroom instruction and discussion the child understands. As the teacher reads aloud to the class, she wonders, "Is Hermana interested? Has she put herself into the story?"

But afterwards, when Ms. Day calls on Hermana and asks how she liked the story, the girl barely speaks. "Good," she says, so quietly that no one else can hear. When Ms. Day then asks how Hermana would feel if she were the boy in the story, Hermana simply looks confused. The more questions the teacher asks, the less Hermana responds. Ms. Day feels frustrated and worried because she has no idea how much Hermana really understands.

THINGS TO CONSIDER

- Have you found yourself in a situation like this?

- What do you think was really happening here?

- What is this teacher trying to assess? Listening? Comprehension? Oral language? Other?

- What else might she try in her effort to informally assess Hermana, depending on her assessment purpose?

- Should she push Hermana harder?

Because Hermana barely responds to Ms. Day's direct questions, the teacher can't tell how much the girl understands. Several things might be going on here. In many more traditional cultures, children are expected to listen but not comment on stories, so it's possible that Hermana has never before been asked her opinion about a story. Similarly, she may have had no experience answering questions that require interpretation of a story, such as imagining herself to be one of the characters. In her home culture, children may not be asked for interpretations of a story's plot or character.

Another source of Hermana's reticence may lie in the teacher's individual questioning of her. Again, in more traditional cultures such as that of Palau, children are more likely to be questioned as a group, with several answering at once. In that classroom environment, a question requiring a one-word answer or a predicted phrase may elicit a choral response from virtually all children. The kind of one-to-one questioning so common to U.S. classrooms is rare or nonexistent, except where a school or set of teachers has adopted U.S.-style schooling. Thus, when Hermana is singled out by Ms. Day, the attention may make her feel uneasy. Finally, there is the possibility that Hermana feels uncomfortable because she is new in the classroom and doesn't know what is expected of her. In all likelihood, her discomfort is both situational and cultural.

It's sometimes impossible to know exactly what's going on with any given student, and it's risky to draw conclusions based solely on a student's cultural background. But, if teachers are to be effective, they must be able to figure out what their students actually know and are able to do. When they approach that challenge with some understanding of a student's culture — when they have developed a degree of cultural competence — they're likely to get more informative results than if, instead, they simply conclude that a student like Hermana, for example, is shy, nonverbal, or "slow."

Deepening Our Understanding of Diversity

How does one begin to develop cultural competence? The first step is recognizing that *everyone* has a culture, and almost every action has cultural underpinnings. It's something of a maxim in multicultural education that until you learn about your own culture you can't really understand other cultures. But doing so is not as easy as it might sound. Much about one's own culture seems so ordinary, so normal, that its cultural foundation is not readily recognized, let alone understood. Developing the ability to see what's going on in one's own culture has been described as "making the familiar strange." Anthropologist George Spindler, who coined that phrase (1988), said the hardest task for him wasn't documenting the practices and values of the other cultures he studied. Rather, it was documenting the cultural practices in a West Coast fifth-grade classroom.

To those who grew up in what has historically been the dominant culture of this country and whose schooling took place in a U.S. school, most classroom activity would probably just look "normal." It would be hard to see the cultural values underlying the ordinary instructional and management strategies of the teacher. Yet, in fact, even what may appear to be relatively unimportant classroom practices can be culturally influenced; for example, how teachers think about treating pencils, erasers, and other materials that have been purchased with school funds. In some cultures, they are treated as community property, while in most U.S. classrooms, they are distributed to students and treated as each child's personal property. Yet a teacher who has taught only in one culture or the other wouldn't likely recognize the treatment of classroom materials as a culture-based practice.

Becoming sensitive and knowledgeable educators able to meet the needs of diverse groups of students requires learning to recognize both the dominant culture, which informs much of U.S. classroom practice, and nondominant cultures, in which large numbers of students have been raised. Especially important is understanding the potential internal conflicts that can arise for students when these cultures are at odds in the classroom. Developing a perspective on these potential culture clashes is a necessary process if we are to make instruction and assessment fair and effective for our students.

English language learners and immigrants are not the only students who may experience such conflicts. Extensive research shows that African American, American Indian, and Alaska Native, as well as White students from poor and/or rural settings, are not well served by our present instructional and assessment practices (Ball, 1997; Delpit, 1988; Deyhle, 1987; Estrin & Nelson-Barber, 1995; Heath, 1983; Hollins, 1996). Among the reasons are differences between the experience base children bring with them from home and what's demanded of them in school. For instance, Heath (1983) showed how children who had learned to tell stories with a beginning, middle, and end at home were more readily understood and positively evaluated by their teachers. A different pattern, based on another cultural tradition, was not accepted. Similarly, middle-class, mainstream children who typically come to school knowing the alphabet and how to spell their names fit in better with teachers' expectations (Valdés, 1996).

Differences between the forms and uses of language children learn in their home communities and those expected in the classroom can lead teachers to underestimate children. When teachers are unfamiliar with children's experience base or ways of using language, they are unlikely to understand how most effectively to instruct and assess these students. And if they don't understand — or even recognize — the inherent strengths of students' culturally based communication or behavior patterns, for example, teachers will be unable to help students draw on those strengths to become more successful learners.

Sometimes the beliefs, policies, and practices of those who design and run the schools unwittingly perpetuate unequal relationships between members of immigrant and other minority groups and those of the dominant culture. For example, the very mechanisms schools use to involve parents may actually prevent them from becoming involved. When school systems require parents to participate in individual parent-teacher conferences, they may inadvertently exclude some parents who are uncomfortable exposing their own lack of knowledge of the language or of how schools are run. Undereducated parents may find it difficult to participate actively in parent-teacher organizations; hence their perspectives will be missing from conversations about how to improve schooling for their children. Alternative ways of convening parents, such as in small groups with opportunities for informal social exchanges, may bring in parents from heretofore unrepresented groups. Without conscious consideration of ways of involving parents, the same old methods for involving them will likely prevail, and those who know the "rules of engagement" are probably going to continue to dominate the conversation and any consequent decisionmaking.

Race, gender, language, ethnicity, family history, personal experience, socioeconomic status — all these, and more, factor into the education experience for both students and teacher. All have implications for how students approach learning and how teachers approach teaching, not to mention what teachers' expectations are for individual students or groups of students. For example, on the basis of unconscious stereotypes, a teacher may wrongly assume cultural and experiential impoverishment on the basis of a student's financial impoverishment or cultural difference. Such misperceptions are bound to interfere with effective teaching and assessment. The challenge, of course, is to be attuned to all those factors that make up the cultural foundation of an individual, whether teacher or student, while, at the same time, steering clear of stereotyping. *A caution*: While working to expand our knowledge of students' cultures, we must take care not to stereotype the members of any particular group. Gaining insight into potential strengths and values that students may bring from their own culture is important. But the effort must be balanced by the recognition that, within any single culture, the beliefs and practices of individual members can greatly vary.

Assessment as a Cultural Phenomenon

Every culture has accepted ways of evaluating children's development, and what's acceptable can differ from one culture to another. For example, not all cultures engage in formal, on-demand assessment of children's skills or learning. Thus, some immigrant students may need time to develop an understanding of the assessment they encounter in U.S. classrooms. The same may be true for American Indian students growing up in traditional communities where, generally speaking, they are not expected to perform any set of skills publicly until they know they are competent. In such communities, requiring them to do so would be asking them to risk ridicule (Deyhle, 1987; Swisher & Deyhle, 1989). Because of such culture-based differences, teachers must be prepared and willing to use a variety of assessment techniques and formats with their non-mainstream students, including informal observation along with a range of more formal measures. Assessment formats reflect particular ways of thinking, and a student's home culture is a key factor in the degree to which certain formats can accurately assess his or her progress. For instance, a true-false item calls for the kind of categorical thinking that some cultures actually teach their children to avoid.

Given the degree to which many teachers use direct questioning of students as a means of informal assessment, it helps to understand some of the cultural factors, as well as gender expectations, that may influence a student's manner of response. For example, a girl who has been raised in a home where females are expected to be deferential may hesitate to raise her hand, speak out in class, or even respond easily when directly questioned. A teacher who doesn't understand the possible roots of the girl's hesitancy could assume that she either doesn't know the answer or is uninterested in the lesson. In another example, many cultures teach children to give due deliberation to any question and respect to all feasible answers. In oral discourse, Japanese people will pause when asked a question because it is thought rude to rush into an answer before respectfully considering the query. To a teacher unaware of this, a slow-to-respond student may appear unsure of an answer, whereas the student may, in fact, simply be polite.

A Framework for Understanding Cultural Differences: Individualism and Collectivism

One broader way of thinking about cultural differences as they relate to education is to reflect on the degree to which people are raised with an orientation either to the group (e.g., family, community, classroom) or to the individual. It turns out that this basic value difference leads to a constellation of cultural features that can be the source of conflict in the classroom. A framework of individualism and collectivism to guide thinking about cultural differences is used here because it has proven to be very useful to a wide range of educators in understanding their students and themselves (Trumbull, Greenfield, Rothstein-Fisch, & Quiroz, in press).

Collectivistic cultures, such as American Indian and Alaska Native, Micronesian and Polynesian, those of Mexico and Central America, Asian and African cultures, are more oriented toward group success. In contrast, individualistic cultures, such as those of the United States, Western Europe, and Australia, emphasize individual success. The table below shows the principal features of individualism and collectivism. Although these orientations are presented here as dichotomous, in reality no person or group is completely individualistic or completely collectivistic. It is a matter of the relative emphasis on one or the other set of values.

Table 1: Individualism vs. Collectivism
(Adapted from Trumbull, Greenfield, Rothstein-Fisch, and Quiroz, in press)

Features of Individualism	Features of Collectivism
• Fostering independence and individual achievement	• Fostering interdependence and group success
• Emphasizing an understanding of the physical world through direct exposure to objects — often out of context	• Emphasizing an understanding of the physical world as it enhances human relationships
• Promoting self-expression, individual thinking, personal choice	• Promoting adherence to norms, respect for authority/elders, group consensus
• Associated with private property	• Associated with shared property
• Associated with egalitarian relationships and flexibility in roles (e.g., upward mobility)	• Associated with stable, hierarchical roles (dependent on gender, family background, age)

How do these orientations play out in education? Most basic, perhaps, a teacher's relative inclination toward individualism or collectivism influences expectations about everything from student behavior to how students learn. In fact, much of the research about learning styles, as well as other education research, "has as its ideological base, the primacy of the individual and individual differences. This perspective is consistent with Western views which elevate and celebrate individual strivings above collective ones" (Ladson-Billings, 1991). Not surprisingly, school culture tends to reflect this perspective. The degree to which students and their families either share this orientation or, conversely, have a more collectivistic approach to life affects much about their own views of schooling — and how likely they are to feel in sync with what's going on in the classroom.

The Rights of the Individual Versus the Needs of the Group

As we have already noted and will reiterate throughout this publication, no single set of values is shared by all members of any culture. The diversity within cultural groups is often as great as diversity across cultures. Even so, the *general* tendencies toward certain values from one culture to another can be remarkable. Consider the responses when, in a recent study by Quiroz and Greenfield (2000), the following classroom "problem" was posed to parents at two different schools:

VIGNETTE: THE JOB SCENARIO

It is the end of the school day, and the class is cleaning up. Salvador isn't feeling well, and he asks Emanuel to help him with his job for the day, which is cleaning the blackboard. Emanuel isn't sure that he will have time to do both jobs. What do you think the teacher should do?

One study site was a school with a primarily European American student population. There, the dominant response from parents was that the teacher should find a third person to do Salvador's job, presumably someone who had the time. This response reflects the more individualistic values of not infringing on others' rights, of protecting an individual's task assignment, and of maintaining an individual's choice — in this case, whether to help or not.

The second study site was a school serving a predominantly immigrant Latino population. There, the vast majority of parents — nearly 80 percent — said that Emanuel should help Salvador, a response reflecting an assumption that human beings are responsible for helping group members, for contributing to the unity and welfare of the group.

THINGS TO CONSIDER

So, how does the framework of individualism/ collectivism help us understand these different response patterns? Well, the usual assumptions from an individualistic perspective would be: 1) each person has a task; 2) each person is responsible for that task and that task alone; 3) if someone needs help, he/she can ask for it, but no one is obligated to offer it — particularly if it interferes with his ability to do his own job. The assumptions from a collectivistic perspective would be: 1) tasks may be routinely done by a certain person, but there is no reason they can't be shared; 2) if someone needs help, you help, even if it inconveniences you. It's easy to see from this research example how a relative emphasis on the individual versus the group could lead to different solutions to numerous daily problems in classrooms.

These general collectivistic or individualistic orientations have important implications for how students learn, solve problems, and behave in school, as well as how their learning can most effectively be assessed. Many educators assume that all students would take a similar approach to the concepts of individual work and group responsibility. But students are influenced by how they look at the role of the individual and the group in society. In many cultures, parents teach their children to work together, to help each other. As educators, we must recognize that many students — including most immigrant populations, American Indians, Alaska Natives, Native Hawaiians, and others — tend to be much more oriented toward the group than toward the individual. The degree of their concern for others extends to how competitive they may want to be academically — at least publicly. For them, individual performance is generally valued only to the degree it contributes to the group's well-being, whether that group is the family, the community, or their fellow students. As a result, in order not to embarrass or shame a peer, a student who knows the correct answer to a question may resist offering it after another student has answered incorrectly.

For such students, instruction or assessment that focuses tightly on individual progress or individual demonstration of learning is not always appropriate. Moreover, an overemphasis on individual assessment means the teacher is not helping students draw on a major strength that many from group-oriented cultures bring to their schooling: the ability to work together. When designing assessments, we need to consider the collaborative strengths of students from collectivist cultures, as well as the likely preference of students from cultures that emphasize individual effort and responsibility. Assessments that play to both strengths give students opportunities to show what they know and can do, while also challenging them to stretch.

Catherine Daley is a teacher-researcher with the Bridging Cultures Project (described on page 25) and a second-grade teacher in Los Angeles. Her largely immigrant Latino students are encouraged to complete practice tests for the Stanford-9 Achievement Test together. Children discuss aloud with each other why a certain answer is better than another. Of course, when it is time to take the real test, she tells them the rules: tests must be completed individually with no help from anyone else. This approach might not work as well in a group of students socialized to individualistic norms.

Self-Expression Versus Respect for Authority

The following example, from the work of Greenfield, Raeff, and Quiroz (1996), shows how people — in this case a teacher and a parent — at different places on the collectivistic-individualistic continuum can sometimes perceive and respond to the same situation in very different ways:

VIGNETTE: CROSSED WIRES

> *A European American teacher enthusiastically reports to an immigrant Latino father that his daughter is "outstanding" — speaking out, expressing herself, taking an active role in class. But the father is distressed: he has taught his daughter not to stand out, to be quiet and respectful of the teacher, and to be considerate of other children. What does this mean, he wonders. Is his daughter failing to understand important expectations for behavior?*

THINGS TO CONSIDER

> The problem here is that the teacher and parent have very different ideas about what makes a good student, yet neither recognizes how different these ideas are. The teacher is reporting what she considers to be exemplary behavior that would make any parent proud. But a father who has taught his daughter not to "show off" or stand out from the group will be distressed by this behavior.

Parents in many cultures teach their children to be quiet and respectful as learners in school (Delgado-Gaitan, 1994; Valdés, 1996). Given that, is it fair to evaluate these children on the basis of their ability to respond to questions individually in front of the class? Perhaps even competitively? It depends on the child, of course. The girl in the above example had clearly responded to the expectations of school rather than to those of her father, but this does not mean she experiences no conflict in doing so. Many students who had been raised similarly would understandably feel constrained in their ability to respond to such assessment methods. Students apparently respond in different ways to the conflicting demands of school and home. Some learn the norms of the school and become alienated from their families because they are not behaving in the expected ways. Some do not take to the norms of the school and may be judged less capable than they are but experience less conflict with their families. And some seem to become bi-cultural, balancing demands of home and school — observing the norms of each setting to the degree they are able. Of course, culturally aware teachers can help students to become bicultural.

The cultural difference we discuss here is not trivial, because much classroom assessment is informal, conducted through questioning or discussion. A typical teacher-student interaction in a U.S. classroom is one in which the teacher asks the questions, an individual student is called upon to respond, and, then, the teacher evaluates the response. While this may seem fair on the surface, it's actually quite unfair to students who would respond better to nonconfrontational, group questioning. Those from cultures with different norms of communication may not be comfortable with this format. This problem has been documented by teachers working with American Indian students (Swisher

& Deyhle, 1992), with Alaska Native students (Eriks-Brophy & Crago, 1993), and with Native Hawaiian students (Au & Kawakami, 1994).

Integrating Versus Separating the Cognitive and the Social

One of the contrasts between individualism and collectivism shown in Table 1 has to do with how the physical world is regarded. In collectivistic cultures, objects and other elements of the physical world are valued for the role they play in human relationships. For instance, a toy is an opportunity for sharing — for interacting with another person. When children learn about the physical world around them, it is generally in the context of a human relationship — in activity with a parent or other family member. They may never be asked by a parent to talk about objects or aspects of the physical world (like weather phenomena or plants or animals) independent of the social context in which they experienced them. If such children go to school in the United States, they are likely to encounter the alien expectation that they discuss and think about objects out of context — stripping the social meaning from their experiences and knowledge. Ideas, themselves, are often treated like objects to be manipulated out of context. For a person with collectivistic values, such a decontextualized approach to knowledge and learning may well seem oddly disconnected from real life. He or she will naturally tend to relate past knowledge in terms of social (particularly family) experiences and approach new learning in terms of its possible social meaning.

VIGNETTE: THE FIELD TRIP

An example of how children from a collectivistic culture may tend to integrate the social and the cognitive/academic is illustrated in the following vignette from the classroom of an elementary teacher who has participated in the Bridging Cultures Project. That research-and-development project, involving seven Southern California teachers, investigates how knowledge of students' cultures can lead to better instruction and home-school relationships (Trumbull, Rothstein-Fisch, & Greenfield, 1999).

Ms. Altchech's fourth-grade class is anticipating a field trip to the Ballona Wetlands Park near their Los Angeles school. In preparation, a wildlife docent from the park has come to their classroom for a second time. When, during his first visit, the docent asked the students what they know about various animals they were likely to see on the trip, they routinely answered with stories about family-related animal experiences. On the second visit, the docent lets a couple more of these stories go by and then announces, "No more stories." Ms. Altchech knows that what the docent wants is a "scientific discussion," with no "extraneous" commentary. But her students are largely from immigrant Latino families, and their cultures do not always stress the separation of content knowledge from social experience. So she isn't surprised when the docent's next question is met with silence.

Later, after the docent has left, she invites her students to tell their stories. To help her students bridge between those stories and the science that will be helpful for their upcoming field trip, she models a way for them to think analytically about their stories, to extract science information from their personal experiences with birds and other animals. She constructs a T-chart on the board, with elements from the students' stories on the left. Then, she asks her students to help her identify the "scientific information" in their stories. For example, she uses a student's comment that "the hummingbird's wings moved so fast" to draw out information about the bird's metabolism and feeding habits. The result is that students are participating and the science lesson is being taught.

The following graphic organizer is adapted from the discussions in Ms. Altchech's classroom.

MAKING ASSESSMENT WORK FOR EVERYONE

Table 2: T Chart Example

Story	Animal	Description	Habitat(s)
"I saw a hummingbird in my grandma's yard. The hummingbird's wings moved so fast..."	Ruby-throated hummingbird	Tiny (about 3 1/2 inches long); iridescent plumage and red throat; long, slender beak; wings beat rapidly; bird can hover in the air.	Marshlands and woodlands, North America
"I saw a dark blue bird when I was at the park with my brother..."	Stellar's Jay	About 8 inches long; blackish brown and dusky blue plumage.	Woodlands, North America

THINGS TO CONSIDER

Ms. Altchech's instructional strategy helps bridge the discourse style used by her immigrant Latino students and the discourse style required in most classrooms. With this strategy, she capitalizes on one of the children's strong cultural values: the value of family. This is evident in the fact that most students relate stories that involve trips or other family activities. So important is this cultural value to their students that, according to all seven Bridging Cultures teachers, any discussion, question, or other learning activity having to do with family engages students more than just about anything else.

DID YOU KNOW?

"Discourse style" refers to the form that communication takes, depending on the context. Often in the classroom, students are expected to use an academic style that is more formal than everyday speech and more restricted in terms of topic.

Ms. Altchech's approach can serve the needs of both instruction and assessment, assuming that she makes clear in her own mind what she is assessing and her criteria for what counts as "good" performance. In this, it's typical of the ongoing informal assessment in which teachers engage as they teach (blurring the lines between instruction and assessment). She is most likely making mental notes of which students can contribute information for the chart; at the same time, because she knows that not all students are comfortable speaking out in a group, she will provide additional opportunities to assess their knowledge.

This approach could easily be translated to a formal assessment strategy. She could ask students to write a story themselves and then use a graphic organizer (like a matrix or simple chart) to record salient pieces of information. She could simply ask students to think about a time when they had experienced something and then organize certain concepts in a graphic organizer. By framing the question in this way (prompting students to connect to personal experience) rather than just going directly to a request for content knowledge, she is using a more culturally friendly strategy. By the way, graphic organizers can also be useful in helping English language learners, whose literacy skills are still developing, to express what they know.

The strategy used by Ms. Altchech is not particularly complex, but it requires some understanding of students' communication styles, as well as knowledge of strategies for bridging between different styles. For students whose home culture does not separate the cognitive from the social, it's not a matter of being *unable* to learn the rules of standard academic discourse; it's simply that they have learned a different discourse style, one that is valuable in its own right.

The Bits-and-Pieces Problem

A related conflict has to do with what teacher/researcher Vicky Dull has called "the bits-and-pieces problem" (Nelson-Barber & Dull, 1998). In school, students are often asked to talk or write about what they have learned in discrete content areas, such as math, science, and social studies. More rare is an integrated, cross-subject approach to content, with students asked about the big picture. Moreover, students are most often asked to respond with short, disconnected answers to narrow questions that are not related to each other in any apparent way. This arbitrary breakdown of continuous life experience and knowledge into discrete content areas and small doses is an alien concept to many. Such an instructional and assessment style is not harmonious with the ways of life in many traditional communities, including, for example, the Yup'ik of Alaska.

Dull uses berry picking to illustrate why this "bits-and-pieces" approach would seem so foreign to her students and to many others: "We go out in the fall and pick berries until the freezer is full or until it snows. If we picked berries the way teaching is done, there would not be enough to last a month — pick a cup here, pick a cup there. The same with hunting, fishing or any other task. In real life, we start a task and complete it rather than doing it in bits and pieces" (Nelson-Barber & Dull, 1998).

THINGS TO TRY

Write the vision or mission statement for your school. The following examples are two very different missions with different implications for students.

School 1. Our students will become independent, lifelong learners, creative problem solvers, self-confident risk takers, able to collaborate with others, as well as be capable in multiple dimensions.

School 2. We envision a deep and abiding respect for their culture, which leads them to care for one another and seek success for the family. We wish to nurture a deep sense of responsibility for the society in which they live — a commitment to caring for the environment; placing a priority on preserving and protecting it.... We wish this so our children, and our children's children, will have the capacity to cherish the past while being prepared for the future.

Your School Vision

What cultural values are implicit in your statement?

Are there words or phrases that might be misunderstood by people from different cultures? How could they be clarified or changed? Do they reflect not

MAKING ASSESSMENT WORK FOR EVERYONE

just misunderstanding but an underlying disagreement over values? If so, how could common values that everyone can endorse be identified?

One option for checking common meaning is to invite a colleague from a different cultural background to review your changes for clarity and appropriateness. Do you share the same view of the meaning of the school vision? Bear in mind, however, that anyone who has been through many years of formal education in the United States (no matter what culture originally) has probably acquired mainstream values. A better exercise would be to ask a parent from a different cultural background to discuss it with you. A short exercise like this also points to the need to include people from different backgrounds at the beginning of the process of crafting mission statements for a school or district, not after the fact. Of course, *how* they are included can make a lot of difference in whether their voices will be heard.

Gender as a Source of Bias
in Assessment

Although rarely raised in the same conversation as language, ethnicity, or, even, the broader issue of culture, gender should also be included in our thinking about diversity. As noted earlier, gender-specific expectations can vary greatly from one culture to another. When those held by a teacher are at odds with those of a student, it can impede learning. Thus, for teachers, it's important to keep in mind that their own gender-related expectations about students may not coincide with how students are expected to behave in their home cultures.

Even within the same culture, gender-related expectations can vary greatly, and they are often so deeply ingrained as to be imperceptible to those who have them. In some U.S. classrooms, for example, teachers tend to give more attention and reinforcement to boys than girls (AAUW, 1992). According to recent research, teachers are often unaware of this phenomenon until and unless they systematically monitor and assess their own practices (Sadker & Sadker, 1994).

Further complicating the gender issue is previous research noting differences in how girls and boys learn or perform, specifically for mathematical abilities, verbal abilities, and spatial abilities (Jacklin, 1989). These differences have declined and nearly disappeared in recent years. Although researchers have failed to identify a precise reason for this change, a host of factors other than true cognitive differences are most likely responsible. Consider again, for example, the fact that many teachers unconsciously tend to give more attention and reinforcement to boys than to girls.

On the other hand, boys are subject to teacher biases against certain kinds of behaviors (as are girls, when they behave like boys). Disproportionate numbers of boys get referred for special education on the basis of their activity level or what is perceived as aggression. This has resulted in a great over-representation of African American boys, in particular, in classes for emotionally disturbed students. Here is a case where culture and gender intersect. In African American culture generally, a higher activity level among boys is tolerated or even encouraged than within the dominant European American culture. So, when European American teachers and teachers socialized to European-American norms observe such an activity level, they may well interpret it with reference to their own values and determine that it is deviant. While this is not strictly an issue of assessment, it has to do with teachers' evaluations of students and the educational and life consequences that flow from these evaluations. Not incidentally, students' grades sometimes suffer when teachers use behavior or comportment as one component of a grade. Most assessment specialists agree that behavior should be graded separately and that academic grades should reflect academic performance alone (e.g., Wiggins, 1998).

Like students from collectivistic cultures in general, girls tend to do better in instructional environments that promote cooperation and collaboration. Research suggests one reason there are fewer women in careers based on mathematics and science is that the "cultures" of such careers are so "masculine" (Eisenhart, Finkel, & Marion, 1996). Mainstream American culture has created stereotypical understandings of the roles of men and women. Masculinity has come to symbolize the orientation to pursue power and achievement over the empathic aspects of life, while femininity has come to symbolize the pursuit of quality of life over power and achievement (Garcia, 1998). Features of these cultures are undoubtedly already present in the high school and college courses that girls take. In addition, girls tend to do less well than boys (FairTest) on many high-stakes examinations (e.g., PSAT, SAT, ACT).

THINGS TO TRY

- Consider how you pair and group your students for most lessons and assessment opportunities.

- Plan some times for group work because girls often thrive in situations where they can work collaboratively.

- Also, plan times when girls can work in groups with other girls. This empowers girls to solve problems on their own and prevents situations where boys take over because they assume they have greater experience.

- List some other ways you can use class grouping to improve participation for all students.

Ideas to improve participation:

How could you determine whether a particular strategy has been successful for various students?

Motivational Barriers to School Success

Sometimes important impediments to school success go unrecognized in students. Theorists have suggested that because of different social histories, some students may find themselves in conflict with the mainstream agenda in the schools. For example, students whose cultures have been denigrated or whose ancestors were forcibly drawn into American citizenship (such as American Indians or African Americans) may experience extreme personal conflict over developing the language and academic habits of people they consciously or unconsciously think of as their "oppressors." Such feelings can interfere dramatically with motivation and, hence, performance. They may not trust that the "system" will do right by them (Fordham & Ogbu, 1986). Such students may, for example, stay out on "test day," because they believe that tests can only harm them. In a large high school in an urban district in California, administrators and teachers were troubled when more than half of their students didn't show up for state-mandated testing. Students explained that they could see nothing to gain and much to lose by participating. They believed that the tests weren't fair, that they would likely do poorly, and that the resulting scores would only be used to punish them and their school in some way.

DID YOU KNOW?

Some studies on women's grades in college-level communications courses suggest that female-specific patterns of communication may get rewarded with higher grades than male-specific patterns (Hughey, 1984). According to accepted criteria for communicative competence, women are actually more successful than men on the whole!

Just as students must trust that the education system has their interests at heart, they must also trust in themselves. They must believe they have the ability to learn, be confident that their efforts can lead to success. Teachers must help students see initial failures as opportunities to learn and help them focus their efforts on attainable goals. We are not suggesting that "failure" be avoided or ignored. That view, notes motivation researcher Martin Covington (1998), "assumes that failure per se causes loss of esteem and self-respect. Quite the contrary, failure can act as a positive force so long as it is properly interpreted by the learner." He suggests that "rather than focusing on failure as the culprit, educators should arrange learning so that falling short of one's goals, which inevitably happens to everyone, will be interpreted in ways that promote the will to persist."

Covington's studies of student motivation confirm that students' beliefs about the causes of their success or failure deeply affect their future attainment. Students who attribute their successes to luck and their failures to lack of ability — forces outside their control — are often actually motivated to withdraw in order to avoid failure. On the other hand, students who see successes and failures as a natural part of the process of moving toward valued goals that they believe themselves capable of attaining are often motivated to greater effort. Once students understand the source of success or failure — that it is not just a matter of luck or, even, ability — they often begin to believe that they can control their own achievement. Teachers can take an important role in helping students both understand the importance of effort and the need to weather occasional failures.

Covington's research is a reminder that how students view assessment processes and results is at least partly under control of their teachers. Teachers' ability to recognize and build on student strengths in both instruction and assessment encourages students to see themselves as competent and capable of navigating the ups and downs on the journey to academic success. Offering students varied assessment tasks, as well as choices in the way they respond, is consistent with the characteristics of good assessment, and it allows students to draw on their strengths.

Related to motivation and effort is *interest.* Anastasi (1990) has written about how motivation, interest, and effort contribute to students' development of aptitudes and proficiency in particular areas. As a student (or anyone) chooses certain activities over others, particular skills get enhanced (to the exclusion of others). This seems to lead students to seek additional experiences that draw on these developing skills. It becomes the schools' job to identify the aptitudes or proficiencies that students have, build on those, and encourage the student to move into new arenas — to develop new aptitudes.

VIGNETTE: JOSEPH'S STORY

The following vignette shows how motivation can impact assessment.

Joseph is the most challenging student in the eighth grade. His sullen attitude and lack of motivation frustrate each of his teachers. He goes through each day with his head down and his hands deep in his pockets, defying anyone who tries to reach him. He had moved to the small mid-western farming town midway through the previous year and clearly seemed to have a hard time fitting in. Other kids were scared of him, and he did not seem to have made any friends. His teachers guessed from his skin color that he was Hispanic or Native American, but they did not know if he was still learning English and had not been able to obtain much information from his family.

Assessment after assessment has shown Joseph to be at the lowest percentiles in both reading and math. He scored at a first-grade reading level on the state reading test, and his teachers wonder if he can read anything at all. They are considering a referral to special education.

Finally, Ms. Watson, his language arts teacher, calls his old school in Oklahoma. When she speaks with Joseph's guidance counselor there, he has nothing but glowing remarks and claims that Joseph had been performing above average in all his subjects. He is very surprised to hear about Joseph's low grades and discipline problems, and he asks to speak to him. After Ms. Watson has put Joseph on the phone and starts to walk out of the room, she overhears him say, "Why should I do any work? The white man controls everything in this town, and I'll never have a future here. What's the point?"

THINGS TO CONSIDER

In this example, Joseph's motivation to learn is getting in the way of his performance. Even though he may be very capable, he has simply decided not to perform, which means that his assessment results are completely invalid. They do not show accurate information about his abilities. Joseph doesn't believe that his effort will be rewarded, and while he may have a basis for his beliefs, this attitude will not be productive for him.

A Sociocultural Approach to Assessment

As was said at the outset, this publication espouses a sociocultural approach to assessment — one that acknowledges the influence on teaching, learning, and assessing of culture, language, gender, and other social factors and aspects of student identity. A traditional psychometric assessment approach seeks to standardize conditions of administration and scoring in order to insure reliability, that is, the likelihood that equivalent assessments given to the same student will result in the same or similar performance and that, broadly speaking, scorers will score the same assessments similarly. Reliability is especially important when trying to compare students' performances. But validity — the assurance that the results of an assessment will accurately reflect students' learning — is as important as reliability. In fact, there is a strong tension between standardizing assessments so that they will be reliable and making them culturally valid by accounting for context. So, at times, the goals of a psychometric approach and the goals of a sociocultural approach to assessment seem to pull in different directions.

DID YOU KNOW?

Psychometrics, the science of measurement of skills, knowledge, and abilities, has traditionally been concerned with development of formal assessments that meet strict criteria for validity and reliability, often through use of sophisticated statistical techniques.

By context, we mean not only the classroom environment and the students' in-school experiences, but also sociocultural factors that influence learning and performance, such as students' backgrounds, home experiences, languages and dialects, and gender. It's precisely these things that a sociocultural approach to assessment takes into consideration. We don't propose that teachers ignore traditional psychometric methods. Rather, we encourage teachers and other assessment developers to consider sociocultural factors when designing or modifying assessments, when identifying an array of assessments to use with their students, and when evaluating students' performance on any assessment.

Table 3: Approaches to Testing

Traditional Psychometric Approach	Sociocultural Approach
• Emphasizes individual psychological processes (implication is that learning is an individual psychological event/process)	• Emphasizes social aspects of learning — community, home, school (recognizing that an individual's ways of learning and demonstrating what has been learned are influenced by how he/she has been socialized)
• Controls for context effects by using items based on content most students are likely to know	• Contextualizes assessments (takes into consideration background differences)
• Strives for objectivity/reliability (as well as validity)	• Strives for validity, authenticity
• Often relies on decontextualized (sometimes unrelated) questions/prompts/items	• Either embeds assessment in instruction or relies on an integrated set of questions that deal with a single topic
• Standardized administration to avoid influence of external factors on performance	• Administration varied to accommodate student differences
• Student performance understood without necessary reference to external factors (unless conditions of administration have been corrupted)	• Student performance evaluated/understood in light of sociocultural information about the student, the school, the course of study
• Bias dealt with statistically, by adjusting scores to reflect factors that interfere with validity	• Bias dealt with in advance by evaluating appropriateness of tasks or items for given students; also may be dealt with while scoring student performances by score annotation; interpretation and use of assessment outcomes may be modified on the basis of understanding the student's background

Issues in Large-Scale Assessment

Large-scale standardized assessment is assessment conducted by states (and sometimes by national entities) to get a sense of how students are doing in comparison with peers across the state or nation. These assessments are mandated, so a teacher cannot simply opt her students out of participation in them (although there are procedures that parents can invoke to pull their children out).

It is not practical for developers of large-scale assessments to take into account every student's or even every district's context. That would mean an inordinate number of assessments and a lack of comparability across them (meaning that their scores could not be aggregated or compared). Nor can the administration and scoring of large-scale assessment be modified extensively without diminishing a test's reliability. But, because these assessments are not directly related to what students have learned and are not adapted to students' learning and communication styles, they may not provide accurate information about students.

Large-scale assessments are typically based on traditional psychometrics, whether they are norm-referenced or criterion-referenced. Even so-called "alternative" large-scale assessments, such as the statewide portfolios used in Vermont and elsewhere, adhere to psychometric principles and do not factor context into design, administration, or scoring. There *is* a trend now within the psychometric community to look for ways to make assessments fairer for English language learners and others. Most efforts to date have focused on accommodation, or the provision of a range of supports during administration (extended-time or untimed administration, re-phrased instructions, availability of dictionaries or calculators). But some psychometricians are seeking greater changes that would affect the whole way tests are developed (e.g., Solano-Flores, Trumbull, & Nelson-Barber, 2000).

There are many reasons to be concerned about the lack of validity of large-scale standardized tests for English language learners and students who are not from the mainstream. One is that decisions, such as college eligibility, are made at least in part on the basis of these tests. This is distressing, when research suggests that these tests predict that minority students will do worse than they actually do in college. For instance, the ACT (American College Testing) test is not a good predictor of college success for many minority students (Myers & Pyles, 1992; Rodriguez, 1996). They often do better than the tests predict. There are similar concerns for girls. Although men outscore women on the SAT (Scholastic Assessment Test), which is intended to predict first-year college grades, women actually get better college grades (including when matched for courses at similar universities) (Neill, 1997a).

VIGNETTE: MARIA'S STORY

In junior high, Maria was an honors student. However, when it came to taking the CTBS (California Test of Basic Skills), Maria wasn't very successful, and on the basis of this test, she was excluded from advanced classes in high school. Of greatest consequence, she felt, was the fact that she was tracked into lower-level mathematics classes rather than those that her peers with the same track record were entering — and that she had hoped to enter. Maria continued to get good grades, but her confidence was damaged by the school's judgment that she wasn't capable of succeeding in the more advanced math classes. Finally, she had the opportunity to take a math test on which she performed well, and she was then permitted to move into a better math class, where she also did well. But when it came to the SATs, Maria again had difficulty performing at a level high enough to qualify her for the schools she was interested in.

When Maria reached community college, she was required to take a series of placement tests. She scored poorly on the literacy test and was placed in a remedial class. This was a shock to her. She had done well in English in high school, loved literature and writing, and knew she could succeed in a regular freshman English class. Refusing to accept the test's assessment of her ability, she insisted on taking the regular English course. Maria's persistence paid off. To make a long story short, she eventually graduated with a Ph.D. from a prestigious California university and has a thriving research career.

THINGS TO CONSIDER

As you may have guessed, Maria's first language was not English. To this day, she considers English her second language and herself a learner of English. Despite her obviously strong intellect and motivation to achieve, she believes her vocabulary is still not equivalent to that of a native speaker. When Maria was a student, her language status could be expected to have an effect on test performance, particularly a timed test normed on students unlike her. However, it is important that we not assume that language differences, such as Maria's, are necessarily a deficit. Maria is now a gifted writer who expresses herself well in both English and Spanish.

What if Maria's school had looked at other indicators of Maria's ability (e.g., her grades, her teachers' judgments)? Given her desire, what would have been lost by allowing her to try the advanced mathematics course? Finally, what might have happened to a student who didn't have Maria's perseverance and confidence to question what the test scores meant about her abilities?

In Maria's case, her own convictions led her to challenge other people's judgments about her capabilities. But there was little she could do to challenge her SAT scores. While clearly not predictive of her abilities, they nonetheless limited her choices for higher education.

Concerns for fairness in assessment should lead to careful examination of the effects of tests and other assessment practices on students, including potentially flawed predictions about their future success and foreclosure of opportunities they might otherwise be able to take great advantage of. Because test scores and grades can narrow students' subsequent opportunities, students should be given the benefit of the doubt in cases where clear decisions about their achievement or ability cannot be made.

While classroom teachers cannot always choose whether or how to administer certain tests, such as state-mandated assessments, they control how they evaluate the results, the weight they give to them, and how they talk about those results with students and their parents. In doing so, it's important to keep in mind that if the backgrounds of their students differ markedly from those of the hypothetical students in the minds of the test developers, their students' performance cannot be considered a valid index of ability or learning.

Classroom teachers who have been educated in a traditional psychometric paradigm often attempt to design assessments that follow patterns and principles they observe in large-scale, standardized assessment. They may create sets of unrelated questions, standardize their administration, and develop scoring schemes to produce a "normal curve," as do developers of large-scale tests (especially norm-referenced tests). Although these practices are grounded in teachers' efforts to be fair and objective, they are neither necessary nor justifiable in classrooms of 25 or 30 students. Teachers actually have great control over the kind of assessments they use to inform day-to-day instructional decisions, to provide insight into student strengths, and to generate formative feedback for students during the learning process. It's here that a sociocultural approach to assessment is always most appropriate. In the coming chapters, we'll talk more specifically about how to choose, develop, or adapt assessments that accommodate the cultural diversity in today's classrooms.

Summary

Decisions about how to address equity challenges in assessment are easier to make in the abstract. Real-world situations are usually more complex than lists of principles and guidelines would suggest, and teachers often have to make on-the-spot interpretations of student behaviors.

This section provided an overview of the research in the areas of cultural diversity, as they relate to assessment. Some of the most important concerns for ensuring equitable assessment for all students include an indepth understanding of the difference between individualist and collectivist cultures, the unique issues surrounding gender, motivation, and what it means to have a sociocultural approach to assessment. As has been stated, a sociocultural approach to assessment offers the best possibility for ensuring valid assessment outcomes. In the next section, the discussion of the key issues and findings continues, this time with a focus on linguistic diversity, recognizing that culture and language are intertwined, and any division of the two is artificial.

SECTION II

Language Issues in Assessment

All languages have structure, and all people use structure when speaking. No language can be superior or inferior, only different in the sense that it fits the needs of different groups. A child coming to school may speak a native tongue that is quite different from the standard English generally used in American schools. These differences may go well beyond simple dictionary definitions or diverse syntactical structures. They can affect the impressions youngsters give their teachers about their intellectual abilities, their attitudes, and even their social acceptability.

Wilma S. Longstreet, *Aspects of Ethnicity: Understanding Differences in Pluralistic Classrooms,* 1978.

As stated previously, assessment is a cultural phenomenon. The ways students are assessed in U.S. schools are by no means universal. Assessment is also in most instances a linguistic process. Assessment is dependent on language for giving instructions, for framing actual prompts or test items, and very often for the actual responses students are to give. Even so-called "nonverbal" tests, such as the Raven's Progressive Matrices or other visual-spatial tasks, often require that students have the mental language to conceptualize the problem or hold certain ideas in memory (Oller, 1992; Roth, 1978).

Language is intimately tied to culture, and separating them is quite artificial. Language was actually discussed to a considerable extent in Section I, in terms of how students participate in conversation or discussion in the classroom, culture-based conventions for posing and asking questions, and cultural variations in using language to show what one has learned. In this section, there is an exploration of assessment of English language learners, and a discussion of the parallels between English language learners and dialect-learners. There are also a limited number of examples related to gender, showing how language use in assessment may affect males and females differently.

How Culture Shapes Language Use: Implications for Assessment

Depending on their backgrounds, students may be inclined to communicate in ways that are quite similar to what's expected in school or, conversely, quite different. More economically privileged families, for example, tend to use language in the ways schools demand, so their children will likely be more familiar with it. In particular, middle-class parents often ask their children to explain past events or talk about upcoming events. This "decontextualized" language use, in which the immediate topic of conversation is not present or self-explanatory, but exists in the past or future, has been associated with success in reading

(Snow, 1983). After all, to comprehend a text, the child needs to be able to rely on language alone. There is no immediate, real-life context to clarify the meaning of a sentence, as in face-to-face communication.

In another example, consider that some cultures equate wisdom with speaking very selectively and value listening over speaking (Philips, 1983), while other cultures, such as the dominant U.S. culture, equate power and knowledge with the active use of language in social situations (Greenfield, Quiroz, & Raeff, 1998). The latter, of course, more closely reflects what's expected in most classrooms. In similar contrast, some groups use language with children primarily to socialize them to expected behaviors, while other groups attempt to engage small children in talking about what they observe or experience — again, not unlike how language is used in schools (Snow, 1983). These very different ways of socializing and interacting with children can be expected to engender different skills — some matched to school expectations, some not.

It's not uncommon to make assumptions about people based on how they communicate. As educators, we need to be continually vigilant that our assumptions about our students are accurate. The following vignettes are just two examples of how students can be misperceived when teachers and other educators do not understand — or even recognize — that they have a different, culturally based, communications style.

VIGNETTE: SIGNS OF SUCCESS

A small group of students from Alaska's St. Lawrence Island take part in a national competition that involves designing and constructing a model to solve an environmental problem. During the competition, teams from many other states are seen animatedly discussing the problem and debating strategies. The St. Lawrence team members, however, seem to talk very little among themselves. Instead, as they construct their model, team members contribute quietly to the work. To observers, little appears to be happening. Many of them conclude that the team has stalled, is bored, and isn't likely to generate anything of interest. But when the time comes for competition participants to show their work, the solution presented by the St. Lawrence students surprises the judges with its elegance and power.

THINGS TO CONSIDER

What strengths contributed to the success of these students? Until the end, competition observers did not see the social-interaction indicators they had traditionally equated with success. Teachers also expect certain indicators to provide evidence of students learning. We must take care not to misinterpret student work when their ways of learning do not match what we expect to see. The cognitive strengths of the Alaskan students were hidden by their reliance on nonverbal communication, and those observing the team were limited by their own cultural experiences and perceptions. The absence of overt verbal communication among team members was interpreted by the observers as limited interaction and enthusiasm. It is clear that the observers were wrong. But what *was* behind the team's apparent lack of communication?

Anthropologist and intercultural communication researcher Edward T. Hall (1977) has studied communication differences across cultures. His studies of the ways in which culture conditions us to perceive our world, and the others in it, provide important insights into ways we can, at times, "not see" or "not hear" what another is communicating.

One of the differences Hall has identified has to do with the amount of explicit information people provide when communicating about a topic. How much do they specifically explain about any given subject? In some cultures, members do not provide much elaboration; they don't

DID YOU KNOW?

- High-context cultures tend to use communication strategies in which most of the meaning is embedded in physical and nonverbal means.

- Low-context cultures, by contrast, tend to use communications in which meaning is made explicit through details and elaborate verbal or written messages.

need to because they share extensive common experiences and values. This kind of communication is referred to as *high context*. By contrast, if the experiences and values within a group are far more diverse, communication *requires* more explicit elaboration and detail. This style is known as *low-context* communication. In all likelihood, the St. Lawrence Island community has a norm of high-context communication, as reflected in the team's behavior.

VIGNETTE: DARREN'S STORY

Darren, an African American, is new to a second-grade classroom composed largely of European American students. His teacher (also European American) has divided her class into heterogeneous reading groups, and she randomly assigns him to one. During the meeting time for his reading group, she attempts to determine his reading level. She says, "Darren, would you like to read the first page?" He shakes his head. She is surprised because students don't usually refuse, but she lets it go. Other students read, and then she asks him a second time, "Darren, why don't you read the next page?" He shakes his head again. She looks at him sternly, wondering if he is going to be a discipline problem, or whether his reading skills are so poor that he can't manage the text. "Darren, please read the next page now." Darren complies and reads fluently, with a clear voice. The book actually appears to be way too easy for him. The teacher is confused by what has just occurred.

THINGS TO CONSIDER

When Darren doesn't respond as she expects him to, his teacher initially worries that he might have a bad attitude or poor reading skills. In reality, any number of things may have been going on. Darren may have been shy or nervous about reading in front of a group on his first day at a new school. Because the teacher phrased her requests as questions, he may also have thought that he had a choice about responding. Many African American students are accustomed to hearing commands in the form of assertive statements rather than as questions (or indirect requests) at home. Teachers who do not realize this often mistake a student's noncompliance as a negative attitude or lack of knowledge/competence.

Different Oral and Literate Traditions

Just as different groups may use different dialects of the same language, so too they may differ in other aspects of how they use language and communicate meaning. There are differences that have been called "paralinguistic," because they are not directly part of the language code. For example, students may use different kinds of intonation and levels of volume as they speak to one another. Are there highs and lows, or do voices sound somewhat monotone? Do they "sound" excited? Agitated? Uninterested? It is remarkable how we unconsciously assume interest level or emotional content from these paralinguistic features. For instance, Navajo speakers tend to use much lower volume and less variation in pitch, sounding monotone to the inexperienced listener. But these features cannot fairly be interpreted to mean lack of engagement with a topic or lack of emotion.

Speakers differ also in the use of gestures, how near they stand to one another, whether they focus directly on "the point" or "talk around it," and numerous other features. All these differences in the ways we communicate what we know and who we are, as well as what we care about, are deeply rooted in our linguistic/cultural identity.

Patterns of text organization differ from culture to culture. A typical Western European and American pattern of argument is to state a thesis (e.g., via a topic sentence) and then support that thesis with details (evidence). When a student begins (orally or in writing) with a series of details and builds up to a conclusion, we may perceive that his/her strategy is immature or deviant. In fact, it is an equally logical strategy common in many other cultures.

Native people, unlike middle-class European Americans, are likely to tell a story to children without asking them to offer their interpretations of events as the story is told. Native children are expected to make their own sense of the tale without the kind of discussion or questioning common in classrooms. Through years of hearing a story repeated, their interpretations will steadily mature, without this discussion.

For many Pacific Island cultures, storytelling is a primary means of communicating cultural values, the history and relationships of family, important knowledge of natural phenomena, moral lessons, and more. In this tradition of family storytelling, stories do not end. Retellings add information, characters, and things to learn. Different storytellers may introduce different points of view about the same event. Each session is intended to provide a piece of the whole picture and leave listeners ready for another telling.

Teachers need to be aware of the different possible ways of relating information or telling stories, if they are to fully understand children from nondominant cultural backgrounds. It is important for teachers of diverse student populations to know something about "sociolinguistics," the science of the social aspects of language. Otherwise, differences in children's language can lead teachers to unintended biases about what children are capable of learning.

Conventions for telling stories, something children in U.S. schools are asked to do as early as kindergarten, vary tremendously among different cultural groups (Heath, 1983; Michaels, 1981). Some children use a "topic-associating" or episodic style, in which a story is composed of a string of personal anecdotes. The relevance of the anecdotes to the topic may seem obscure because there is no evident beginning, middle, or end as commonly thought of. This style is typical of many African American students (Heath, 1983).

When working with some African American children, especially from urban areas, majority culture teachers can have trouble seeing the point(s) a child is making and predicting where a story is going. Some teachers are more accepting of children who use a storytelling approach known as *topic-centered* rather than the *topic-associating* style. A topic-centered approach to writing a story establishes a primary topic and structures the story around it.

African American teachers can be helpful to non-African American teachers in understanding and interpreting topic-associating children's accounts, because even excellent non-African American teachers have difficulties with this approach to storytelling (see also Ball, 1997). They do not perceive it as having a pattern because the pattern is so different.

The Ball research illustrates the value of having teachers from different backgrounds get together to evaluate student work and to talk not only about the common standards they hold, but about how to interpret

DID YOU KNOW?

Researcher Arnetha Ball had four European American teachers and four African American teachers, all enrolled in the same graduate program of a highly regarded private university, evaluate the writing of six fifth-/sixth-grade students. Three of the students were African American, two were native English-speaking Hispanic students, and one was European American. All students were considered academic achievers, with one African American student and the European American student described as "high achievers." The teachers were trained to use a holistic rubric, as well as scales evaluating different aspects of writing. On average, European American teachers gave higher scores to the European American student than to the other students, while the scores of the African American teachers did not differ by ethnic group, in general. However, the African American teachers were more impressed with the texts written by the high-achieving African American student. *All* the teachers tended to evaluate essays written in what Ball describes as "standard academic organizational patterns" more positively.

Ball notes that the African American and Hispanic students structured their writing not only according to standard academic patterns, but also at times according to other patterns common in the oral language of the groups they came from. It is likely that the European American teachers did not recognize these patterns as legitimate or desirable (or even see them as patterns, perhaps), while the African American teachers did, which could account for why they didn't penalize students for using them. Nevertheless, it appears that all eight teachers had an "ideal" in mind, represented by the standard academic organizational pattern.

(Ball, 1997)

differences in performance that originate in cultural and linguistic differences. As the Ball example demonstrates, a recognition of differences doesn't have to mean a lowering of standards; rather, it may call for eliminating unnecessary penalties in judging students' work.

As is clear from this example, it is not only English language learners whose writing may be misjudged by some teachers, particularly when teachers from one cultural background are scoring the writing of students from another cultural background. There are cultural differences in both oral and written discourse patterns. Many decades ago, Bartlett (1932) studied the narrative patterns of some American Indian groups and was surprised to discover that a good story was structured in "fours." There were four episodes, or four opportunities for a protagonist to solve a problem, or four deeds a hero needed to accomplish. Just think of how different this is from the accepted rhythm of the typical Western European-based fairy tale (with three bears and three chairs and beds, or three pigs, or three attempts to solve the usual problem). Not only that, but the beginning, middle, and end of American Indian narratives were not readily evident to someone outside the culture. To the uninitiated, the stories seemed formless. We become so conditioned to hearing a familiar pattern over and over again that we find exceptions to it strange: a two-episode story sounds incomplete; a four-episode story sounds too long. There is, of course, nothing inherently superior to a story with a particular number of episodes or even a "clear" beginning, middle, and end.

Some literary traditions focus much more on setting than on plot, others heavily on character. But imagine a middle school student's grade on a story-writing assignment if he spent 50 percent of his space setting the scene or 75 percent on character development. A teacher unfamiliar with any of these traditions can only judge writing based on them as deviant from the norms she does know. Acknowledging the validity of other writing or speaking conventions does not preclude teaching additional conventions. Students do need to learn the discourse patterns of the mainstream U.S. culture.

Table 4: Language Patterns
(Adapted from Bennett and Bennett of the Intercultural Communication Institute, 1993)

LINEAR:	**CIRCULAR (CONTEXTUAL):**
Discussion is conducted in a straight line, developing causal connections among subpoints towards an end point, stated explicitly. Low reliance on context.	Discussion is conducted in a circular movement, developing context around the main point, which is often left unstated. High reliance on shared context.
Let's get right to the point!	*Once you have the whole picture you'll know what I mean!*
DIRECT:	**INDIRECT:**
Meaning is conveyed through explicit statements made directly to the people involved, with little reliance on contextual factors such as situation and timing.	Meaning is conveyed by suggestion, implication, nonverbal behavior, and other contextual clues; for instance, statements intended for one person may be made within earshot to a different person.
What you see is what you get!	*What you get is what you manage to see/hear!*
ATTACHED:	**DETACHED:**
Issues are discussed with feeling and emotion, conveying the speaker's personal stake in the issue and the outcome.	Issues are discussed with calmness and objectivity, conveying the speaker's ability to weigh all the factors impersonally.
If it's important, it's worth getting worked up over!	*If it's important, it shouldn't be tainted by personal bias!*

Our challenge as educators is to help students walk successfully between two or more forms and patterns of communication. We must teach them to know when to use the conventions and structures of each.

The Dialect Issue

A *dialect* is one version of a language that differs systematically from another version of the same language. Everyone speaks a dialect, and no single dialect of English — or any other language — is superior to another, according to its complexity or ability to communicate whatever its speakers need to communicate to each other. However, some dialects are accorded greater or lesser *social* value than others according to the status of the groups that speak them. Among some of the broadly recognized dialects that tend to be devalued by members of the dominant society are the Cockney dialect in England and, in the United States, Ebonics, or Black Vernacular English, and the New York City dialect (Wolfram, 1981). Dialects vary according to pronunciation, syntax, and word meanings, as well as in features of pitch, volume, and pacing. Dialects also generally differ in conventions, such as how stories are structured and told, rules of conversation, how questions are posed and answered, and how various forms of written language are organized.

Traditionally, dialects have been viewed as mutually intelligible versions of the same language. In other words, despite variations in pronunciation or usage, a speaker of Southern English can generally understand a speaker from the Northwest. Numerous people speak more than one dialect, choosing the most appropriate one based on the situation or the person with whom they are speaking. In fact, most of us speak differently at home or in casual conversation with friends than we do at work or in more formal situations — moving from more formal to less formal speech. But for some people, these differences are greater because they speak two distinctly different dialects.

The home language of many African American children offers an important example of the complexity of dialects and of how a dialect can operate much like a foreign language for many native-English-speaking students. Although teachers cannot be expected to be linguists, they do need to have some basic understanding of their students' dialects so they can make sense of students' oral and written communication.

Known as "Black English Vernacular," "Ebonics," "African American Vernacular English," or "Black Language" (Perry & Delpit, 1998; Fillmore, 1997), this dialect or language (scholars argue over the designation) is like all other linguistic systems in that it has rules and is capable of serving all of the intellectual and social needs of its speakers. Black Language has multiple forms — oral and written, formal and informal, vernacular and literary (Perry, 1998). Its form and use have been influenced by West African languages, as well as by the social circumstances surrounding African Americans' histories in the United States. For example, deletion of the final consonant in a consonant cluster (wes' for west or col' for cold) brings English words more in line with the form of words in some West African languages (Smith, 1998). That said, Black Language speakers can certainly learn to hear these final consonants and spell words in "school" ways.

The oratorical styles of rhythm, rhyme, metaphor, and repetition used by African American preachers are some of the other distinctive elements of Black Language (Perry, 1998). Teachers can capitalize on these aspects of language in their instruction by encouraging students to use these elements in their creative writing assignments (poetry, essays, or narrative). They can provide opportunities for classroom presentations in which students explicitly use rhetorical strategies from their home dialect (e.g., a persuasive speech). In assessment, recognition of rhetorical strategies that come from what students have been exposed to in their communities adds to fairness in grading and scoring. "Standard" patterns are not always required, particularly when effective communication within a certain context is the goal.

Black Language is distinguished by many other conventions as well, including particular structures for storytelling or narrative writing (Ball, 1997; Michaels & Cazden, 1986; Heath, 1983). Although teachers cannot be expected to be linguists, they do need to have some basic understanding of their students' dialects, so they can make sense of students' oral and written communication. If a student uses an unfamiliar narrative structure in telling a story, a teacher may immediately assume that the student is using a defective "mainstream" approach. But the student may actually be using a fully developed strategy associated with his or her home dialect or language. Similarly, when a student uses grammar or spelling that reflects the dialect he or she has learned, these differences need to be understood not as errors that indicate learning problems, but as alternative forms that are correct within a different system. Students need to learn the counterparts of these forms in the new dialect, which in the case of school is what's known as "standard academic English."

If students don't use the kind of language expected in school, they need to learn how; but that does not mean they must give up their first language or dialect. Rather, they can become proficient in two dialects. In addition, we want to stress the parallels between bidialectism (proficiency with two dialects) and bilingualism (proficiency with two languages). In fact, those African American children — and others — who do not speak the "mainstream" English dialect face much the same challenge as children learning a completely different language, even though in the case of African Americans, their dialect and the "mainstream" dialect are largely mutually intelligible.

VIGNETTE: A STORY FROM OAKLAND

In an interview printed in "Rethinking Schools" (see Section VI), Oakland, California, fifth-grade teacher Carrie Secret describes how her approach to teaching English has shifted to one in which the language and culture of her African American students are valued equally with standard academic English and the mainstream culture that dominates in most schools.

"Our mission ... continues to be: embrace and respect Ebonics, the home language of many of our students, and use strategies that will move them to a competency level in English.

She describes the change: "In the past, I used the 'fix-something-that-was-wrong' approach. I was always calling for the children to say something correct or to fix something to make it right. I now approach the same task from a different perspective that has a more positive affect on my children.

"Some days I simply announce: 'While you are working, I will be listening to how well you use English. In your groups you must call for translation if a member of your group uses an Ebonic Structure.' Some days I say, 'Girls, you are attending Spelman, and, boys, you are attending Morehouse College.... Today you use the language the professors use and expect you to use in your classes, and that language is English.'

In the midst of teaching the language that provides access to the world outside their home community, Secret also makes sure students value their home language. "We read literature that has Ebonics language patterns in it. For example, last year in fifth grade we read Joyce Hansen's Yellow Bird and Me, *and in fourth grade we read her book* The Gift Giver. *The language was Ebonic in structure. The language was the bonding agent for students. The book just felt good to them.*

"When writing, the students are aware that finished pieces are written in English. The use of Ebonic structures appears in many of their first drafts. When this happens I simply say, 'You used Ebonics here. I need you to translate this thought into English.' This kind of statement does not negate the child's thought or language."

THINGS TO CONSIDER

There are many different ways to communicate, and, as educators, we must value them all, while, at the same time, help students know how and when to use the language of the dominant culture. Which communication patterns are you most comfortable with? Do you know the styles common in the cultures of your students? How do you decide when it is acceptable to use "nonstandard" language and when "standard English" is required in your own classroom?

Lisa Delpit, an expert on culture and dialect, reminds us that standard English is the language of power and business. When we do not equip students with the skills they need to speak and write standard English, we place them at a disadvantage. Carrie Secret demonstrates how we can both recognize and respect students' language strengths *and* learn what students need in order to master the "standard" dialect.

Gender, Language, and Assessment

Language style and use are also associated with gender differences. A quick look at the differences in the experiences of boys and girls in the same classrooms provides immediate evidence that all students do not have equal opportunities to take an active part in whole-class and small-group work. When girls are recognized, they rarely get to say more than a sentence or two before a boy interrupts and takes over the conversation. Many girls also put themselves down by beginning with a disclaimer when answering a question in class. For example, they may say, "I don't know if this is right, but..." Further, teachers respond differently to boys' and girls' requests for help, being more apt to coach boys to get the answer themselves while giving girls the answer directly.

Likewise, boys are more likely to be instructed how to perform tasks while girls often have tasks done for them, and boys tend to receive feedback related to a task, the content, or thought process. Girls are more likely to get feedback based on the appearance of their work. Girls sometimes get graded up because they communicate better (Hughey, 1984; Hughey & Harper, 1983). Boys may get graded down on the basis of handwriting (Sprouse & Webb, 1994; Sweedler-Brown, 1993) or, as mentioned earlier, even behavior (Bennett, Gottesman, Rock, & Cerullo, 1993).

THINGS TO TRY

Such recognized biases in schools are just a part of the sets of experiences that tend to limit the expectations and perceptions of each gender. Some programs are addressing the needs of girls more directly. The "Teaching SMART" program in Rapid City, South Dakota, has a model program for helping girls in mathematics and science (Vobejda & Perlstein, 1998). Some insights from the program include techniques that more fully engage girls in learning. Try some of these techniques in your classrooms:

- Wait five seconds after asking a question before calling on a student to answer — teachers are likely to see more girls raise their hands. The boys' hands typically shoot up immediately, but gradually, this practice assures a better balance. Perhaps some boys who don't routinely respond will also start to do so.

- Don't always let a group decide who will lead and who should record (write on the chalkboard, keep minutes, etc.). Experience shows girls will almost always end up recording because they have nicer handwriting.

- Call upon all students whether or not their hands are up.

- Help students develop alternative ways of communication in which both boys and girls are given the same opportunity to talk and be listened to.

What did you notice when you tried some of these techniques? Did the communication patterns in your classroom change? If so, how? What are the implications for assessment?

Understanding Students' Language Proficiency: Focus on Second-Language Learners

Whatever else might affect students' communications patterns, for students who are not native English speakers, there is also the question of language proficiency. Can they understand and use English well enough to be accurately assessed in English on their understanding of content? Other aspects of communications notwithstanding, the integral role of language itself in teaching and learning makes it imperative that teachers have a solid understanding of their students' English language skills. Consider what can happen when, instead of relying on assessment data, teachers rely on their assumptions about students' language.

VIGNETTE: FALSE ASSUMPTIONS

The following example describes the experience of an education consultant who works with teachers and students in schools. In his own words, he describes a surprising experience he had in one school in which erroneous assumptions about students' language altered a teacher's expectations of students.

"I was on time. This was my chance to try out with students the electricity assessment that I had been developing for the last two months. Ms. Gallagher came to me, smiling:

'I'm glad that you're from Mexico,' Ms. Gallagher said. 'I'm concerned about two Hispanic students I have. They don't understand a word of English and I'm afraid they're getting bored. Would you mind working with them? I don't have tests in Spanish. Maybe you can tell me how they're doing in science.'

"When I try out my assessments in schools, I usually have students work in pairs anyway. From observing their interaction, I can tell how they interpret the directions provided and what kinds of thinking and problem-solving strategies they use in doing the assessment. No, I did not have any problem working with them.

"As I walked with the kids down the hallway to the corner of the school's gym where I had set up all my materials, I tried to melt the ice. I introduced myself and told them where I grew up — in Spanish, of course. Then I asked them to tell me where they were born. After exchanging glances, they tried to respond in Spanish, but they couldn't. I could tell they were uncomfortable that they were not fluent in Spanish. We switched to English.

"As they engaged in the science task they interacted all the time in English, and they had no problem reading and writing in English. In fact, their English wasn't any better or worse than that of any other kid in the same school.

'This is fun,' said one of them as the bell rang. So engaged were they connecting batteries and bulbs that they didn't mind missing recess.

"As I drove back to my lab, I wondered how many opportunities to learn had been denied to these kids because their teacher had erroneously assumed they only spoke Spanish. Then I had a scary thought: These students might be tested in the future in Spanish, under the assumption that they do not understand a word of English."

THINGS TO CONSIDER

How can we account for this nearly unbelievable situation? For starters, instructional and assessment practices are often a reflection of teachers' perceptions of other individuals and other cultural groups. Perhaps the students did not voluntarily speak up in class, and the teacher, assuming they spoke no English and thinking she was being helpful, never called on them because she didn't want to put them "on the spot." The students might not have even realized that the teacher thought they spoke no English. And had they known, they might still have done nothing to correct her misperception — especially if their families had come from rural areas in Mexico where, as is true in many traditional communities, students and parents do not question the decision of a teacher, who is considered powerful and authoritative. Possibly, too, the parents, themselves, were not proficient in English and would have found it difficult to speak with the teacher.

Whatever the reasons for this misunderstanding, it would have been avoided entirely with appropriate and timely language assessment. Determining a student's proficiency in English should be a first step in deciding whether to gauge his or her learning with an English-based assessment. If a student isn't fully proficient, an assessment in English cannot be expected to yield valid results. Unfortunately, determining if a student has greater proficiency in English or in another language isn't as easy as one might think.

The Challenge of Assessing English Language Skills

The necessity for all students to become fully proficient in "standard" English is clear, as is the need to assess their progress in doing so. Because demonstrating what one has learned is heavily dependent on language proficiency, it's critical that teachers be able to accurately judge students' proficiency and the degree to which it either supports or impedes students' ability to show what they know in the academic realm.

One study of how to accurately determine English proficiency found that different measures of proficiency produced a different pattern of classification. In other words, students were classified at different levels of English proficiency depending on the source of information used (Solano-Flores, Ruiz-Primo, Baxter, Othman, & Shavelson, 1994). On one kind of test, a student may score as "fully English proficient," while on another, the same student may score as "limited English proficient." Clearly, then, it's important to use multiple sources of information in assessing language proficiency. In addition to a formal assessment, teachers may well want to draw on more informal assessments, such as observations in both social and academic situations and parent reports of language use at home.

There are different types of proficiency, and Olmedo (1981) notes that when testing members of linguistic minority groups on academic learning, "it is essential to understand the kind and degree of bilingualism of the individual being tested." Conversational fluency is not the same as academic fluency. On the playground, an English language learner might chatter away in English with his or her friends, but that doesn't mean the child's English language skills would be adequate for an academic test. In a similar vein, a native Spanish speaker, for example, could score well on one assessment of his native language skills, but if the assessment didn't address *academic language* proficiency, the results could *falsely* predict greater success with Spanish than is warranted. Academic language proficiency is heavily dependent on having used a language for academic purposes. When children cease learning academics in their first language at school, that language may not continue to develop as a tool for academic learning — unless opportunities outside of school support such language learning.

If determinations about English proficiency are based on insufficient or superficial information, a student may be improperly identified as English proficient. If so, student performance would be assessed without taking into account any language limitations, and the student's achievement would *look* worse than if the student had been assessed in his or her first language. Conversely, without a thorough assessment, a student who is actually proficient in English could be improperly identified as an English language learner, akin to the experience of the two children above whose teacher thought they spoke no English. One result could be that teacher expectations about the student's performance would be lowered, and the student might not be given the opportunity to adequately demonstrate his or her learning.

Distinguishing Between Language Proficiency and Academic Proficiency

The following vignette demonstrates some of the issues to consider in academic assessment of English language learners.

VIGNETTE: THE HISTORY ASSESSMENT

Mr. Strauss's fourth grade has just finished a unit on California history. He wants to assess his group of largely immigrant Latino students on how well they have understood the role of the Spanish missionaries in colonizing California. He intends to capitalize on their interests and make the assessment motivating, so he creates an open-ended question with room for some choice in response. He cues the students to some elements of knowledge that he does expect to see in their writing. He gives them 50 minutes, so that they can think about what they want to write first. Here is his assessment prompt:

"There were many players in California history who had a lasting influence on our state. Among these were the Spanish missionaries, particularly Father Junipero Serra. Write an essay of at least two pages on the Spanish missionaries, explaining what they did and how it affected California and the people who lived there at the time. You might want to imagine that you were alive in those days. Tell what you think are the pros and cons of the actions of these missionaries. What was good, and what was bad? How have their actions affected the California of today?"

Mr. Strauss knows that for most of his immigrant Latino students the actions of the Spanish missionaries are very personally meaningful and positive (even though he has had them do research on the effects of the missionaries' actions on the California Indians). After all, these missionaries brought Christianity and literacy to the New World. He wants to assess what they have learned and encourage them to consider all the historical evidence. He hopes he will elicit different

MAKING ASSESSMENT WORK FOR EVERYONE

points of view, and then students can discuss aloud why they took the perspective they did. But this is the first time he has given an extended writing assessment. Usually he gives quizzes that require short answers. He isn't prepared for the limited output he gets from his students. Most of them produce only a few sentences, and those are not connected well to address the questions in the prompt. This is their first year in an English-only classroom, but they all did well on their language proficiency test, and he knows they were very involved in this particular unit.

THINGS TO CONSIDER

What is going on? Mr. Strauss has matched his assessment to what he has taught. He has fairly clear ideas of his learning targets, and he believes he has chosen an assessment method that will allow students to show what they know. He has considered how to make the assessment tap students' points of view and interests. Why have they done so poorly? After all, this particular history should be easy for them to connect with on a personal level. These are some of the possibilities:

- Mr. Strauss's assessment relies very heavily on written language proficiency. Students who have been transitioned to English-only instruction may be proficient in oral language but lag behind in writing skills (in part because of instructional practices).

- On-demand writing tasks — where students don't have time to make outlines and drafts but go almost directly to a final product — are often difficult for students required to write in their second language. Process writing, which has been widely adopted and may be what students are used to, provides for planning and multiple drafts and usually includes peer support. Writing an essay on a complex topic in 50 minutes is an entirely different task.

- Mr. Strauss has nicely given a context to his prompt. He didn't just launch into a direct question. However, in order to comprehend the prompt, the student has to read some fairly complicated sentences and grapple with at least four questions. Students reading in a second language are likely to take longer to get an accurate sense of the overall problem and formulate a plan for responding to it than native English speakers.

- When students write in a second language, they may have to pay undue attention to the mechanics of writing — something that takes attention away from monitoring the overall product (how well they are communicating or addressing what they meant to, how well their argument is stacking up, etc.).

Assessments designed for second language learners can go wrong in so many ways. Sometimes the directions on a test are ambiguous or require understanding of complex syntax. This is troublesome because, if a student does not frame a problem correctly from the outset, his or her solution is likely to be flawed (Durán, 1985). In the case of Mr. Strauss and his students, one of the problems may have been that the assessment prompt, or set of questions, was just too linguistically complicated. Students had to wade through a lot to get the full picture of what Mr. Strauss expected them to do.

But even if they understood the prompt and had a lot of knowledge about the topic, creating a formal essay would be very demanding for students who have just been transitioned to English language arts. The reality is that even students who pass language proficiency tests at high levels are still developing as users of English, and they cannot be expected to perform like native English speakers. Mr. Strauss could have scaffolded the assessment task by having students brainstorm in small groups, make an outline of the main points they wanted to address, and use a graphic organizer (just a simple T-chart, like Ms. Altchech used) to list pros and cons before writing the actual essay.

Sometimes teachers choose oral assessment for the reasons outlined above. But oral assessments are not always easier than written ones. Instructions given orally can put too great a demand on memory. When giving instructions or posing a question orally to students who are still mastering English, there are several ways teachers can adjust the language demands. They can slow their speech, give context cues, and relate what they are saying to students' past experience (Watson, Northcutt, & Rydell, 1989).

Teachers need knowledge of how language factors may cloud the picture of academic achievement and how to create assessments that minimize this confusion. They need skills in mediating — or adjusting — the administration of assessments so performances will reflect the true learning of students. Another very simple step Mr. Strauss could have taken would have been to walk his students through his assessment prompt and have some of them paraphrase what they thought they were asked to do.

Responding to Student Writing Errors

Much assessment *is* done through writing, and it's natural to notice student errors in writing (whether writing is the object of assessment or the vehicle for assessing learning in another subject area). But not all errors merit the attention they receive (Leki, 1992; Valdés, 1991). When it comes to evaluating student performance, teachers need skill in determining which kinds of student errors indicate learning problems and which are simply normal developmental blips along the way to language mastery.

There need to be established criteria for what should count as *serious* errors. For instance, even though omission of articles (as in, "My family had picnic this weekend.") grates on the ears of many English teachers, they need to realize that this is a relatively trivial error. In addition, when teachers are familiar with students' first languages, they can look at student work with an understanding of how the first language is "coming through," versus focusing unduly on errors (Sweedler-Brown, 1993). In the case of articles, for instance, many Asian languages do not use them at all. Even English language learners who have progressed to "advanced" status as English speakers and writers may continue to struggle with these issues. General education teachers can benefit from working closely with those who teach English as a second language or bilingual teachers. Both groups speak and/or know a great deal about the languages of their students.

The same benefits can be derived from collaboration between African American teachers familiar with Black Language and their non-African American colleagues. Students who exhibit features of Black Language in their writing are also learning a second code, and similar understanding needs to be brought to bear by teachers.

Assessment Adaptation and Translation Issues

When a student performs poorly on an academic assessment, we often do not know if the performance reflects poor learning or simply an inadequate mastery of language (García & Pearson, 1994; Hamayan & Damico, 1991). A student may have met requirements for English-only instruction but still take longer to process ideas in English than in his or her first language. For this reason, a timed test or time-limited assessment of any kind may penalize an English language learner. Vocabulary in a second language may be less developed than that of a native speaker. A person may know a word such as "credit" or "bark" but not know all the common meanings or the connotations of the word.

Students who speak English as a second language may perform differently on an assessment, depending on which language they are allowed (or choose) to use. In an investigation on the use of monolingual (English-only or Spanish-only) and bilingual (English and Spanish) response formats in science performance assessments, Solano-Flores, Ruiz-Primo, Baxter, and Shavelson (1992) found evidence suggesting that not only test format but also the language chosen for responses are factors in student performance.

DID YOU KNOW?

It has been suggested that language minority students' schooling aptitude is underestimated if testing is conducted only in English. On the other hand, when an assessment is translated from one language to another, its validity is seriously jeopardized. Its level of difficulty may change, or it may be assessing something entirely different from the original from which it was translated (Olmedo, 1981).

In another investigation, Solano-Flores, Ruiz-Primo, Baxter, Othman, and Shavelson (1994) attempted to obtain more accurate information on language proficiency. They examined three types of data on English proficiency: standardized English proficiency scores provided by schools, patterns of English use in different sociocultural contexts, and patterns of use in bilingual test formats (for example, reading the items in one language and responding in another). They found that each measure of English proficiency produced a different pattern of classification. In other words, the students were classified at different levels of English proficiency depending on the source of information used (Solano-Flores, Ruiz-Primo, Baxter, Othman, & Shavelson, 1994).

The main implication of these results is that any decision about a student's English proficiency should be made only after different sources of information have been carefully examined. If decisions about student English proficiency are based on insufficient or superficial information, a student may be improperly identified as English proficient. Her performance will be assessed without taking into account her language limitations, so her achievement will look worse than if she were assessed in her first language. Conversely, an English-proficient student may be improperly identified as an English language learner. Expectations about her performance will be lowered, and she will not be given the opportunity to adequately demonstrate her learning. Even "accepted" approaches to assessing English language learners can give inaccurate results unless the students' sociocultural context is taken into account.

In this era of testing, assessments are being modified for use with students for whom the instruments weren't originally created. Among these modifications are test accommodations, such as changes on administration procedure or administration time, which may be made for English language learners or students with certain disabilities. There are also test adaptations, such as format changes or translation. The quality and validity of the scores produced when accommodations are used are still under investigation.

One of the most common adaptations for English language learners is translation. In fact, many assume that the whole issue of language proficiency in assessment can be avoided simply by translating tests into the language in which a student is most proficient. But that's a risky assumption. Studies in which different language versions of the same assessment are used show that even a single word whose translation is slightly inaccurate may produce unintended interpretations of an item and alter its psychometric properties, giving an advantage to students tested in the assessment's original language.

There are also some sociocultural reasons for why even a perfectly translated assessment may, nonetheless, yield inaccurate results. In one study of bilingual assessment formats, researchers created a Spanish version of assessments developed in English by using a standard translation process commonly accepted as valid (Solano-Flores, Ruiz-Primo, Baxter, & Shavelson, 1992). In this process, an experienced translator translated the original assessments into Spanish; a panel of bilingual scholars reviewed the Spanish versions and translated them back into English to monitor retention of the original meaning; and, finally, the Spanish versions were refined based on a series of try-outs with a sample of Spanish-speaking students.

From the scholarly point of view, the translation was accurate and the grammar impeccable. But some Latino English language learners were unfamiliar with some Spanish words that the researchers had *assumed* were part of the students' everyday language. Because the assessments had originally been developed in English, the sociocultural background of the English language learners hadn't been considered during the development process. The scores of these English language learners would have been considered dependable because the standard translation procedure had been used, but, in reality, the assessments would not have been valid because, for these particular students, the assessment inadvertently tested students' Spanish vocabulary knowledge rather than their academic content knowledge.

This is one more reminder that when the sociocultural background of minority students is not properly considered, even commendable efforts intended to promote equitable testing may yield flawed results from assessments of dubious validity.

Because a translated version of an assessment does not undergo the same process of development and refinement as the original, the overall quality of the translated version may be inferior. Some researchers are investigating the limitations and possibilities of a model for concurrently developing content area assessments in English and Spanish. The skills and knowledge to be assessed are specified, with the content and format for each assessment task agreed upon. Then, when assessment developers make a change in one language version of the task, (e.g., English), they make an equivalent change in the other language, (e.g., Spanish). That way, at the end of the process the two sets of assessment tasks are comparable across languages (Solano-Flores, Trumbull, & Nelson-Barber, 2000).

VIGNETTE: EXAMPLES OF ADAPTATION ERRORS

What follow are examples of the wide variety of adaptation-related errors that have been found in tests, with an explanation of the circumstances that led to these particular errors. All these examples come from tests that have been translated from English for Spanish-speaking English language learners. But, as you'll see, such errors could easily arise in translations for other languages as well.

- *A science prompt for second-graders shows an illustration of a crab and asks the student to indicate the crab's pincers. The prompt is translated as: "Señala la panza del cangrejo." The translator meant to write "pinza" (pincer), but instead wrote "panza," which means "tummy" or "belly." The inadvertent substitution of one vowel significantly changed the meaning of the prompt.*

- *A reading diagnostic test in English, considered appropriate for first-graders, is translated into Spanish to diagnose reading skills of Spanish-speaking English learners. The English word "bat," which is monosyllabic and has three letters, has to be translated as "murciélago," which has four syllables and 10 letters. Although the translation is correct, any conclusions that can be made about native Spanish speakers based on this translation would be objectionable because of the differences in the reading levels.*

- *A science test that has been available in English for several years is translated to serve native Spanish speakers. To ensure comparability across languages, the format and appearance (e.g., number of pages, location of items and illustrations) of the Spanish version must be the same as the format and appearance of the English version. Because printed Spanish takes about 25 percent more characters than printed English, the only way the translator finds to meet these requirements is to reduce the font size of the text in the Spanish version. Although the two language versions have similar appearances, the Spanish readers may have more difficulty reading the test because of the small font size.*

- *A mathematics test that required one year to develop is about to be printed. The publisher is then asked to produce a Spanish version that will be given to English language learners during the same administration period. The company hires only one translator, who is given one week to deliver the Spanish version. With such a tight timeline, the wording of the prompts cannot be reviewed and refined as carefully as it was for the English version. As a result of the rush, several errors are made. For example, in a series of word problems in the Spanish version, the last sentence of the text is missing. Yet two of the five multiple-choice items still refer to that sentence. The mistake is only noticed and corrected long after students have been assessed and placement decisions made based on the assessment results.*

THINGS TO CONSIDER

Determining the best way to assess English language learners, even those who have been judged English-proficient, is difficult. Teachers may want to offer students choices in the languages of the assessment wherever possible.

No equitable testing can be attained if the first languages of minority students do not receive the same treatment as English throughout the assessment development process. Obviously, translation and other adaptation procedures need to be improved.

Summary

It is clear that we have many issues to consider in order to ensure fair and useful assessment of our students' learning. Understanding students' culture-based differences in ways of using language, students' language proficiency, and how language is involved in the whole assessment process are keys to valid assessment. For some students, it may take years to make sense of and be comfortable participating in the kinds of interchanges considered routine in American classrooms. By that time, many of them will have been lost to the system — or, at the very least, misjudged. Other methods need to be cultivated with such students as early in their schooling as possible to equip them with the skills that will enable them to navigate successfully between their own culture and that of school.

Assessments can reveal what students know and can do at a given point, or they can actually obscure students' learning. In particular, when a student produces nothing or very little on a test, it is difficult to know what is going on. Does he or she really not have the skills or knowledge necessary to perform well on the test? Or is the assessment not doing its job?

Unfortunately, it is often easier to blame the student than the assessment, even though we need to look to both for explanations about low performance. Even if the problem lies with the student, distinguishing among causes can be difficult. Less than optimal learning can be caused by the following student factors (among other things):

- A mismatch between student language needs and language of instruction

- Lack of effort

- Lack of ability

- Lack of motivation

- A learning disability

- Conscious or unconscious resistance (when a student's individual social identity seems to be threatened by what he or she is required to do to participate in the classroom)

The assessment factors we have identified are those that interact with student factors. It is, of course, possible to have an assessment that is invalid on other grounds: the developer may not have selected a set of questions or tasks that adequately sample the domain being assessed, and wrong conclusions may be made about a student's competence in the domain (let's say mathematical reasoning). Or the assessment may be too difficult for nearly all students, on the basis of what has been taught. Here, we are concerned with assessment factors that can lead to misjudgments about students' opportunity to learn or student differences from "mainstream" expectations that have nothing to do with the skills being assessed.

When teachers are knowledgeable about how language, culture, and a host of other factors interact with assessment, they can take steps (and support their districts to take steps) to improve the ways assessments are designed, administered, scored, and interpreted.

Defining Good Assessment

We must arrange school learning so that it encourages more varied achievement goals than the narrow set of values often associated with competitive excellence and high standardized test scores at all costs. We must also learn to respect alternative ways for attaining excellence — for the sake of the group, for tradition, and for honor. Moreover, these changes must be made without doing violence to the fundamental academic mission of all schooling, that of providing students with the subject matter skills necessary to thrive, not merely survive. Finally, in the process of reform, we must not ask students to give up their cultural and ethnic identities.

Martin V. Covington, *The Will to Learn: A Guide for Motivating Young People,* 1998

Section III focuses on the criteria for high quality assessment. Five keys to quality are described with detailed explanations, examples, and classroom strategies. The following vignette provides an example of a situation in which the teacher has assessment questions and could benefit from understanding the keys to good assessment.

VIGNETTE:
MR. JONAH'S CLASSROOM ASSESSMENT CHALLENGE

It's October, and Mr. Jonah, an eighth-grade science teacher, is planning a unit of study on electrical energy. Last year's visit to the local power plant provided a real-life context for the conceptual understandings the students were developing and also served as a starting point for investigating the impact of electricity on the daily lives of the community. His assessment plan last year included keeping electrical energy learning logs, recording observations at the power plant, and drafting, then refining, questions to use while interviewing older members of the community. At the end of the unit, students presented their learning at an Energy Fair through oral presentations and written reports with models and charts.

This year, Mr. Jonah plans to involve his students in developing criteria for evaluating their learning logs and interview questions. He's also pondering ways to gather good information about several new students who have recently enrolled. He's had a difficult time interpreting their written work and is worried that they may be unable to complete the reports that were a central feature of last year's unit assessments. He's fairly sure that two of the students have very limited experience writing in English. Another has lived in this country all her life, but her writing, while lengthy, seems unorganized with lots of starts and stops and ideas that seem to disappear. A fourth student's writing is often unrelated to the topic. Mr. Jonah sees some difficult assessment challenges ahead.

THINGS TO CONSIDER:

- How can Mr. Jonah make sure that these students understand what's expected?

- How will he interpret and use the work they produce? What decisions can he make about adjusting instruction and judging their progress?

- Which forms of assessment will give them the best opportunity to show their learning while providing good evidence about the expectations he's set?

- How many samples of their work will he need to make confident judgments about their learning?

- What are potential barriers to good assessment: features of the assessment that contain biases or lead to mismeasurement?

Like Mr. Jonah, many educators struggle on a daily basis to determine what their students truly know and are able to do. They want to use their assessments to provide insights into the skill and knowledge of their students and to guide their next steps in classroom instruction and assessment. Before they can move their students toward improved knowledge and performance, educators must be able to assess effectively the work of their students.

Building on the groundwork laid in Sections I and II, this section provides a foundation for ensuring that any assessment we use to gain insights into the learning of our students is of high quality and adheres to standards for assessment defined in the work of Dr. Richard J. Stiggins, author of *Student-Involved Classroom Assessment, 3rd Edition*

(Merrill, 2001), and his colleague, Dr. Judith Arter, both of the Assessment Training Institute, Portland, OR. Dr. Arter was principal author of *Improving Classroom Assessment: A Toolkit for Professional Developers: Toolkit98,* a previous publication of the nation's regional educational laboratories (See Section VIII). In addition to information about each standard, which we are calling Keys to Quality Assessment, we add sociocultural implications. For each key we provide an example of cultural and linguistic issues to consider, guiding equity questions, and things to try for sharpening mastery of these keys to high quality.

FIVE KEYS TO
QUALITY ASSESSMENT*

KEY 1
What?
Clear and
Appropriate
Learning Targets

KEY 2
Why?
Clearly Focused
and Appropriate
Purpose

KEY 3
How?
Appropriate Match among
Targets, Purposes, and
Method of Assessment

KEY 4
How Much?
Sufficient Sampling of
Student Work to Make
Sound Inferences
about Learning

KEY 5
How Accurate?
Fairness and Freedom
from Biases that Distort
the Picture of Learning

---

* Source: Stiggins, R.J. (2001). *Student-Involved Classroom Assessment, 3rd Edition.* (Columbus, OH: Merrill, an imprint of Prentice Hall.) Adapted by permission.

Clear and Appropriate Learning Targets. *WHAT* do we want to assess? What knowledge, skills, reasoning ability, products, and habits of mind are essential for student success? Do students understand what is expected of them? Is the knowledge or skill that students are expected to demonstrate in the assessment influenced by cultural and linguistic factors?

The first key to good assessment is having clear and appropriate learning targets. A learning target is a chunk of content clear enough and specific enough to both define what to teach and to let students know what they need to learn. Learning targets can be generated by the teacher or by others outside the classroom. They are called many things: content standards, benchmarks, outcomes, learning goals, objectives, essential learning requirements, competencies, learning expectations, and more. Effective learning targets are characterized by a strong relationship between targets and state or district standards, a match between targets and a specified amount of curriculum, and a clarity that allows students and others to understand what the targets mean. If we're not clear about our learning targets, our students will not be clear in their responses. Our job is to define in crystal clear terms **what** is to be learned.

As we develop targets, it's important to consider:

- Is the target clear enough that a group of teachers would agree on the range of knowledge, skills, and performance implied by the target?

- Would they agree on what to teach and what to assess?

- Have we clearly defined our expectations not only for ourselves, **but for our students**? (Regional Educational Laboratories, 1998)

For example, it's easy to agree on a target like "communicates well," but what does this mean? What types of communication? In what contexts? Effective student learning targets are specific enough to enable everyone — teacher, student, and parent — to share the same understanding of what knowledge and skills demonstrate mastery.

But this requires just the right amount of specificity. For instance, as an appropriate classroom learning target, "geography of our state" is too broad — it's really a topic that's likely to have multiple targets within it — and could be a whole year course! By contrast, "the length of the Columbia River" is too narrow a target — not of high enough importance to warrant much teaching time (although this depends on your overall goals for student learning and what core knowledge is an essential foundation for additional learning).

Types of Learning Targets*

There are many different ways to categorize learning targets for students. Categorizing helps us thoroughly think through what we want students to know and be able to do (in other words, clarify targets) and helps us determine if we have a good mix of learning targets.

- **Knowledge and Understanding:** What facts do students know outright? What information can they retrieve? What do they understand? The assessment challenge is to develop knowledge and understanding targets that are at the heart of a discipline — those worth learning and assessing.

- **Reasoning Proficiency:** Can students analyze, categorize, and sort into component parts? Can they generalize and synthesize what they've learned? Can they evaluate and justify the worth of a process or decision? The assessment challenge for reasoning targets is to define the difference between doing these things well and doing them poorly.

- **Skills:** We have certain skills that we want students to master such as reading fluently, working productively in a group, making an oral presentation, speaking a foreign language, or designing an experiment. The assessment challenge for skills targets is to define, in clear words, what it means "to do something well."

- **Ability to Create Products:** Another kind of learning target is student-created products — tangible evidence that the student has mastered knowledge, reasoning, and specific production skills. Examples include a research paper, a wooden table, or artwork. The assessment challenge for product targets is to describe and define the characteristics or dimensions that make for a quality product.

- **Dispositions:** We also frequently care about student attitudes and habits of mind, including attitudes toward school, persistence, responsibility, flexibility, and desire to learn. The instructional challenge is to generate a classroom environment where students actively choose to engage in the learning and perform at their best. The assessment challenge is to define these and know how to use results to motivate students to want to learn.

---

*Source: Stiggins, R.J. (2001). *Student-Involved Classroom Assessment, 3rd Edition.* (Columbus, OH: Merrill, an imprint of Prentice Hall.) Adapted by permission.

VIGNETTE: THE STORY OF A MISUNDERSTOOD TARGET

In the example below, the teacher has a specific learning target in mind, but her students do not seem to be aware of what the teacher is looking for as she assesses them.

Ms. Schwartz is a high school English teacher. Her students are studying a novel. Periodically, as her students work through the novel, she asks questions in class. She uses this questioning as an informal assessment to gauge their understanding. During the questioning, the students give her very general answers; they do not provide details from the novel that reflect significant knowledge about the book.

As a means of checking their knowledge through another type of assessment, this week she gives her students an essay question. When she examines the results, she finds that students were able to make solid generalizations, but they still do not back up these generalizations with supporting details. Her conclusion, based on her two assessment processes, is that these students lack understanding of the novel either because they aren't reading the assignments or they read without comprehension. She is not sure what strategy she needs to use to get her students more deeply into the reading — or get them to read it at all! She decides to bring it up at the next grade-level meeting.

In her work session with other grade-level teachers, Ms. Schwartz discusses her concern about this lack of effort and skill to the other teachers. Several of the teachers begin to discuss the cultural background of many of the students in this class. Ms. Schwartz had not been aware that the students she teaches are from a culture that prizes communicating meaning with as few words as possible. If fact, in this culture, providing extensive detail is viewed as disrespectful of others, because it implies that the writer assumes that the audience can't "get it" without extra help. To be a powerful communicator in these cultures is to be able to communicate the gist of the idea or concept with as few words as possible.

THINGS TO CONSIDER

In the case above, the learning target was not explained to students. The teacher's unspoken expectation that clear understanding is characterized by a display of extensive detail is at odds with the definition of what it means to "communicate well" in their culture.

The underlying challenge for this teacher was not just to address the different operational definitions of demonstrating understanding, but to help students bridge between the communication patterns in their home/culture and the expectations in the classroom — to arm students with clear portraits of the learning target, and in so doing, enable them to select the appropriate communication pattern for the assessment.

Many times a target that we consider straightforward and clear is just the opposite. Unless we take the time to get to know our students and their personal context, we may incorrectly assess the level of our students' understanding.

Table 5: Reflective Questions for Key 1

Equity Questions	Some Implications for Action
Are my learning targets clear to **all** of my students?	Discussing your targets with other teachers may help you know if you are using strategies that are ineffective because of culture. Also, talk to your students about their assessments. If their response is not what you expected, ask them why.
Is my learning target important? To **all** of my students? Is it clear to my students and me **how** I will know when they achieve the target?	Ask yourself if you have helped students see how the target fits into the big picture. Connect the target with external expectations and life outside the classroom. What words and processes have you used to communicate your expectations?
Is there prior knowledge that can help my students connect to, and make meaning of, the learning targets?	Help students connect a given target with their experience. Give and ask for examples to clarify meaning and check for understanding. Use conceptual organizers (webs, concept maps) to convey the meaning of the target. Ask students to brainstorm what they know about the target.

THINGS TO TRY

Think of a learning target to improve
(i.e., "communicates well").

When you see this term or phrase, what does it tell you needs to be taught? Is it absolutely clear what you would need to teach?

Is it clear what would be assessed? What would students do to show their learning? When they are masters of the target, what would students know, be able to do, and create/demonstrate? What would you expect to see in students' behavior?

What could you add to the target statement to strengthen and clarify it for other teachers and your students?

Revised/Refined Learning Target:

- **An option for checking common meaning:** Invite a colleague to review your draft target for clarity and appropriateness. Do you share the same definition of the revised target and its importance to student success?

- **An option for student involvement:** When students complete the assignment for the target, have students rate the answers and look at differences and similarities in answers. Ask if some of the ideas are ones they might not have thought of, or if there are some that everyone agrees upon. This can be both an opportunity for insights into differences across cultures and a bridge to shared meaning within the context of the classroom.

Clearly Focused and Appropriate Purpose.
WHY are we assessing? How will the assessment information be used? By whom? To make what decisions? Are there cultural and linguistic expectations that might conflict with the intended purpose of the assessment?

The second key to good assessment is having a worthwhile purpose. Some assessments give students information about their own performance. Students use the results to decide what they'll study, how much to study, whether it's worth studying, what they're good at (or not), and how they might be able to earn their living as adults. Other assessments help teachers change and improve instruction. Still others give administrators, parents, and community members information about individual students or schools that they use in different ways. For example, parents may want to know how their own children are doing while state department officials may use statewide assessments to decide how to distribute resources.

In addition to providing useful information, good assessment does not harm or unduly frustrate our students. Assessment should not be so expensive, time-consuming, or painful that the negatives of the process outweigh the benefits. Ultimately, we want students to understand how they learn, how to evaluate their own performance, and how to undertake the learning necessary to improve their work.

Looking at the variety of users and uses also underscores the crucial importance of balancing large-scale assessments and high quality classroom assessments. After all, it is the day-to-day classroom assessments that most affect decisions made by teachers, parents, and students. What happens if classroom assessments are not well thought-out and executed?

VIGNETTE: THE WRITING CONFERENCE

The following example shows what can happen when a teacher is not clear about the purpose of an assessment.

Mrs. Albert is a seventh-grade language arts teacher. This week she is beginning a unit on essay writing. She has decided that she will help her students to develop their essays through writing conferences. The students will write three drafts on the same topic, and she will conference with them personally about each draft. On the first rough draft, she asks the students to focus on the main ideas for their paper. However, she cautions them to add enough detail so that she knows they can further develop the main topics.

One of her students, Nguyen, is looking forward to this conference. She used brainstorming to come up with her topics and then used clustering to group topics and put them in order. She is excited about the subject matter, and she knows that while she is still behind her class in the mechanics of English, she is very good at coming up with ideas.

When Mrs. Albert hands her paper back, the first thing she notices is all of the marks on the paper for spelling and grammar. In fact, there are so many errors marked on the paper that she is unable to focus on what Mrs. Albert is saying to her. When Mrs. Albert asks her if there are any questions, Nguyen quietly picks up her paper and returns to her seat.

THINGS TO CONSIDER

Using writing conferences to improve student writing is a wonderful tool in the classroom. It is a strategy that allows the teacher and the student to interact one-on-one about the student's work. However, because Mrs. Albert did not communicate to his students all that she would be assessing, this process failed Nguyen. Her pride in her work was gone within seconds. The dismay that Nguyen felt is common when a teacher's purpose changes or is miscommunicated. This causes students to feel confused and frustrated. It is vital that students understand the purpose for their work and that teachers carefully express and follow through on the information they give their students.

Before an assessment can be used to reflect the current capabilities of the students, it must be written and designed in such a way that students can respond effectively with the knowledge that they possess so that the results of the assessment have meaning and can be useful for decisionmaking. If the purpose of the above assignment was to determine how well students are able to express their ideas, then the conference should have focused on ideas. Nguyen was unprepared to discuss spelling and grammar conventions and may have, in fact, believed that she would be able to work on those parts of the paper later. She may have focused exclusively on ideas; therefore, an assessment of her spelling and grammar abilities is unlikely to show what she is truly able to do when she is prepared and tries her best in those areas.

Table 6: Reflective Questions for Key 2

Equity Questions	Some Implications for Action
Why do I use this assessment with my students?	Consider turning your assessment purposes into questions to clarify the kinds of decisions you wish to make on the basis of an assessment. Example: Has my focus on word choice resulted in more vivid words in my ELL students' oral and written stories? Is there a consistent pattern of errors in my students' mathematical problem solving? Which students can benefit from math lab?
What decision(s) will be made on the basis of this assessment? Are my students clear about how the assessment will be used?	Students need to know when assessment is intended primarily to let you and them adjust and improve and when there will be other users of the information. They need to know what kinds of decisions will be made, particularly when high stakes may be attached.
How can I make sure that users outside the classroom don't misuse assessment information about my students? For example, do the users of the information understand the validity issues posed by assessing the content learning of English language learners?	There are many different audiences for assessment information. It is important to consider what information to present and how to present it. Some assessments should be used exclusively within the classroom to promote learning and some should be shared. Users must realize that, for students whose language and/or background experience do not match those of the dominant group, inferences about those students may not be valid.
When do I use assessment activities solely to build student self-assessment skills? How do these occasions differ, if at all, from those in which I assess students to find out what they know and can do?	Helping students understand how they are assessed and allowing them to be a part of the process helps them understand expectations and learn to recognize how to improve their own performances. These are important skills, and research shows this process improves student motivation and achievement.

THINGS TO TRY

The list below was developed by a group of teachers seeking to define the major uses of assessment in their classrooms.

We want our assessments to

- show growth in students' work

- allow all students, including those of various cultural and linguistic backgrounds, to demonstrate what they are able to do

- promote creative and critical thinking and problem solving

- give insights into progress toward our targets

- enable students to manage their own learning

- help determine student grades

- communicate with parents

- provide information to improve instruction

- let us see where our students' work is in relation to standards of excellence

- help us evaluate the effectiveness of program, materials, and approaches

- enable students to show what they know and can do in a variety of ways

(Compiled from the work of teachers at Waialae Elementary School, Honolulu, and Garapan Elementary School, Saipan)

Select 2-3 items from the list that you believe match *YOUR* primary purposes for assessment, or feel free to add to the list. Compare and discuss your priorities with those of your colleagues, parents, students, or others.

My primary purposes for assessment

KEY 3

How?

Appropriate Match
Among Targets,
Purposes, & Method
of Assessment

Appropriate Match Among Targets, Purposes, and Method of Assessment. *HOW* will we assess the targeted learning? Which methods of assessment are most appropriate for each kind of target? Is the method used to address each target designed with consideration of the cultural and linguistic traits of the students?

The third key to high quality assessment is to match targets, purposes, and methods. Good assessment means choosing the best assessment method for the learning target and the population being assessed. Stiggins has provided us with a description of four methods of assessment (*Student-Centered Classroom Assessment, 2nd Edition,* 1997). Each method has strengths and provides insights into one or more kinds of targets. Each also has limitations for use with certain targets and varies in applicability to different purposes.

Assessment Methods

- **Selected Response:** The selected response method provides students with a set of possible answers from which to choose. Common selected response formats include multiple choice, true/false, and matching. In addition, we have included short answer formats here because, like selected response items, they require specific correct answers that can be scored yes/no or right/wrong. The strength of this method is its ability to establish whether students have the knowledge on which further learning can be built. It tends to match best with knowledge and reasoning targets. A limitation is that this method's frequent focus on vocabulary and sentence structure can be inordinately challenging for English language learners.

- **Essay:** This method generally involves using writing as the tool for demonstrating content knowledge, conceptual understanding, and reasoning. Typical formats include traditional content area essays and writing essays. The strength of this assessment method is that it requires students to pull together the bits and pieces that they have learned into a coherent written whole. Again, however, writing may not always be the best way for English language learners to demonstrate their content knowledge.

- **Performance Assessment:** Performance assessment is assessment based on observation and informed judgment. It focuses on what students can do with what they have learned. It generally falls into two categories: products and performance skills. Products include such things as posters, graphs, drawings, videos, models, projects, rebuilt engines, maps, diagrams, computer visuals, etc. When writing itself is the learning target, performance assessment is used to create products that demonstrate mastery of forms of writing such as narration, exposition, persuasion, and so forth. Performance skills that might be the focus of a performance assessment include oral presentations, plays, debates, songs, or lab skills. A strength of performance assessment is that it enables us to assess powerful learning that is often not well assessed using other methods. A limitation is that, without care, students might be asked to perform in contexts that are culturally unfamiliar.

- **Personal Communication:** This method offers us opportunities to view student learning by talking with, and listening to, students. This method helps to uncover student misconceptions, as well as confirm their reasoning, attitudes, and behaviors. Strategies for this method might include asking questions, interviewing, conferencing, discussing, and listening for *their* questions. The strength of this method is that it often allows students to express knowledge without having to worry about the mechanics of writing. Personal communication is often an appropriate way for teachers to follow up and probe beyond the learning revealed in products and performances. A limitation in this method is, again, cultural — do we interpret nonverbal and interactional information correctly?

VIGNETTE: MR. WASHINGTON'S STORY:
"WHY DON'T THE GIRLS SPEAK?"

In his ninth-grade geometry classroom, Mr. Washington has just started a new unit on circumference and diameter. He decides to assess students' prior knowledge of the topic by asking the class several questions and writing their answers on an overhead entitled K-W-L. K is for what students already know, W is for what they want to know, and L is for what they will learn by the end of the unit. While he asks questions and calls on the students who raise their hands, he makes notes about who answers in his grade book.

At the end of class, he looks at his notes and realizes that almost all of the answers came from the boys in his class. He is dismayed that the girls do not seem to know anything about the topic.

MAKING ASSESSMENT WORK FOR EVERYONE

THINGS TO CONSIDER

Simply asking questions of the whole class and calling on students who raise their hands may not always be the best way to assess what students know. Researchers have frequently found that boys tend to put their hands up faster than girls do when they are asked a question. Many girls do not raise their hands until they have organized their thoughts, often not until after a boy has already answered. Or something else entirely may have been going on in Mr. Washington's class to create bias that he was not aware of. Teachers need to be aware of these potential gender differences, as well as other sources of bias, in order to create mechanisms to prevent them from happening when they create assessments.

Perhaps allowing everyone to share with a neighbor while he walked around the class and made observations or allowing everyone to write their prior knowledge on note cards would have given Mr. Washington a better sense of the class's prior knowledge and interest level. Finding the appropriate match between target learning, purpose, and method can be challenging but is an important key to effective student assessment.

DID YOU KNOW?

Studies have shown that teachers typically wait only nine-tenths of a second for students to answer questions. This rapid pace favors males, as males are more likely to jump into classroom conversations first. If teachers increase wait time to three to five seconds, it will give girls and other students more of a chance to participate. The wait time also allows for more right answers and more creative answers. Research also shows that the time between a student's answer and the teacher's reaction to that answer is only a split second. Increasing this second wait time will give the teacher a better opportunity to respond more meaningfully to girls' contributions. (For more information about gender issues in the classroom, see the Web site: www.girlscount.org)

Table 7: Reflective Questions for Key 3

Equity Questions	Some Implications for Action
As I think about a specific assessment I've given recently, was there a good match between my purpose, the kind of learning target, and the assessment method? Would I change anything?	Thoughtful reflection on your own practice is one of the most effective ways to make changes that will help your students and give you better information. As you continually question whether you chose the best assessment methods for your targets and purposes, your assessments will improve.
Do I use a good mix of methods? Are there any methods that I use very infrequently? Why?	Some students will respond to some methods better than others will. In particular, linguistic or cultural issues may make some methods more effective than others. It is a good idea to use a wide variety of methods throughout your teaching.
Which methods might not be effective for English language learners? Why?	Assessments that rely heavily on reading and writing English will be challenging for English language learners. Using them is fine if you are assessing English language development. If you are assessing for other content areas, however, students may know much more than they are able to express. Helpful guidelines may be to provide many opportunities for clarifying instructions and to create prompts that are easy to read and stated in simple syntax.

THINGS TO TRY

Think of a learning target. (For example, "Knows the Causes of the Civil War")

Learning Target:

How would you normally assess this target (selected response, essay, performance assessment, or personal communication)? What kind of information about the students' knowledge of this target would this assessment give?

How?   *What information:*

Choose an assessment method that you do not normally use. What kind of information about the students' knowledge of this target would this assessment give?

How?   *What information:*

An option for checking common understanding: Discuss your ideas with colleagues. They may have different ideas about how to best match up targets, purposes, and methods. Discuss your results with students to see if they agree with your choice of methods and the types of information you can gather from the assessment.

KEY 4

How Much?

Sufficient
Sampling of
Student Work to
Make Sound
Inferences
About Learning

Sufficient Sampling of Student Work to Make Sound Inferences About Learning. *HOW MUCH* will we collect? Do we have enough varied samples of student work to make good judgments about current proficiency related to the target learning? Have we chosen sufficient and varied assessment examples that allow the students to take advantage of their cultural and linguistic strengths?

Assessment is a broad term that should refer to more than a single test or a single sample of work. To be able to assess accurately what a student knows and is able to do for any given learning target, teachers should analyze enough samples to make confident inferences about student learning. In fact, larger, more complex learning targets may require more samples. For instance, a single assessment such as a single sample of writing or a single math problem would not enable a teacher to infer writing or problem-solving competence. Much evidence would need to be gathered to draw confident conclusions.

In addition to choosing a sufficient number of samples, a teacher should also consider the ways culture and language influence student performance. For example, although we frequently think of selected response items as the way to test for knowledge, perhaps students can exhibit the same knowledge through visuals, webs, maps, drawings, or graphs. Perhaps some work can be produced collaboratively. Depending on the target, samples from multiple occasions and use of different methods help contribute to a clear picture of student performance. A good assessment plan offers a representative sampling from a variety of tasks that is large enough to permit the teacher to make accurate inferences about student learning.

VIGNETTE: MINERS AND THE GOLD RUSH

In the vignette below, a teacher uses only one assessment to assess student learning and finds that he may not have the information he needs.

Mr. Salena, a fourth-grade teacher, has developed a unit called the "Story of the Gold Rush." He and his students have spent weeks studying the routes to the California Gold Country, the supplies needed by the early settlers, and the impact of the Gold Rush on the population of California. They have read books and examined artifacts from the time period. Finally, Mr. Salena has asked his students to write a story from the viewpoint of a miner.

When Mr. Salena reads the answers of the students, he is very disappointed in their stories. They reveal very little about the journey to California; on the other hand, they are unusually creative, and many of the stories are actually parables that present lessons in life to the reader. Mr. Salena thought he had been very clear in explaining to the students that he wanted a story about the Gold Rush. He is disappointed that he is going to have to reteach the material and develop a new assessment.

THINGS TO CONSIDER

When Mr. Salena made this assignment, he was trying to garner the interest of his students as well as assess their knowledge about the California Gold Rush. But he failed to consider that his students might see this assignment from the viewpoint of their culture rather than as a social studies project. In the culture of his students, storytelling is used as a tool of communicating expectations, religion, and etiquette to children; stories are used to communicate ideas and concepts, not facts. The children did tell stories; however, they created stories that fit their experiences with storytelling, not the stories that Mr. Salena expected.

Because this is a single assessment and because the students have responded in a manner he didn't expect, Mr. Salena does not have a clear idea of the depth of understanding that his students have about the Gold Rush or its impact on California. In reality, his students may know much more about the Gold Rush than they have displayed in their assessment, but it is impossible to know without additional samples. If this project was one of several assessments, he would have a clearer vision of his students' knowledge.

These stories do serve a purpose that Mr. Salena did not intend. They have provided him with an opportunity to get to know more about the way his students think, and therefore how they learn. Though this one event will not provide him with all the information he needs, it will help him to know about his students' sociocultural perspectives and strengths and how these should figure into future assessment plans. These stories might also provide a bridge to create an environment of sharing and interest that will help him in future assessments.

Table 8: Reflective Questions for Key 4

Equity Questions	Some Implications for Action
Do I remember a time when I felt uncomfortable because a decision was made based on too little information?	This is an indication that multiple assessment opportunities are important. A student could be sick, tired, or distracted on any given day, so that even if the assessment was created perfectly, they may not perform to the best of their abilities. We certainly want to give them another chance.
Are my students given multiple opportunities to show what they have learned, and through multiple kinds of assessments?	For students from nondominant language and cultural backgrounds, getting an adequate sample of performance is a challenge because it is likely that without significant changes, many assessments will yield less information about these students than they do for "mainstream" students.

MAKING ASSESSMENT WORK FOR EVERYONE

THINGS TO TRY

Below is the start of a plan for gathering samples of student work related to a reading standard. After examining the standard, its key components, and the beginning of the plan, add your ideas about additional sources of evidence that will provide a good sampling of information about student progress toward the standard.

Reading Standard	Making Sense of Standards	Key Features of the Standard	Performance Indicators
Read a range of literary and informative texts for a variety of purposes	"Range" is the ability to read a wide variety of texts for a variety of purposes. Reading a range of texts helps students deepen their knowledge of reading and of their world.	Types of text: • Literary • Informative • Functional Purposes: • Literary experience • Gain information • Perform a task	There is evidence of breadth. The student has read: • At least 25 books • A balance of literary and non-literary works • At least 3 different genres or modes • At least 5 different authors

(Adapted from National Council of Teachers of English, 1996)

Sampling Plan

Preliminary list of assessment sources for collecting samples:

✓ Reading interview

✓ Booklist/log

✓

✓

✓

Some Cultural and Linguistic Considerations

How will students contribute to the evidence of their reading range?

What are some texts that reflect the language and culture of your students?

What sources in the family and community can contribute to the picture of students' reading range?

Evaluate Your Plan: Does this plan ensure that you'll gather enough information of the right kind, so you can draw confident conclusions about student achievement? What else would you want to know, and what evidence would you need?

KEY 5 **How Accurate?** Fairness and Freedom from Biases that Distort the Picture of Learning

Fairness and Freedom From Biases That Distort the Picture of Learning. *HOW ACCURATE* are the assessments? Do they really assess what we think they're assessing? Is there anything about the way a target is assessed that masks the true learning of a student or group of students? Do we know the strengths that students bring to learning and use those strengths in our assessments?

Even when we design our assessments so that we know exactly what we are assessing and why we are assessing, we've picked just the right way to assess these things, and we know how much to assess; unfortunately, it's still possible to end up with assessments that don't work — for your purposes and/or for your students. Have you ever tried to engage students in an instructional activity and found that they did not learn what you expected them to learn? The instructions weren't clear, there wasn't enough time, students didn't have all the prerequisite skills, or students did not react to the learning sequence the way you envisioned they would.

The same thing can happen in assessment. These "things that go wrong" are called sources of mismeasurement, bias and distortion, or invalidity. The result is that the information from the assessment doesn't mean what we think it means. Such biases can have serious consequences because a grade or certification of competence is only as good as the assessments upon which it is based. What happens if the ability to read the instructions interferes with a student's ability to demonstrate math skills? Or, the necessity to write a response interferes with how well a student can demonstrate the skills needed to set up a scientific experiment? These are serious potential sources of bias and distortion.

When the first four keys are addressed equitably, bias and distortion can be limited. However, as can be seen from the questions and vignettes above, any assessment can contain sources of bias and distortion, not just the so called "objective" instruments. We tend to think of standardized tests as containing the greatest bias and distortion in the classroom because these assessments do not take into account students' experiences, nor do they often correspond closely with local curricula. However, as can be seen from the questions above, any assessment can create bias and distortion, not just objective instruments. The following table indicates some of the most common sources of bias and distortion.

Table 9: Possible Sources of Bias and Distortion in Student Assessments

Sources related to the assessment itself	• Too much reading or writing on an assessment designed to assess something besides reading or writing • Unnecessarily difficult or unfamiliar vocabulary used in instructions • Assessment in a language that is unfamiliar to the student • An assessment method that doesn't allow students with different learning styles to do their best • Unclear instructions • Attempts to make a problem more "real-life" that result in a context more familiar to some groups of students than others • Rater bias or untrained raters for performance assessment • Performance criteria that don't cover the most important aspects of performance or that are vague • Irrelevant clues to the right answer, more than one right answer, or unnecessarily convoluted questions on multiple choice tests • Narrowly defined criteria that recognize only one way to be excellent
Sources related to the student	• Student is tired, hungry, sick, or distracted for some other reason • Student is not used to the format, timing, or other logistics of the testing situation
Sources related to the environment	• Noisy or distracting environment • Assessment administrator who projects a negative attitude toward the assessment

VIGNETTE:
MS. PONCIANA'S STORY: "SAVING THE TURTLES"

Ms. Ponciana and her students are in the midst of a unit that is structured around this core question: How can we preserve and care for turtles found on our reef and encourage others to do the same? One of the targets for this unit is to strengthen students' knowledge of turtle habitat and how it's changing as a result of human use of the reef environment. Her hope is to also move her students to care deeply about the preservation of the turtle and, because of that caring, to be disposed to use their knowledge to guide the actions they take themselves.

It is early in the unit, and Ms. Ponciana wants to gauge the current attitude of her students toward the unit topic. She has been using personal communication — questions that she's given small work groups to discuss and report — as the method of gathering initial information about student knowledge of, and disposition toward, endangered turtles.

But, as she focuses in on one group, she realizes that there's a student who has not spoken at all. Rowena and her cousin, Charlie, are newcomers from the Federated States of Micronesia. He's taking part. Rowena appears to be disengaged from the discussion. In the midst of the discussion, she is silent. Ms. Ponciana is frustrated. Surely Rowena, who comes from an island where turtles are greatly valued, has ideas to add to the group's work. Why won't Rowena contribute?

THINGS TO CONSIDER

Judging silence as disinterest or lack of knowledge can result in biased assessment. Different cultures have different expectations of behavior, communication, and respectful action that encourage different behaviors. For example, in the scenario above, Charlie and Rowena are from a culture where females do not speak when they are in a group with a male relative. Grouped with other girls or in a mixed group without a male relative present, Rowena would have the opportunity to express her ideas during the discussion. If Ms. Ponciana had changed the composition of the work groups in the classroom, Rowena would have been able to express herself.

DID YOU KNOW?

Grouping by gender can play a role in assessment accuracy in settings where the expectations and experiences of girls result in limited participation. For example, there is evidence from recent efforts to encourage more girls to go into mathematics and science that, when grouped together for hands-on science activities, the males in the group tend to dominate and girls' contributions are little recognized.

Table 10: Reflective Questions for Key 5

Equity Questions	Some Implications for Action
If the target is an academic skill or concept, can it be separated from the student's language as a target of assessment? Do I use words in defining the learning targets that are outside the experience of some of my students or that might have different meanings for them?	Consider that some targets may be language-dependent. Second-language learners may function differently vis-à-vis the target from native speakers. Check for multiple meanings of key words in your targets — ask students, colleagues, community and family members for help. Stick to the simplest language that can convey clearly the meaning of your targets.
How does culture impact assessment methods?	Like language, culture can have a profound effect on assessment results. Teachers need to be aware of the norms for the different cultures in their classes, so that they do not create assessments that will confuse or frustrate students. Some students may respond better through group work, demonstrations, or exhibitions versus paper and pencil tasks, and some choice over when they will show what they know.
Do I know enough about my students' cultures and the strengths they bring to learning?	Invite families, cultural organizations, and students themselves to describe and give examples of the strengths in their culture.
Am I unconsciously biased against particular students because of the ways they use language, their dialect, or their pronunciation?	Try to look beyond the words of the students and focus on what they are communicating. Collect multiple papers from ELLs and compare them to find trends and traits. Use this information to help in assisting the students and in determining when the student has more knowledge that his/her paper reveals.

THINGS TO TRY

Think of a time when you were not able to get the information you needed from an assessment.

Your assessment:

What were the possible biases or sources of mismeasurement on this assessment?

What do you think went wrong, and how do you think you could change your assessment in order to get the information you need?

Summary

Think back to Mr. Jonah's classroom. He was concerned about new students whose writing was very limited or appeared rambling and unorganized. A simple diagnosis of "having problems" is the common reaction of most teachers; however, if we take the time to look at the students, we find that there are sometimes other issues that affect student success. We should always ask ourselves if there are cultural or linguistic expectations and patterns that result in students failing to do well on an assessment. Perhaps the topic of the writing is outside their experience. Perhaps it's the need for expressing knowledge in written form when having little mastery of English writing skills is the barrier. Mr. Jonah's written science report requirement may actually mask the learning of the two students who are English language learners. Requiring an essay written in English will not give accurate information about the science targets if the students do not have the necessary vocabulary and writing skills. Though it may be true that a child may be slow to develop writing skills, it is still important for us to look at the whole picture of the student.

For us, good assessment is about more than creating solid evidence of the status of student work. Although we must pay attention to the quality of our assessments, we must also attend to the impact assessments have on student motivation to learn. Good assessment, and the feedback that it can provide, leads to improved instruction and opportunities for students to learn.

Good assessment at any level is characterized by

KEY 1

What?

Clear & Appropriate Learning Targets

Key 1: Clear and Appropriate Learning Targets.
WHAT do we want to assess? What knowledge, skills, reasoning ability, products, and habits of mind are essential for student success? Do students understand what is expected of them? Is the knowledge or skill that students are expected to demonstrate for the assessment influenced by cultural and linguistic issues?

KEY 2

Why?

Clearly Focused & Appropriate Purpose

Key 2: Clearly Focused and Appropriate Purpose.
WHY are we assessing? How will the assessment information be used? By whom? To make what decisions? Will the cultural and linguistic traits of the user interfere with the intended purpose of the assessment?

KEY 3 **How?** Appropriate Match Among Targets, Purposes, and Method of Assessment	**Key 3: Appropriate Match Among Targets, Purposes, and Method of Assessment.** *HOW* will we assess the targeted learning? Which methods of assessment are most appropriate for each kind of target? Is the method used to address each target designed with consideration of the cultural and linguistic traits of the students?
KEY 4 **How Much?** Sufficient Sampling of Student Work to Make Sound Inferences About Learning	**Key 4: Sufficient Sampling of Student Work to Make Sound Inferences About Learning.** *HOW MUCH* will we collect? Do we have enough varied samples of student work to make good judgments about current proficiency related to the target learning? Have we chosen sufficient and varied assessment examples that allow the students to take advantage of their cultural and linguistic strengths?
KEY 5 **How Accurate?** Fairness and Freedom from Biases that Distort the Picture of Learning	**Key 5: Fairness and Freedom From Biases That Distort the Picture of Learning.** *HOW ACCURATE* are the assessments? Do they really assess what we think they're assessing? Is there anything about the way a target is assessed that masks the true learning of a student or group of students? Do we know the strengths that students bring to learning and use those strengths in our assessments?

Using Students' Cultural and Linguistic Strengths to Build Good Assessments

We learn ... primarily by building on our strengths. It is important for teachers to encourage students to see what has potential, what has strength, what can be developed.

Donald Murray,
A Writer Teaches Writing, 1985

The previous sections built the rationale for equitable assessments, and Sections IV and V are "how-to" oriented. Section IV describes how to consider the five keys of good assessment and students' strengths in designing and interpreting assessments. There are examples from a variety of schools and cultures as well as practical steps for individual settings. The following cartoon shows how difficult it can often be to know what all students are thinking and learning.

Is this your classroom reality?

THINGS TO CONSIDER

- What do you see?

- What's happening here?

- Where do the students' varied mental pictures come from?

- Have you been in a situation where you weren't sure that students were all seeing and hearing your lesson in the same way?

- How can we understand what they see and understand?

- As the teacher tries to build assessments around her students' strengths, what challenges does she face?

Now, think about the young people we work with each day. Understanding students' cultural and linguistic backgrounds can give clues to what to observe and the kinds of questions to ask in order to clarify how they are interpreting lessons. Even within a single culture or language group, there is great variation among students. Each student brings unique knowledge, goals, ways of learning and expressing what's been learned into the classroom. To make the most of students' assets, educators need to know what these assets are!

The previous sections introduced the concept of sociocultural and linguistic impacts on assessments and the keys to quality assessment. This section focuses on strategies for building good assessments based on the keys and student strengths.

MAKING ASSESSMENT WORK FOR EVERYONE

A CAUTION

As you read the "how-to" suggestions below, please keep in mind that we are not suggesting in any way that standards be lowered for students with different backgrounds. Rather, we're holding students to the same high standards, but assessing them more accurately. We recognize that their developmental profiles may vary as a result of differences in language, culture, race, gender, and socioeconomic level.

In order to create and use high quality assessments in the classroom, educators should begin with student strengths and should follow the keys outlined in Section III:

Key 1: Clear and appropriate learning targets

Key 2: Clearly focused and appropriate purpose

Key 3: Appropriate match among targets, purposes, and method of assessment

Key 4: Sufficient sampling of student work to make sound inferences about learning

Key 5: Fairness and freedom from biases that distort the picture of learning

Key 5 is particularly important because, unfortunately, even when Keys 1-4 are done correctly, bias can still creep into assessment. Creating or "fixing" those assessments to make them work for everyone involves many decisions about the assessment tasks themselves. This section offers "how-to" suggestions and examples for making those decisions.

How to Make Assessment Work for Everyone: Connecting Assessments to Student Culture and Experience

How do culture, language, and environment influence students' different ways of knowing and the kinds of knowledge they have? There are obvious differences based on the environments in which students have been raised. Students who have lived in cold, mountainous areas will likely know about particular animals that are adapted to that kind of habitat. Students from a Pacific island cannot be expected to have the same firsthand knowledge. Their knowledge base is more likely to include ways of conserving precious water where there are few trees and intense heat, the varieties of root foods that can survive the onslaught of a typhoon, and where and when to catch particular kinds of fish. Students raised in an urban environment may have little firsthand knowledge of rural farm animals, coming to school with much more experience of mass transit and large hospitals, for example. One obvious assessment implication has to do with the choice of assessment tasks developed to elicit information about learning and how teachers interpret "incorrect" responses.

Consider the following strategies to help design and improve assessments:

- Show the assessment question, task, or assignment, as well as proposed scoring criteria, to teachers who have knowledge and experience with the culture of your students

- Also, share your assessments with teachers who have had long experience on the campus and discuss potential student responses

- If you have teachers of English language learners in your school setting, invite them to take a "critical friends" look at your draft assessments and suggest ways to more fully call upon students' culture and experiences

- Ask former students to review your assessment questions, tasks, and criteria for potential context biases and misunderstandings

- Ask parent volunteer(s) to review your assessments for things that might be unfamiliar or unclear to students

- Ask current students to explain the reasons for their answers to gauge their understanding of the assessment

VIGNETTE: THE BIRDS

This example from Toolkit98 *by the Regional Educational Laboratories shows what a difference student background can make in student responses.*

Test Item: Four birds were sitting on a fence. A farmer threw a stone that hit one of the birds. How many birds were left on the fence?

Item developers expected the mathematical answer 3. Farm children knew that if there was a stone thrown toward the fence, no matter how many birds were hit, ALL would fly away. Based on their experience, their (correct!) answer was 0.

THINGS TO CONSIDER

Student knowledge base and life experience is a significant strength that we, as educators, need to capitalize on. At the same time, we must realize that students do not all come with the same experiences. Do you use test questions similar to the one above? Are you confident that all your students interpret your test items in the same way?

The ways to connect assessment with students' culture and experience are as varied as the students in any classroom. One approach that has been successful in a number of different settings is contextualizing performance tasks within the realities of students' lives outside the classroom. When we contextualize performance tasks, we create assessment activities and questions that reflect the culture and background of our students. For example, in a rural setting, a reading comprehension passage about farm activities may be appropriate.

How to Make Assessment Work for Everyone: Ensuring Diversity in the Ways Students Can Respond

One way to assure that assessment accurately portrays learning is to offer students choices that enable them to call on their strengths to best show their knowledge and skills. Keeping the target clearly focused, students can be offered choices in

- the tasks to which they respond;

- the ways in which they respond (orally, in writing, with visuals, etc.);

- the language in which they respond;

- when they want to respond, based on when they feel ready;

- whether the assessment is presented to them orally or in writing; and

- whether they may seek input from their peers and then refine their work.

It's especially important to clarify for students the assessment criteria and expectations. What does "respond" mean? Do all students have to contribute to class discussions for them to "participate" in learning? Is it important for students to present their work in front of the group or class? Is it OK for a student to let others share his/her work? Does each student need to take a turn reporting? Leading a group? Participating in learning is an area that can be a minefield for students — and for teachers.

Part of the challenge is to clearly separate "participation" as a target in and of itself from participation to gauge knowledge or skills. If the latter, then valid assessment requires allowing students varied, culturally appropriate ways to participate.

Given the cultural and linguistic richness that students bring to learning, it's important to offer a variety of ways for students to demonstrate their progress and achievement. Assessments may be chosen or designed by way of learning styles, multiple modalities, or multiple intelligences, among others, as long as these variations enhance ability to obtain accurate measurements of what students know and can do.

VIGNETTE: THE CIRCULATORY SYSTEM

One useful way of thinking about ways for students to show what's been learned is to consider multiple intelligences as vehicles for approaching learning and ways to display that learning in assessment. Intelligences can be tapped to develop or select performance tasks. Remember that almost all of these ways of showing learning do not operate in isolation from one another. Several are often combined with others as students are creating products and performances.

The following example shows how a teacher who applies the research on multiple intelligences in her teaching has given her students a variety of ways to demonstrate what they've learned.

To help her English language learners master some key vocabulary (and concepts) about the circulatory system, Ms. Thomas has her students make small posters — each with one of the key terms. One group of students becomes the system itself, physically positioning themselves around the room, each holding one of the posters. The other group of students is the blood, circulating through the system and passing key components on their journey. As the "blood" moves through the system, the students in this group call out the name of each component as they pass by. To acknowledge success, the student holding the poster in question raises it in the air for all to see. Students learn the functions of the various components, and their journey focuses on describing what each component of the circulatory system contributes.

THINGS TO CONSIDER

This activity utilizes visual-spatial, bodily kinesthetic, interpersonal, and naturalist intelligences to help the students learn vocabulary about the circulatory system. Is this typically the way teachers approach teaching vocabulary? What would be the positive and negative aspects of assessing in this way? Think about your classroom; do you have students who have a preference for a specific kind of assessment? Are there ways that you can use assessments that involve multiple intelligences?

Further, think about when you allow choice with your own students. Are some responses "better" than others? Why do you feel that this is so? What is the strength of each response? How could you, as a teacher, help each of the students above improve and build their own strengths?

In analyzing the various ways students can respond, we should also consider the use of time. Rigid time limits on classroom assessment lead to questions about the purpose of the assessment. *Is it to gain accurate information about learning? Or is it to see who comes up with an answer fastest?* When students who are bridging languages and culture are faced with time limits, the accuracy of the assessment can be seriously compromised. When the target is one that is time dependent — like the task that firefighters face when responding to a blazing home — then, of course, time is a major factor. But for students who may well understand or be able to produce a high quality product given additional time, flexibility is an essential option for good assessment.

How to Make Assessment Work for Everyone: Ensuring Clear Criteria

The criteria that educators utilize when assessing student performance are a significant part of assessment. As in the above examples, cultural and linguistic factors play a role. For students from different backgrounds, certain criteria may not make sense and may make it difficult for them to know how to improve their work.

Useful criteria make learning targets clear for all of us — students, teachers, and parents — assuring that the first key to good assessment is in place. Our concern is that criteria that may seem clear and obvious to some students — and to us — may be very fuzzy for students from language and cultural minorities. In this case, our second key to quality, knowing the users of assessments and assuring that our purpose is clear to all, will not be met. For all students, the keys to good assessment should be used and an emphasis on clear and appropriate learning targets and clear and appropriate purposes should result in clear and appropriate criteria.

Criteria are clearest when students are involved in developing, trying out, and refining them. One strategy for involving students in developing criteria as well as for making meaning of criteria is to help them see criteria in the world around them. There are four simple steps teachers can go through with students to help them influence and understand how their work will be assessed (adapted from Gregory, Cameron, & Davies, 1997).

1. Students should brainstorm all the possible attributes of any given assignment.

2. Students should sort the subsequent lists of attributes into like responses, then create and label categories. The class should discuss whether some of the things on the list are really personal preferences rather than required components. Each category may become a trait.

3. For each trait, the class should brainstorm what constitutes high, medium, and low performance on the trait. This forms a rubric made of criteria that can be used to score student performance, indicating strengths and areas for improvement.

4. The class should try out the criteria with work samples, and then add, revise, and refine as needed.

Even when there's an existing scoring guide or rubric, time spent helping ALL students understand criteria will pay off in improved performance.

When students are encouraged to brainstorm traits and to define high quality for themselves, the result is often healthy discussion about different interpretations of quality. These differences that are revealed in the brainstorming and discussions are both insights for the teacher and ways to help all students come to a better understanding of the particular learning target.

VIGNETTE: THE SUBSTITUTE

The following example shows how students can be involved in the creation of criteria (Culham, 1999). The teacher in the vignette uses the steps listed above.

Ms. Nelson is preparing the students in her Brooklyn math classes for work on problem solving. In the next few weeks, students will be expected to work on several different complex, multifaceted problems. She plans to assess their results using the following criteria or traits: conceptual understanding, strategies and reasoning, computation and execution, insights, and communication. She has rubrics for these traits so that students can see where to improve, but she is afraid that if she just shows the rubrics to her students, they will be intimidated and confused.

She decides that before she talks about problem solving, she needs to do more to help her students understand scoring rubrics in general. She wants to emphasize that life is filled with things that can be described and evaluated according to traits. People make these kinds of assessments all the time. Further, she wants her students to see that identifying traits is a way to break something into parts, each of which can be addressed individually, ultimately leading to improved performance overall. She decides to have students develop their own rubric for something very familiar to them: behavior while a substitute is in the room.

This is the scoring rubric that the class develops:

5   *The class's behavior was so wonderful that the substitute would be tickled and delighted to come back to our classroom to substitute again. The students (with maybe one or two exceptions):*
- *Lined up, entered quietly, and went directly to their seats*
- *Had needed materials out and ready*
- *Looked at the speaker, especially the teacher when s/he was teaching*
- *Were quiet, polite, and responsible in dealing with the teacher AND one another*
- *Used class time wisely*

3   *The class's behavior was average. Some times were better than others. More than a few students needed reminders.*
- *The students may have lined up and entered noisily, but quieted down after entering the classroom or being reminded once*
- *Most had materials ready; some did not*
- *More than a few students needed reminders to stop talking when they should have been listening*
- *Some students wasted class time or needed reminders to get back on track*

1   *The class's behavior was so horrid that the substitute would be delighted to NEVER come back to our classroom.*
- *Lining up and entering the room was noisy and chaotic*
- *Few students had materials out and ready*
- *Many students were noisy or inattentive when the teacher was teaching*
- *There were many incidents of students being loud, rude, and/or irresponsible*
- *Very few students used class time wisely*

After discussing and laughing with her students about the above rubric, Ms. Nelson feels more confident about the task of introducing her rubrics for mathematical problem solving. At the same time, she knows further discussion will be necessary to ensure that all of her students understand them.

THINGS TO CONSIDER

If students do not understand how their performance is being scored, it will be difficult for them to know what to do in order to improve. Do all of your students agree on what "good" looks like? Do they understand what the scoring or grading system means? For example, students may not understand the difference between *usually*, *sometimes*, and *little*. Similarly, with many points on a scale, it becomes difficult for teachers and students to have a clear picture of the improvements needed in a piece of work in order to receive a higher score. On a 20-point scale, what's the difference between a 13 and a 14? What does the student do differently next time? Moreover, does the rubric assess what you want it to assess? For instance, a focus on the amount of information may not be appropriate. Does a student whose essay provides *four* major causes of the Civil War demonstrate lesser achievement than a student who assembles *seven* trivial facts? In improving student learning, the way performance is scored can be as significant as the assessment itself. Some rubrics help students easily see what to do to improve while others leave them confused.

Ultimately, we hope students will learn to assess their own work. The process of discussing criteria and then using the criteria to score their own work samples can be a powerful learning experience, helping students to take more responsibility for their own learning. However, not all students from all cultural backgrounds are prepared for, or comfortable with, such levels of self-reflection. Estrin and Nelson-Barber (1995) offer the following list of questions for educators to consider as they develop criteria and assessment plans:

- Are children asked to evaluate themselves verbally outside of school?

- When is it acceptable for a person to claim to have done something well?

- When is it all right for a student to evaluate his or her own work positively?

  — One-on-one with a teacher?

  — With a parent?

  — With a peer?

  — With an older/younger sibling?

- Is it permissible for a student to compare himself/herself to a peer in terms of achievement or performance?

- Is it permissible for a student to compare himself/herself to an external standard?

- How do children know they are getting better at doing something?

- Under what circumstances do people consciously engage in reflection in your setting?

- Under what circumstances do people set goals for the future?

How to Make Assessment Work for Everyone: Balancing Individual and Cooperative Assessments

We want to match our methods of assessment to students' strengths and experience, as well as help students stretch beyond their own comfort zones. As noted earlier, some students are naturally more focused on the success of the group while others are more focused on their individual success. In order to help those students who have to learn to navigate between the expectations of home and school cultures, teachers will need to carefully explore strategies. But it would be beneficial for students whose culture matches that of the school to also learn new ways of participating in assessment. Here are some ideas for addressing both sets of students' needs.

Group work can be configured to provide opportunities for both cooperative and individual effort. The key is to balance both. When tasks are truly collaborative, students may:

- Help each other figure out how to approach or complete the task (or parts of the task)

- Figure out how to share limited resources (e.g., one copy of a newspaper clipping that everyone needs to read)

- Take over for another who can't complete his/her share of the task for some reason

- Express joint ownership of the completed task (e.g., through the way they present or illustrate their results)

While collaborative tasks necessarily require a give and take, they can also be designed to require individual reflection and self-assessment related to progress, challenges, contributions to the group, and so forth. To further stretch students beyond their current strengths, teachers may create activities in which students:

- Combine individual and group assessments into extended tasks including informal assessment of students' entering knowledge bases with cooperative strategies like KWL (what we know about the topic, what we want to know more about, what we learned about the topic), individually web or list things they know about the topic; write in their journal, and so forth.

- Include self-assessments and peer reviews that lead to revision and refinement.

- Document their individual contributions to the overall effort.

- Select pieces of work that are included as evidence of individual learning.

VIGNETTE: MAKING UP LOST TIME

The example below (adapted from work by Sablan, 1994), shows how a balance between cooperative and individual assignments can be achieved.

After a series of storms disrupts the school year, a teacher comes up with the following lesson. It includes opportunities for both collaborative and individual work.

MAKING ASSESSMENT WORK FOR EVERYONE

Setting and Role: *This year's storms have closed your district's schools for several weeks. You are part of a team of students investigating possible actions to complete the school year. It's now February 2, and the final plan is expected to be implemented on March 1.*

Goal or Challenge: *Students must complete 180 days of school to meet state requirements. The proposal currently being circulated would extend classes into July. The Director of Education would like to be able to complete the school year without adding extra days. Your challenge is to investigate the state requirements and come up with two or more alternative plans for meeting the required 180 days by June 18.*

Product/Performance and Purpose: *Create and present a plan to the Director and the School-Community Council at their next meeting. To prepare for the meeting:*
- *Individually, investigate and prepare two or more alternative plans for meeting the required 180 days by June 18. Please refer to state and board of education policies.*
- *As a group, select the one among your plans that the group believes is most effective. Prepare supporting reasons for your selection. Individually, record your thoughts on the group's decisionmaking process in a journal.*
- *Decide how best to communicate your plan to decisionmakers.*
- *Present your plan to the council with a display of the mathematical calculations that demonstrate that your plan will satisfy the 180–day requirement within the time remaining in the school calendar.*
- *Briefly record in your individual journals and describe in your presentation the issues your group dealt with when putting together the plans and deciding which would be most effective.*

Audience: *School-Community Council and Director of Education.*

Criteria for Success:
- *The selected plan will ensure the close of the school year by June 18.*
- *Mathematical calculations are complete and accurate.*
- *Policies and requirements are met by the plan.*
- *Implementing the plan will not require significant additional costs.*
- *Conclusions and recommendations are backed up by data, graphs, and supporting details.*

THINGS TO CONSIDER

Students need to learn to work both in groups and also as individuals. Are your students receiving sufficient opportunities to develop proficiency in both? As we work with students to balance individual and cooperative assessments, we must remember that it takes time. Students may not be able or willing to move quickly from one end of the scale to the other.

Some Final Thoughts

In the midst of reaching all of our students and promoting their success, we need to take care that the tasks we set do not limit our students' ability to show their learning because of our own limited expectations of certain students. Building on student strengths and ensuring quality assessment does not mean "dumbing down." We want our assessments to honor students' diverse strengths WHILE demanding intellectual rigor.

It's also important to give students time to prepare for an assessment. They can be told what will be happening and what the expectations are for performance. This step is particularly important for formal tests that are administered in a relatively standardized way. Students should be allowed to talk about their experiences with tests and ask questions about the upcoming test or the testing process.

In addition, the performance of English language learners and students from nondominant linguistic and cultural groups should be scored by teachers who have an understanding of linguistic and cultural issues. For example, many spelling patterns of transitional bilingual students are understandable with reference to their primary language but almost inscrutable to a reader who does not know that language. "He geib ibriting" may not be read as "He gave everything." The problem extends to understanding students' syntax and their meaning. Confusion about how to mark the past tense ("he didn't wanted") may be understandable, but more complex syntactic errors based on the student's first language may result in incomprehensible answers. Semantic confusions (versus obvious vocabulary substitutions) may lead to wrong interpretations of student ability. A character may be described as "shy" rather than "ashamed" by a student because the same word in Spanish (vergüenza) can mean both shame and shyness. An untrained scorer may conclude that a student has low comprehension rather than problems with spelling, syntax, or vocabulary. It is important to distinguish between *real* indicators of learning problems and features of work that merely represent typical stages of English language learning.

Summary

In this section, we have talked about how teachers can tap into the cultural and linguistic strengths of students. If we could see into the heads of students and see the cartoon captions that were on the first page of this section, building on the culture and language of students would be a much easier process. However, in reality, as teachers we are learning about our students as they learn about us. As teachers we have the responsibility to build an environment where students can succeed.

Knowing how to build on student strengths and use good assessments are increasingly important skills for teachers. In order to truly know what students know and are able to do, we must have high quality systems of assessment in our classrooms. Those systems should include connecting assessments to student culture and experience, ensuring diversity in the ways students can respond, ensuring clear criteria, and balancing individual and cooperative assessments. The next section focuses on how to fix and revise existing assessments.

Repairing and Improving Externally Developed Assessments

Kiyas oche kapetotimak kisteumowin.
[The way we do things is our knowledge.]

Old Metis saying quoted
by Elmer Ghostkeeper

When the starting point is an existing assessment, Section V helps educators evaluate its quality, identify pitfalls for diverse students, and provide specific ideas for getting around the barriers. In the example below, a group of teachers concerned about the district's test banded together to develop an alternative assessment that would meet each of the characteristics of good assessment, to be a more accurate measure of student achievement (Trumbull, Koelsch, & Wolff, 1999).

VIGNETTE: THE REDWOOD CITY ASSESSMENT

In Redwood City, districtwide assessments are given in the fifth grade. By this grade most of the district's English language learners (nearly all of whom speak Spanish as a first language) have transitioned to English-only instruction.

The fifth-grade reading assessment (Performance-Based Assessment — PBA) requires students to read a narrative text and an expository text and respond in writing to a series of questions about them. The prototype PBA, containing 15 questions, addresses standards related primarily to vocabulary, comprehension, summarizing, interpreting literary elements, connecting text meaning to one's own life, and using structural and design elements of books (maps, charts, captions, etc.) to enhance comprehension.

The group of concerned teachers judges that the texts used on the PBAs are at too high a reading level, vocabulary is arcane, and the content and themes are not culturally appropriate for these students. In addition, the directions are too long and visually dense with text, and responses call for considerable writing.

THINGS TO CONSIDER

- The Redwood City teachers are challenged to ensure that all of their students have an equitable opportunity to demonstrate their reading proficiency. However, is there more at stake here than demonstrating proficiency?

- What are the issues they must address as they move through the process of meeting student needs?

- What choices do they have?

Like others facing a challenge to be accurate and fair in the assessment of their students, Redwood City educators had a number of options to consider as they developed the Transitional Performance-Based Assessment for their students. The previous section demonstrated why culture and language should be considered in all aspects of the testing of cultural and linguistic minority students. This section offers practical recommendations for promoting equitable testing when teachers select, use, administer, and develop assessments.

Assessments are usually developed based on assumptions about the values, experiences, beliefs, and learning styles of the students. Some of these assumptions may not hold for the entire population. As a consequence, the way in which exercises are designed, prompts are phrased, and student responses are scored may produce an inaccurate picture of the knowledge and skills of cultural minority students.

One effective way in which teachers can contribute to more equitable assessment practices consists of being critical consumers of assessments. From our perspective, being a critical assessment consumer comprises three activities: knowing the challenges that we need to overcome to improve our assessment practices, being aware that often assessments for minority students are defective because of flawed adaptation and translation procedures, and using certain assessment development and scoring strategies intended to address student diversity.

There are some actions that we can incorporate into our daily practice to promote more equitable testing practices. These actions concern our activities when we review the assessments we use, when we develop assessments of our own, and when we score student responses.

How to Make Assessment Work for Everyone: Reviewing Assessments

Accomplished teachers know very well that developing an assessment is a never-ending process. Assessments for English language learners should not be an exception.

To attain more equitable testing, we need to become critical reviewers of all assessments we use, whether we are the authors of these assessments, we borrow them from colleagues, or we purchase them from testing companies.

In addition to using our own judgment, we can take three actions to review assessments: using external reviewers, interpreting students' responses, and obtaining student verbalizations. These actions should be taken continuously with any assessment, even if it has been used many times in the past and is regarded as "non-culturally biased."

Using External Reviewers

People with different skills and backgrounds can be sensitive to flaws that others may overlook. In addition to colleagues, external reviewers can include translators, content specialists, native speakers of the language targeted, and parents. Use more than one of each. We have observed that many errors made in tests designed for English language learners occur because organizations or development teams rely on the opinion of only one parent or only one native speaker.

Use as many reviewers as possible. Each person may give a different opinion. We will need to use our judgment to decide how the exercises can be improved.

When we review or have someone review a translation, we should always have the original version in English with us. As basic as this idea may sound, many organizations give their reviewers only the translated version. Without the original version in English, the reviewer can review, at the most, the correctness of the language used, not the accuracy of the translation. It is not unusual to run into translations in which the original, intended meaning has been altered, but the scoring rubrics or criteria are the same across languages.

In addition to reviewing language, have reviewers check for cases in which exercises:

- Exclude or offend underrepresented groups (e.g., the characters used are only male)

- Contribute to perpetuating stereotypes about those groups (e.g., the characters are a male and a female with divergent points of view; the male is right)

- Promote the notion that the content area is not open to all groups (e.g., the characters' names in an exercise sound like White, European American names)

- Include descriptions of situations, words, sentence structures, or pieces of equipment that are familiar to only a specific group of students

Interpreting Student Responses

Interpreting English language learners' responses accurately requires a recognition that their native language may strongly influence how they interpret an item and how they respond to it. Being able to identify those influences allows teachers to obtain valuable information of their students' strengths and weaknesses.

VIGNETTE: AN EXAMPLE FROM THE NATIONAL ASSESSMENT OF EDUCATIONAL PROGRESS (NAEP)

Using vocabulary that is age or linguistically inappropriate may result in exercises that penalize certain groups of English language learners. Here is an example provided by Solano-Flores and Nelson-Barber (2000):

One of the 1996, fourth-grade science questions NAEP released reads as follows:

> *"A nail becomes warm when it is tiered into a piece of wood. Tell why the nail becomes warm."*

One student responded as follows:

"because in side of the tree is warm."

Most likely, this student's native language is Spanish. In addition to having a Spanish syntactical structure, the response reflects two typical mistakes made by English learners whose native language is Spanish: confusing "nail" and "snail" and confusing "warm" and "worm," whose sounds they confuse. Because of this and the fact that "tiered into" is unfamiliar to beginning English learners, quite probably the student interpreted the item as if it read:

> *"A snail becomes a worm when it is (?) into a piece of wood. Tell why the snail becomes a worm."*

The student clearly missed the fact that the item was about physics and tried to make up a biology response.

THINGS TO CONSIDER

Although it is impossible to know whether the student would have answered correctly had she or he understood what the item was asking, the example illustrates how an unfamiliar word may cause a student to perform poorly on an essay. It also illustrates how the interpretation of student responses can be used to improve an exercise.

Obtaining Student Verbalizations

The reasoning used by students in their responses reveals whether an exercise is eliciting the intended kind of thinking. Asking students to talk about their responses can help clear up problems in the assessment as well as reveal possible student misconceptions or flawed problem-solving strategies and identify the linguistic and cultural influences that shape student responses.

We can ask the students to tell us in their own words what they think the question or task is about. This strategy allows us to detect possible misinterpretations of the question or task due to inappropriate translation. A good, effective way to improve a question or task consists of asking the students to rephrase it (e.g., How would you ask this question to a friend?).

Also, we should ask students to "think aloud" as they engage in responding to the items. By asking them to describe what they are thinking, we will be able to identify whether they respond to the item as they are expected to.

An alternative to this strategy is the approach of interviewing students individually, right after they have completed the item, and asking them to explain their thinking retrospectively.

How to Make Assessment Work for Everyone: Developing Assessments

Concurrent Assessment Development

Developing two language versions of the same assessment concurrently is the best approach to promote equitable testing when developing an assessment from scratch for English language learners. We should not wait until we have developed the English version to start developing a version in another language. Educators must develop both versions at the same time and with the same team of assessment developers. By allowing both language versions to go through the same process of development (which includes revising the assessments iteratively based on the results obtained from piloting them with the students), we give them equal opportunities for refinement and for capturing sociocultural aspects relevant to language (Solano-Flores, Trumbull, & Nelson-Barber, 2000).

The rationale for concurrent assessment development is that adapting tests to address cultural and linguistic diversity has a serious methodological weakness that prevents testing from being equitable: the process used to develop the original version of the assessment is different from the process used to develop the adapted version. Developing an assessment is a cyclical process. During each iteration, developers observe the students or ask them to talk aloud as they perform in order to gain access to the reasonings they use to solve the problems. Developers also interview students to investigate how well they understand the problems posed and the kind of knowledge and thinking skills they use in solving the problems. In each iteration, developers discuss their findings and create a more refined version of the assessment. Among other things, they may rephrase questions; add, replace, or eliminate words; or include examples in the directions for equipment use (Solano-Flores & Shavelson, 1997). When an assessment

Researchers from the Language and Cultural Diversity program at WestEd are currently investigating the potential and limitations of certain alternatives to translating assessments (Solano-Flores, Trumbull & Nelson-Barber, 2000). They contend that a more equitable testing of linguistic minority students in their first language can be attained only if both the source and secondary language versions are given the same status and are developed concurrently. Their model for concurrent assessment development is currently being tested with bilingual teachers in the Wenatchee School District, in the state of Washington.

is translated from English into another language, this delicate process that allows assessment developers to refine language does not take place for the other language.

Designing Appropriate Ways for Students to Respond

Nothing is trivial when it comes to deciding the characteristics of an assessment's response format — the methods intended to capture the student responses. This is especially the case in situations in which students have different cultural backgrounds. Different cultures tend to produce different ways to interpret and respond to questions. Consider the following cases. They have been identified from observing students with different cultural backgrounds taking science assessments designed for either research purposes or large-scale testing (Solano-Flores & Shavelson, 1997).

- English language learners can benefit from constructed-response exercises that allow them to provide their answers with drawings. They may provide more information if the spaces for drawing are not bounded by boxes.

- Students are more likely to make drawings, computations, and notes on observations and thoughts when the question provides a blank half a page than when it provides half a page with lines to write on. Lines tend to elicit written responses only. In addition, the number of lines suggests that a specific response length is expected. Also, too many lines may have the undesired effect of intimidating some students, thus discouraging them from attempting to write an elaborate response.

- Opposite pages in notebooks with double-sided pages allow students to keep information close at hand. If that information is provided on the left page and the questions are arranged on the right page, students can use the information to answer the questions without having to turn to back pages.

Finding the response format characteristics that best work for a specific cultural group may take a great deal of experience. In this process, we always need to be aware that any decision on the way a question is worded and the physical appearance of the response format is relevant to the testing of English language learners.

Striking a Balance between Reading Demands and Contextual Information

At the beginning of the 1990s, when multiple-choice testing was under scrutiny, high hopes were placed on constructed-response assessments as potential tools for promoting more equitable testing. It was thought that, by their concrete, well-contextualized nature, verbal-linguistic skills might play less of a role than with abstract, decontextualized, multiple-choice, and other traditional tests.

In some cultures, knowledge occurs in a contextualized manner; isolated pieces of information — typical of multiple-choice items — are meaningless unless they are related to a specific situation. Therefore, it makes sense to assume that, for students from these cultural groups, constructed-response assessments can provide a better opportunity for cultural minority students to demonstrate their knowledge.

However, providing too much contextual information to make a task meaningful increases the reading demands and may place those students at a disadvantage if they are, in addition, poor readers.

As with any step taken in the process of assessment development, striking a balance between the reading demands posed by an assessment and the contextual information needed to make its task meaningful takes a good number of tryouts and revisions.

VIGNETTE: BAGELS

In the following vignette, a teacher suspects that a district test may prove challenging for his students.

Mr. Powell, a third-grade teacher in New Orleans, is preparing his students for a new districtwide reading assessment. He just earned his license to teach English language learners, and for the first time, most of his students are from immigrant families. He has a combination of students whose families are from Vietnam and Laos. The district has released a list of books that may be used on the exam. His class has read most of them already, but there are still a few that he wants to make sure they have a chance to experience. One of the books is Mrs. Katz and Tush *by Patricia Polacco. It is one of his favorite books, and he is surprised that he hasn't used it yet with these students. As he flips through the book at home, he notices many references to traditionally Jewish foods. He believes his students will understand the story, given the pictures and context clues, but he is worried that on an assessment with multiple-choice questions, his students may get stuck on the vocabulary and have trouble comprehending the reading passages. He decides to bring in bagels for his class as a treat and a basis for discussion before he reads the book. He wants to demystify the language that will be strange to them as much as possible. Predictably, as he covers the bagels with cream cheese and passes them out, his students stare at him with wonder and ask, "Teacher, what is that?"*

THINGS TO CONSIDER

In this case, Mr. Powell was not able to redesign an assessment that he felt would ensure student success, but he was able to prepare his students for the exam. What further steps would you have taken to prepare your class for this reading test? If Mr. Powell had been on the assessment design committee, what suggestions should he have made?

Using Multiple Forms of Assessment

An increasing body of evidence (Baxter & Shavelson, 1994; Dalton, Morocco, Tivnan, & Rawson, 1994; Ruiz-Primo & Shavelson, 1996) shows that different types of tasks (e.g., multiple choice, short answer, essay, hands on, computer simulations, concept maps) tap into different types of knowledge and skills. For example, a student may get high scores in a hands-on assessment and low scores in a computer version of that assessment, even if both assessments pose exactly the same problem and vary only on whether the student manipulates real or virtual objects. Seemingly parallel ways of designing assessment questions can result in different responses because they require different, unintended skills.

The reasons that account for differences in score due to type of task are still being investigated. A possible reason is that, because of their different experiences and skills, some students perform better on tasks that, say, involve reading long paragraphs; others perform better on tasks that involve manipulating objects; and still others perform better on tasks that involve interpreting visual representations of objects.

Gender and racial differences in performance have been investigated for only a few of the new alternative assessments (e.g., Jovanovic, Solano-Flores, & Shavelson, 1994; Klein, Jovanovic, Stecher, McCaffrey, Shavelson, Haertel, Solano-Flores, & Comfort, 1997). There is scant information on how different tasks elicit from students different styles of thinking and problem-solving strategies depending on their cultural and linguistic backgrounds.

Since each culture promotes different sets of skills and values among its members, it is possible that individuals from some cultural groups may tend to perform better on some tasks than on others. Using a limited variety of assessments in a multicultural classroom may privilege some students and penalize others.

The solution to this potential dilemma consists of using a wide variety of tasks in classroom assessment. This not only renders more dependable measures of student academic achievement, but also ensures that all students are given the opportunity to demonstrate their learning.

How to Make Assessment Work for Everyone: Scoring Assessments

Assessing to Understand (Not Just Grade) Our Students

Alternative, constructed-response forms of assessment allow for focusing not only on the product but also on the process (reasoning) used by students to respond to an item or solve a problem.

Since constructed-response assessments permit a variety of responses varying in degree of correctness, the universe of possible correct responses may be vast and, in many cases, undetermined. This means that some students can come up with unanticipated responses or solutions that are, nonetheless, good.

Unfortunately, probably because of the long tradition of multiple-choice testing in the United States, many American teachers still limit their grading of constructed-response exercises to judgments about the product, not the process involved in the students' responses.

Assessing students based solely on product is not consistent with the rationale for using constructed-response assessments. This may adversely affect students who are different from the mainstream population. This is especially the case for students who, because of their linguistic and cultural backgrounds, may provide their responses in novel ways.

Understanding what students are trying to say before assigning a grade to that response is a good approach to promote equity in the scoring of constructed-response exercises. A careful reading of student responses (even those that at first glance look inadequate) may reveal in some cases that a student has a reasonably good understanding of a given topic but cannot articulate a response in the same way as native speakers of English. In addition, a careful reading of student responses provides teachers with valuable information that they can use to help students improve their written communication skills.

Separating Content Knowledge From Writing Skills

One of the major challenges for objective scoring in large-scale assessment is the difficulty of training scorers to focus on the skill or knowledge that a given assessment intends to measure. This is probably due to the fact that, whereas assessments are supposed to assess knowledge on a specific skill or knowledge domain, educators are used to assessing individuals as a whole. As a result, they may tend to judge an individual's performance based on things that are irrelevant to the targeted learning.

The influence of grammar and spelling mistakes in scoring is a case in point. Teachers may find it difficult to resist the temptation to assign a low score to, say, performance on a science item if it is plagued with grammar and spelling mistakes. Obviously, this tendency may affect English language learners more than other students in the classroom.

Being Sensitive to Cultural Values

Knowing the way cultures view and make sense of the world may lead to more accurate inferences about an individual's capabilities. Cultures' norms may influence the way in which students interpret and solve an item (Kopriva & Sexton, 1999). For example, students may be asked to create a fair race. Students are expected to create a racecourse in which each contestant runs the same distance. Those from cultures that do not emphasize competition may interpret the word "fair" in a different way and create shorter distances for slower runners, as if the item asked them to create a racecourse in which all contestants have equal chances of winning.

How to Make Assessment Work for Everyone: Giving Students Opportunities to Communicate Learning in Their Most Fluent Language

Finally, students who are learning English frequently have trouble expressing their knowledge and skills in English. Their progress in English must be assessed, of course, but their learning in other academic areas must also be assessed. Therefore, in order to truly discover what they know and are able to do, English language learners often need accommodations in assessment, including assessment in native language. The decisions made by Redwood City teachers and bilingual staff continue to provide a good example of how to meet the needs of English language learners.

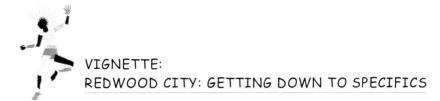

VIGNETTE:
REDWOOD CITY: GETTING DOWN TO SPECIFICS

The Redwood City Department of Bilingual Education became convinced that merely introducing special accommodations for transitional students, such as allowing them to read texts in Spanish as well as English or take more time to complete the assessment if they so desired, would not address students' actual needs. Mediation, such as rephrasing prompts or instruction or responding to student questions, also seemed inadequate to solving what teachers saw as the real problems with the assessments. Staff believed that an alternative assessment specifically designed for students transitioning into English-only instruction was the best answer.

Teachers reasoned that an alternative reading assessment should have the following characteristics:

- *Appropriate texts (in terms of themes, level, and length)*

- *Clear instructions and accessible vocabulary*

- *Response strategies similar to what students had been exposed to in instruction (appropriate for English language learners)*

- *A similar sampling of the district's reading standards to that of the PBA*

- *A format as similar as possible (in terms of numbers and types of items) to that of the regular PBA*

The intent was to create an English reading assessment that would perform the same functions as the PBA, sample many of the same standards, and replicate the PBA in form to the degree possible. It needed to be appropriate for English language learner students in their first year of English reading. The Transitional Performance-Based Assessment would not be comparable to the PBA in any sense of equating of the assessments, but neither would it operate on an entirely different set of premises. In fact, it would be parallel in many ways.

The Redwood City assessment design group decided that to read aloud one paragraph of the reading selection prior to distributing the full passage would improve performance. The group felt strongly that hearing the word in the context of the story would elicit greater involvement in the pre-assessment activities than putting the word on the board and asking students if they knew its meaning. Moreover, reading aloud the paragraph in question provided students with a definition of the word "elaboration." The technique of defining a word through elaboration and description, rather than saying the word and asking for definitions, is commonly used in the teaching of second languages. Thus, the preassessment activity paralleled sound instructional practice. Teachers believed that using this technique in the assessment would put students at ease and lower their anxiety about taking an important test.

THINGS TO CONSIDER

English language learners can be at a wide array of levels of proficiency in English and may need very different accommodations. When is native language assessment needed? When are modified instruction, simplified vocabulary/language, and/or longer time periods appropriate? When should students be allowed dictionaries or interpreters?

Summary

Unfortunately, teachers do not have complete control over all of our students' assessment experiences. We all have to use some external tests and materials as well as submit to large-scale state or district assessment, even though it may sometimes be against our better judgment. Regardless, teachers can still be critical consumers of external assessments and can strive to make student experience as positive as possible. Some things to consider include strategies for reviewing assessments, developing assessments, scoring assessments, and assessing students in their own language.

Finally, when we discover errors in assessments that may potentially affect students from cultural minorities, we should make their creators aware of them. Many errors may go unnoticed by testing companies because they do not get enough feedback from teachers. By providing this feedback on a continuous basis, teachers will make companies realize that they need to improve their translation and cultural adaptation procedures and will contribute to a more equitable assessment.

SECTION VI

Readings to Deepen Our Learning

If you don't respect the children's culture, you negate their very essence.

Embracing Ebonics and Teaching
Standard English, 1997

Additional Reading

Embracing Ebonics and Teaching Standard English: An Interview with Oakland Teacher Carrie Secret

This article is adapted from an interview with Carrie Secret, a fifth-grade teacher at Prescott Elementary School in the Oakland Unified School District. Prescott had been the only school in the system where a majority of teachers had voluntarily agreed to adopt the Standard English Proficiency program, a statewide initiative which acknowledges the systematic rule-governed nature of "Black English" while helping children to learn Standard English. Secret was interviewed by Barbara Miner, managing editor of Rethinking School.

How long have you been a teacher and how long have you been at Prescott Elementary School?

After I left Omaha in February 1966, I was hired in Oakland and assigned to Prescott. Everybody said, "Oh you poor thing, you're assigned to Prescott!" But I've been there 31 years because I refused to be transferred. There had been times when excellent teachers left Prescott, but they were never replaced with the same caliber of teacher.

I've never desired to do anything but teach. I have never desired to leave the classroom for any other position. Teaching is my passion. I've taught every grade in elementary school except kindergarten. I now teach fifth grade with a group of children I've had since they were in first-grade. I have 31 children in my class. One is Lakota Sioux, two are Cambodian, two are Mexican and 26 are African American.

Prescott is one of the Oakland schools that uses the Standard English Proficiency Program (SEP). Can you explain the concepts underlying SEP?

The issue gets clouded because the SEP Programs vary throughout the state. The most powerful difference is that we in the Oakland SEP, under the inspirational directorship of Nabeehah Shakir, dared to honor and respect Ebonics as the home language that stands on its own rather than as a dialectical form of English. We see and understand that our language patterns and structure come from a family of languages totally unrelated to the Germanic roots of English. In some programs, grammar and drill are strong parts. I think our using second language learning strategies has more impact on the students. The view is, "We are teaching you a second language, not fixing the home language you bring to school."

There are three cornerstones to our SEP program: culture, language, and literacy. Our program is not just a language program that stresses how well you acquire and speak English. We emphasize the learning of reading by incorporating a strong literacy component. Another crucial issue is that we push students to learn the content language of each area of curriculum. The Oakland SEP Program is not just a grammar and drill program but a program that emphasizes language and content and encompasses all areas of curriculum.

Children are not empowered simply because they know subject/verb agreement. That is not powerful for children it they don't have content in which to use the language. Yes, we want the children to speak English and have positive feelings about themselves, but that comes about only when the children know content. It doesn't matter how well you speak if you are not able to participate in and use the language of the content areas during discussion times.

The other issue is culture. If you don't respect the children's culture, you negate their very essence. We in the SEP program draw our cultural components from the work of the Center for Applied Cultural Studies and Educational Achievement (CACSEA) at San Francisco State University. CACSEA is under the directorship of Dr. Wade Nobles, a scholar in African and African-American culture and history, and provides professional development programs for teachers of African-American students. CACSEA's program manager and trainer, Augusta Mann, presents staff development sessions for SEP that focus on the culture of African-American people and uses the culture to enhance reading achievement. The program highlights nine cultural aspects that permeate African-American life: spirituality, resilience, emotional vitality, musicality and rhythm, humanism, communalism, orality and verbal expressiveness, personal style and uniqueness, and realness. These concepts are then presented in conjunction with instructional strategies that have proven to be effective for African-American students.

Are there particular times during the school day when a student is required to speak Standard English?

In fifth grade. I encourage the students to practice English most of the instructional time. I say "encourage" because "required" is a word that sends a message that if you don't use English then you are operating below standard. Let's say that in fifth grade, students are requested and encouraged to speak in English almost all the time.

There's a misconception of the program, created by the media blitz of misinformation. Our mission was and continues to be: embrace and respect Ebonics, the home language of many of our students, and use strategies that will move them to a competency level in English. We never had, nor do we now have, any intention of teaching the home language to students. They come to us speaking the language.

We read literature that has Ebonics language patterns in it. For example, last year in fifth grade we read Joyce Hansen's *Yellow Bird and Me*, and in fourth grade we read her book *The Gift Giver*. The language was Ebonic in structure. The language was the bonding agent for students. The book just felt good to them.

When writing, the students are aware that finished pieces are written in English. The use of Ebonic structures appears in many of their first drafts. When this happens I simply say, "You used Ebonics here. I need you to translate this thought into English." This kind of statement does not negate the child's thought or language.

Before I met Professor Ernie Smith, my approach was different. I used the "fix-something-that-was-wrong" approach. I was always calling for the children to say something correct or to fix something to make it right. I now approach the same task from a different perspective that has a more positive affect on my children.

Somedays I simply announce: "While you are working I will be listening to how well you use English. In your groups you must call for translation if a member of your group uses an Ebonic Structure." Some days I say, "Girls, you are at Spelman and boys, you are attending Morehouse College (historically Black colleges). Today you use the language the professors use and expect you to use in your classes, and that language is English."

I once had some visitors come to my class and they said, "We don't hear Ebonics here." But that is because I had explained to my children that company was coming, and when company comes, we practice speaking English. Company is the best time to practice because most of our visitors are from a cultural language context different from ours.

Do you ever allow students to use Ebonics in the classroom?

The word that bothers me is "allow." Students talk. They bring their home language to school. That is their right. If you are concerned about children using Ebonics in the classroom, you will spend the whole day saying, "Translate, translate, translate." So you have to pick times when you are particularly attuned to and calling for English translation.

When the children are working in groups together, say three or four of them, I try to keep them in an English-speaking mode but I don't prevent them from using Ebonics. I want to give them time enough to talk through their project in their comfortable language. It's like a re-write to me. But at some point, they have to present their project to me and these are required to be presented in their best English.

Professor Ernie Smith said something that put things in perspective for me, especially when it comes to how children pronounce words. And that advice is: You do not teach speech at reading time. When children are reading to me, I want to know that they are comprehending what they are reading. So I don't stop them if they don't pronounce words according to the English pronunciation.

But I will listen to the pronunciation and make mental notes. For example, I might note that Girl X and Boy Y are dropping the final "t"s off their words — for example saying "lef" for "left" or "bes" for "best." I then note to myself that I will need to work on that Ebonics feature with the class.

That's another thing — I always do whole group. I don't like programs that single out kids or pull out children. That includes both gifted and talented programs and deficit-model programs.

How do you teach children to understand that they may be dropping consonants when they speak?

I'm lucky in that I have been with these children five years and at a very early age I engaged them in listening to language for the purpose of hearing and understanding the difference between Ebonics and English. However, by the middle of second grade, they were all readers. So at that point it was easy to go to the overhead and show them exactly what they said and then call for the English translation of what they said.

Hearing the language is a crucial step. Children who speak Ebonics do not hear themselves dropping off the "t" for instance. You have to teach them to hear that. So we do a lot of over-enunciation when they are small. I also do a lot of dictation where I will dictate a sentence and have the children write what I said, by sound only. I also try to always point out what is Ebonics speech and what is English. Children must first hear and develop an ear for both languages in order to effectively distinguish between the two.

Do you have any tips for teaching reading to Ebonics speakers?

One of my best approaches with young readers is that I read to them a lot. When they were in the early grades, I read when they come in at 8:30, I read after the first recess, I read after lunch, and I read after the second recess. In first grade, I actually read through the reader that they are going to be using. So by the time I give them their readers, in about mid-October, they are not afraid of the book. They know that words are only something that someone else has said and written down.

We also do a lot of home reading in our school: this is part of a school-wide program called the "Just Read" program. Every day, the children take home a book and someone is expected to read to them.

I still read to my children in fifth grade. And they are always reading, whether a book, or for a report, or researching information. I also continue to stress reading for pleasure. Basically, I give the children a lot of language and oral listening — and it's attentive listening and inclusive listening where they have to respond back to me so that I know they are listening.

I am strong on phonics, but I embrace, enjoy, and like whole language. But I am also just as strong on phonics. In first grade, I start dictation right away, giving them phonetically pure words to spell back to me or write back to me. And our kindergarten teachers have done a good job preparing the students for us and have explained certain phonics principles, like short vowels and long vowels. They also give the children certain sight words that we want the children to recognize and certain sight words that we want the children to read.

In the early grades, I do a lot of word flash card drills, phrase drills, sentence drills, which may be from the stories I am reading to them. We also have another drill called "read the word, write the word." We sit in a circle and read from a state-developed word list that was developed for each grade. We take a column a day and we read them and write them, and that becomes a standard homework assignment.

I also want the children to move into critical thinking and content. I am one who believes that everything can be taught at one time. So, for example, we have a phonics book that has a lot of pictures for identification and sounds. After the children have completed the page, they have to go back and group at least four pictures together and tell why they grouped them together. Or they might group four pictures that belong together and one that doesn't and explain why. I might also make a connection between the lesson and the children's lives. I will say, "How would you connect the picture to your life, and why?"

How do you use Black literature to help children learn Standard English?

A lot of people emphasize using Black literature and then translating it. I no longer use this strategy because we were always translating Ebonics to English, but rarely, if ever, English to Ebonics. That tended to negate in my mind the equality of the two languages.

I use the literature because of its cuitumi essence, its beauty. I want the children to be proud that Toni Morrison and Alice Walker are great writers and that Maya Angelou spoke at the President's inauguration. I am not about to take a beautiful piece of Ebonics literature and then translate it into English. You cannot enjoy Langston Hughes if you are worried about translating him. The beauty of our language gets lost in the translation.

It is necessary for our students to become aware that our greatest models for excellent writers wrote fluently in both English and Ebonics. There are beautiful pieces by Langston Hughes and Paul Laurence Dunbar in English as well as in Ebonics. I had students read the *Antebellum Sermon* by Dunbar which is straight-up Ebonics, and then read *The Seedling,* which is straight-up English. I also use writings by Jeremiah Wright, a minister out of Chicago who delivers magnificent and powerful sermons that contain African and African-American history. He speaks with a rhythm, with an emotional vitality, as he uses high level vocabulary in his sermons. Hearing him speak, nearly all the children get the message from context. However, they are required to go back and pull out the vocabulary and research each new word. This is a powerful way to get children to use new vocabulary.

These kind of writings tend to fortify children and also give them a lot of language. I believe in giving children a lot of adult, intellectual language rather than "See Spot run" language. I also try to address the culture of all my children. For example, we have read *To Destroy You Is No Loss* by Joan Criddle and *The Clay Marvel* by Minfong Ho, which are about the Cambodian children. We have read *Daniel's Story,* a story about a Jewish child in a concentration camp, and *Remember My Name,* a book about the Native American's Trail of Tears experience.

How do you organize your school day?

In the morning, I do a centering opening based on the CACSEA program. Research has shown that if you get children's adrenaline flowing, they get that natural high and then you can teach them anything you want for the next hour and a half. Basically, that 90 minutes is the only time I teach the whole group. The rest of the morning and afternoon, the children are in independent- or small-group work study mode.

When they come in the morning, we start by standing behind our chairs and we do some recitations out of our poetry readers. All of these are self-enhancing pieces of poetry, something that touches the children so they get the joy of being in the classroom. After reciting the poetry, we sing songs. We use a variety of music that touches the spirit of the child. For example, we have used *I Believe I Can Fly,* or Whitney Houston's *Step by Step,* and *To Be Loved,* or some Sweet Honey in the Rock. We have used Sounds of Blackness, classical jazz, and even some Bach,

Beethoven, and Mozart. We may even do some African dance movement to music by Herbie Hancock or Quincy Jones.

When the energy is high I say, "Now go inside yourself and find your perfect peace and decide what you want to get out of the day and promise yourself that you will get it." Then I tell them to say my name and request what it is they want from me. I think that is very important, because they have the right and the responsibility to keep me straight, just as I try to keep them straight. I am there because an adult has to be with the children but I try not to have a hierarchy. There needs to be a mutual respect between the teacher and students. My relationship with the students is a high priority with me. We are strongly bonded by love and trust for each other, our affectionate feelings transcend the classroom and extend out to the families and communities of my students. We outright love and care for each other.

After the centering, the children write in their journals. Sometimes it is on whatever they choose. Sometimes I check to see if they are internalizing a piece we are working on, such as the sermon "What Makes You So Strong?" I ask them to answer that question as it pertains to them, to see if they understand the essence of what makes a person strong. They may write on "What Makes You So Strong Black Child?" or "Cambodian Child" or "Black Teacher." They have to look for the resilience and the strength in themselves and in other people. Can they identify it? Can they pick it out? We write in our journals for about 10 minutes. After that I tell them, "Now I am getting ready to teach and what I teach you have to remember for the rest of your lives." They take notes — they've been taking notes since they were in first grade — in their record-keeping book.

I try to connect my teaching to African proverbs, principles of Kwanzaa and the Virtues of Maat, or a piece of poetry, or a recitation we are working on. A good example is "What Makes You So Strong." The piece refers to 200 million people lost in the Atlantic Ocean during the Middle Passage from Africa to slavery in the West. From that, we talked about the different oceans of the world and the continents they touch, and from there we read books on the Middle Passage, and from there they did an art piece that showed the root of the Middle Passage and the triangular trade from Africa, to America, to England. From there we went into the study of triangles, which led into geometry.

We did more reading on the Middle Passage and slavery, for example Amos Fortune's *Free Man.* I read excerpts from *Roots* by Alex Haley, where Kunta was in the Middle Passage. From that we went to other history resource books and did a quick come-back report — where different children read different books and come back with what they found. I used the Middle Passage as the basis for the daily oral language lesson, where I write a sentence with a lot of errors that the students have to correct.

We also used the morning recitation as the basis for a math lesson on estimates. I designed a lesson called "Wipe Out." I have them look at different estimates on how many people were lost in the Middle Passage, because in each source (music, sermon, poem, book) there are different numbers ranging from 70 to 200 million. Using a selected estimate, they determine how many countries would be "wiped out" if they lost the same number of people using the present day population. We worked it with Mexico, United States, and African countries so that the children could understand exactly what the numbers meant and the impact of the Middle Passage loss.

After the whole-group teaching ends (the students all have the schedule, which is my weekly lesson plan), I tell the children, "I have taught all that I am going to today. Now it is up to you." They know the work they have to do that day, either by themselves or in groups of two, three, or four.

What has been the most encouraging aspect of the Ebonics controversy? The most frustrating?

What is most encouraging is that parents who were ashamed to come to school and talk their language, and parents were actually ashamed — they lost that. They told me, "You know, Miss Secret, until Ebonics came I wouldn't come over here." It was of benefit to the community as well. Even my mother told me, "You know, Carrie, I wish I had only known I had to learn English better, and that it wasn't that I was using bad English."

Then the other thing that I thought was really important was the support that came from our Superintendent, Carolyn Gettridge, and the school board members, especially Toni Cook. They really took a bold stand in the cause for African-American education.

The downside of the debate is that there were African Americans who were so ashamed, so afraid, and so paranoid about what we were doing in Oakland. I don't blame the media for this. My job is to teach and the media's job is to sensationalize news. But I do blame those of us who picked up for the media and helped them do their job.

It bothered me that in 1997, scholarly African Americans did not tell the media, "Let me take the time to go to the source and talk to someone in Oakland before I talk to you." That bothered me more than anything.

Clarifying Terminology

Theresa Perry and Lisa Delpit

Following are definitions of some of the terms used in the debate on Ebonics. The definitions are based on the most commonly accepted usage of the term in linguistics and educational literature.

Dialect: "A regionally or socially distinctive variety of a language, identified by a particular set of words and grammatical structures.... One dialect may predominate as the official or standard form of the language, and this is the variety which may come to be written down." David Crystal (Ed.), *A Dictionary of Linguistics and Phonetics.*

Vernacular: "(Refers) to the indigenous language ... of a speech community, e.g., the vernacular of Liverpool, Berkshire, Jamaica. etc.... Vernaculars are usually seen in contrast to such notions as standard, lingua franca...." David Crystal (Ed.), *A Dictionary of Linguistics and Phonetics.*

Slang: "The nonstandard vocabulary of a given culture." Wayne O'Neil, "If Ebonics Isn't a Language, Then Tell Me, What Is?"

Standard English: "...the variety which forms the basis of printed English in newspapers and books, which is used in the mass media and which is taught in school." George Yule, *The Study of Language.*

Standard Black English: "...(Has) the grammar of standardized, textbook, or educated English and phonology which is less like that of [Ebonics] ... but with intonational patterns that in some way identify the speaker as Black.... Standard Black English is identical [except for stylistic features] to other written standard speech varieties, while spoke SBE often identifies the speaker as Black." Shirley Lewis, "Practical Aspects of Teaching Composition to Bidialectial Students: The Narrative Methods," in *Writing: The Narrative, Development, and Teaching of Written Communication.*

Black English: A dialect of English, spoken by descendants of enslaved Africans in the United States, which has its own grammar and rules of discourse.

Ebonics/Black Language/African American Language: "...Linguistic and paralinguistic features which on a concentric continuum represent the communicative competence of the West African, Caribbean, and United States slave descendents of African origin." Williams, R.L., *Ebonics: The True Language of Black Folks.* See also the article by Ernie

Smith ... in which he notes that in the hybridization process of English and African languages, it was the grammar of the Niger-Congo African languages that were dominant, and the extensive word borrowing from the English stock does not make Ebonics a dialect of English. Smith also notes that Eurocentric scholars "lack any logical reasons for using vocabulary as their basis for classifying Black American speech, while using grammar as their basis for classifying English."

African American Vernacular Tradition: "In African American literature, the vernacular refers to the church songs, blues, ballads, sermons, stories, and in our own era, rap songs that are part of the oral; not primarily the literature (or written-down tradition of Black expression.... What would the work of Langston Hughes, Sterling Brown, Zora Neale Hurston, and Ralph Ellison be without its Black vernacular ingredients? What for that matter would the writings of Mark Twain or William Faulkner be without those nine elements? Still this material also has its own shape, its own integrity its own place in the Black literacy canon: the literature of the vernacular." *The Norton Anthology of African American Literature.*

Resources on Ebonics

from Theresa Perry

Smitherman, Geneva, *Talkin and Testifyin: The Language of Black America* (Detroit; Wayne State University Press, 1986). This wonderful book is still the best introduction to the study of Black Language available. It is required reading for teachers who work with African-American children.

The Norton Anthology of African American Literature, edited by Henry Louis Gates, Jr. and Nellie V. McKay. Too many teachers have never read African-American literature. Those who have read individual works have not systematically explored the tradition and come to understand how it draws upon the vernacular language of African Americans. This anthology is where teachers who work with African-American children can find direction in their study of the African-American literary tradition.

Hoover, Mary Rhodes, *Super Literacy* (Benicia, CA: Onyx Publishing Co., 1996). *Super Literacy* is a fast-paced, multi-faceted curriculum methodology for teaching reading, writing, and speaking to African-American students, and other students for whom English is not their first language. This phonics inclusive approach to literacy is based on the premise that no singular methodology will develop the high level of literacy skills that African Americans want for their children. It emphasizes multiple approaches to developing fluency in reading, writing, and speaking, including daily affirmations, oratory, literature, linguistic-based phonics instruction, content area reading, comprehension, test-taking activities, and memorization. These curriculum materials were initially developed by Mary Rhodes Hoover for the Nairobi school almost 30 years ago, and they have been used in school systems around the country. They were recently used as part of the Standard English Proficiency Program in Oakland. Mary Rhodes Hoover is a professor of education at Howard University who specializes in African-American language and literacy. She is available for consultations and can be reached at Howard University, School of Education, 2441 Fourth St., NW, Room 132, Washington, DC 20059, 202-806-7343.

from Wayne O'Neil

Let me recommend not books but the following two quite different types of material for teachers to look at:

1. For more discussion of the Ebonics issue from the point of view of linguists and expanding on the issues raised in my article, I suggest:

   a. Geoffrey Pullman's "Language that dare not speak its name," *Nature*, 27 March 1997, 321-322.

   b. The Linguistic Society of America's "Resolution on the 'Ebonics' Issue" (see page 27).

   c. Charles Fillmore's "A linguist looks at the Ebonics debate" at: http:// parents.berkeley.edu/current/ebonics.html.

2. But to get an understanding of the madness out there on this issue and the sometimes frightening racist energy spent on it, I recommend that teachers turn to the Internet, do an "Ebonics" web search, and thus get a sense of how important it is to bring the Ebonics/Black English/African American English issue into the realm of rational discussion. For it is likely that their students are seeing the web material and its racism, misinformation, and miseducation.

from Mary Rhodes Hoover

Delpit, Lisa, *Other People's Children: Cultural Conflict in the Classroom* (New York: New Press, 1995). Gives an excellent background on issues related to language and literacy.

Hoover, Mary; Dabney, N.; & Lewis, S., *Successful Black and Minority Schools* (San Francisco: Julian Richardson, 1990). Describes successful literacy programs, where students test at and above grade level, for Ebonics speakers.

I would also recommend Geneva Smitherman's *Talkin and Testifyin: The Language of Black America,* which remains the best summary of African American Language/Ebonics.

from Terry Meier

Dandy, Evelyn, *Black Communications: Breaking Down the Barriers* (Chicago: African American Images, 1991). For teachers and future teachers, Dandy's book provides a great introduction to the topic of Black Language/Ebonics. She includes many classroom examples that teachers can relate to easily and that spark much discussion about effective teaching practice.

I would also recommend, as others have, Lisa Delpit's *Other People's Children: Cultural Conflict in the Classroom* and Geneva Smitherman's *Talkin and Testifyin: The Language of Black America.*

Gender Equity:
Still Knocking at the Classroom Door

David Sadker

*Gender equity? Oh, yes, that was big a few years ago. Today, girls'
home economics and boys' shop are gone.*

*Girls get better grades. Girls are more likely to get into college,
whereas boys are more likely to get into trouble. Why all this
attention to girls? Boys are the ones in trouble.*

Title IX? Wasn't that repealed?

Many educators are confused about gender equity. Is it still a problem?
Is it more about political correctness than about educational
effectiveness? Wasn't that battle fought and won years ago? Until 1980,
Ivy League schools such as Columbia University did not even admit
women. Today, the majority of college students are women. Perhaps we
should declare victory and move on.

Michael Kazin, in his forthcoming book *Like a Civil War: The United
States in the 1960s* (Oxford University Press, in press), helps educators
understand the cultural context surrounding educational equity. Kazin
writes that in the war between liberals and conservatives that
characterized the 1960s, the conservatives actually won most battles.
Today's cultural landscape is littered with their mantras, now part of the
national conventional wisdom: Government is too big, taxes are too high,
affirmative action is unfair, business is overregulated, and school choice
will improve education. But conservatives did not win all the battles.
Kazin believes that the decade's most successful social crusade was
feminism, a movement that restructured U.S. society.

Commentators now proclaim on the air-waves that gender bias no longer
exists, except for the men who are victimized by feminists. Their efforts
are not without success: Today the word *feminist* carries as many
negative as positive connotations. So what is an educator to believe?

Those who believe in gender equity face an uphill struggle. Each time I
begin a training program to help educators detect and eliminate bias
from their classroom teaching, I am reminded of what some call *gender
blindness* (Bailey, Scantlebury, & Letts, 1997, p. 29). Often I show a
videotape with subtle, if pervasive, gender bias. Asked to evaluate the
tape, most teachers miss the bias. After practicing some rudimentary
coding of classroom interactions, we go back to the tape. Surprise,

surprise! Now the gender bias is overwhelming. No longer political or personal, the bias has become a research reality, *their* reality, and the teachers are motivated to create equitable teaching strategies. But why the initial gender block?

In Failing at Fairness, Myra Sadker and I described "a syntax of sexism so elusive that most teachers and students were completely unaware of its influence" (1995, p. 2). Teacher education and staff development programs do little to prepare teachers to see the subtle, unintentional, but damaging gender bias that still characterizes classrooms.

But subtlety is not the only reason for the persistence of inequity. A false sense of accomplishment has also taken root. We have made wonderful advances, especially in the area of access to schools, courses, and careers. Although bias is less problematic today, it still permeates and influences our classrooms.

What is the salient and current research on gender progress and problems in schools? What are the disturbing cultural developments that have distorted and politicized educational equity? To answer these questions, I will borrow a device used by a late night television host: a top 10 list.

The Top 10 Gender Bias Updates

Update #10. Segregation still thrives in U.S. schools. Title IX has breached the walls of the Citadel and the Virginia Military Institute, and females are now admitted to all tax-supported educational institutions. Too often, however, courses of study and careers remain gender-specific.

- The majority of females major in English, French, Spanish, music, drama, and dance, whereas males populate computer science, physics, and engineering programs.

- A recent study of 14 school-to-work programs revealed that over 90 percent of females cluster in a few traditional careers: allied health careers, teaching and education, graphic arts, and office technology (American Association of University Women Educational Foundation, 1998, p. 88).

- Although almost half of medical and law students are female, they are concentrated in a few "female friendly" (and lower-paying) specialties (Sadker & Sadker, 1995, p. 194).

Update #9. Public schools are now creating single-gender classes and schools. More than a century ago, most schools were gender-segregated. Some private schools still are. And the research on their effectiveness, at least for the girls, is compelling, if not universally accepted. In response to this research and to the pressures of assertive parents (usually of girls), public school districts have openly and sometimes surreptitiously created their own single-gender classes or schools. Is this a positive or a negative development?

If we were to carefully implement and research a limited trial of single-gender public schools and classes, the findings could improve public coed schools for boys as well as for girls. However, the current approach has the potential to fractionalize our society. In short, creating single-gender classes and schools is not a substitute for ensuring equitable public education for all our students.

Update #8. Gender-related safety and health concerns continue to plague females. One hundred years ago, the argument against female education centered on health. Doctors warned that education redirected blood initially destined for the ovaries to the brain. The result: Educated women would be less likely to reproduce and more likely to go insane. The doctors' prescription: Keep girls out of school. Bizarre, but a sign of how people viewed female health issues. Today, our attention to more genuine and pressing health risks.

- Twenty percent of school-age girls report being physically or sexually abused, and 80 percent report experiencing some form of sexual harassment.

- Although research shows that physical activity leads to higher self-esteem and lifelong health benefits, girls are only half as likely as boys to participate in physical education.

Update #7. The dropout rate is not what we think it is. Most educators know that boys repeat grades and drop out of school at higher rates than girls. However, few realize that girls who repeat a grade are more likely to drop out of school than male grade repeaters. When girls drop out of school, often because of pregnancy, they are less likely to return and complete school than boys. In 1995, for example, approximately one-third of Hispanic females between 16 and 24 had not completed school and had not passed a high school equivalency test. Boys drop out with a "crash," whereas girls drop out more quietly, more quickly, and more permanently.

Update #6. For girls, gifted programs are often "early in and early out." Elementary school gifted programs identify girls in equal or in greater numbers than boys. However, by 10th grade, girls begin to drop out of these programs at a higher rate than boys. Boys are more likely to take math and science gifted programs, whereas girls populate gifted programs that focus on language arts. For both girls and boys, gifted programs often reinforce gender segregation.

Update #5. Gender bias also affects males. Because men earn more money, manage most organizations, and dominate both government offices and sports arenas, many Americans assume that men are the victors in the great gender divide. In fact, sexism harms — and Title IX protects — both genders. Boys are stereotyped into gender roles earlier and more rigidly than females. Three out of four boys report that they were targets of sexual harassment — usually taunts challenging their masculinity. Males who express an interest in careers typically thought of as "feminine" also encounter social pressures. The percentage of males in elementary teaching, for instance, is smaller today than when Title IX came out a quarter of a century ago.

Although females receive lower grades on many high-stakes tests, males receive lower course grades (American Association of University Women Educational Foundation, 1998, pp. 27-33). Males are less likely to have close friends and are more likely to endure alienation and loneliness throughout life. Males, after all, experience higher mortality rates through accidents, violence, and suicide. From schoolyard shootings to low humanities enrollments, boys act according to negative male stereotypes, and educators need to discourage this influence.

Update #4. Classroom interactions between teachers and students put males in the spotlight and relegate females to the sidelines. Studies of teacher discourse underscore male dominance in the classroom. Teachers unconsciously make males the center of instruction and give them more frequent and focused attention. Although some boys do not want this attention, and some girls may not notice or may even desire this lack of attention (Feldhusen & Willard-Holt, 1993), the impact on both genders can be costly. Increased teacher attention contributes to enhanced student performance. Girls lose out in this equation. African American girls, for example, are assertive and outgoing when they enter school, yet they grow more passive and quiet through the school years (American Association of University Women Educational Foundation, 1998, p. 49). Boys reap the benefits of a more intense educational climate.

Update #3. The math and science gender gap is getting smaller. The idea that boys outperform girls in math and science has received national attention, and that attention is paying off.

- During the 1990s, female enrollment increased in many math and science courses. Honors as well as advanced placement courses showed enrollment gains.

- Girls are now more likely than boys to take biology and chemistry courses, whereas physics is still a male domain. Boys, however, are more likely to take all three core sciences — physics, chemistry, and biology (American Association of University Women Educational Foundation, 1998, p. 13).

- Tests continue to reflect a gender gap, particularly high-stakes tests like the SAT. Although the gap has decreased in recent years, males continue to outscore females on both the math and verbal sections of the SAT. Boys outscore girls on math and science achievement tests, whereas females outscore males on the verbal section of the ACT. Although girls take more advanced placement exams in all courses except math, science, and computers, boys earn higher advanced placement scores and are more likely to receive college credit (American Association of University Women Educational Foundation, 1998, pp. 35-41).

Update #2. A new gender gap exists in technology. Certainly, the greatest change in education in recent years is the technology explosion, with the majority of U.S. schools now connected to the Internet. But boys are more wired into this revolution than girls are.

- Boys enter schools with more computer experience than girls, and girls know it. Girls rate themselves significantly lower on computer ability.

- Stereotyping is alive and well in the tech world. Girls are more likely to enroll in word processing and clerical courses, whereas boys are more likely to enroll in advanced computer science and computer design classes. Both print and Internet resources continue to promote sex stereotyping, with males portrayed in powerful and prestigious technological positions (Knupfer, 1998).

Update #1. Some political forces are intent on reversing many gains in educational equity made during the past decade. Thirty years ago, when Myra and I first began to research gender bias, we thought that the task was pretty straightforward. First we would objectively analyze schools to see whether bias really existed. If we found bias, we would then document the inequities and work on solutions. We thought that armed with knowledge, people would want to change. Not so simple.

Educational equity is a political issue. Ultraconservatives have created "educational research" to discredit the decades of studies documenting gender bias in schools. The Women's Freedom Network is one such group that sponsors attacks not only on the research but also on the integrity and motivations of the researchers. With generous private funding and contracts with talk show hosts, news commentators, and even mainline periodicals, these "media experts" launch their attacks.

In the past, the enemies of equity spoke more openly about their beliefs: the "natural" roles of men and women, the "biological destinies" of each, even biblical references to explain the "second-class" status of females. A new day requires new tactics. The Internet and the media do not evaluate the qualifications of researchers. As a result, individuals who make up in colorful commentary what they lack in research qualifications attack the lifework of competent researchers. I regret the ultimate cost that such tactics have on the lives of children.

Cultural Support of Sexism

After practicing techniques to identify the subtle gender bias embedded in her classroom behavior, a teacher education student at the University of Wisconsin wrote:

I really didn't think [gender bias] was very prevalent, particularly because it can be so subtle. I especially didn't think I would ever do it. But ... I had also called on the boys more, not realizing. They were being quiet, instead of noisy, and I called on them to reward them they could pick out the next book. Yet the girls had been good the entire time, yet I hadn't called on them, at all. (Lundeberg, 1997, p. 59)

What is unusual about the story is not that the student could not see the bias; rather, it is that she was enrolled in a teacher education program that included such fundamental research in her training.

In a recent national study of mathematics and science methods professors, Campbell and Sanders (1997) found that two-thirds of education professors spent less than two hours teaching about gender equity and that they rarely provided practical classroom strategies to neutralize bias. More than half the professors were satisfied with limited treatment. Why has teacher education been so slow to teach about and respond to gender bias?

One explanation may be the social resistance to feminism, female concerns, and even gender studies. In one study, students taking 17 different courses received a Sociology of Gender course syllabus developed and taught by a fictitious Wendy Barker. The students rated the syllabus. Many students indicated the course as imbued with bias, promoted a political agenda, and contained exams and papers that were too subjective. Although all students showed a bias against the female instructor, the bias was strongest among male students. When a similar group of students received the same syllabus, this time developed and taught by William Barker, a fictitious male, the evaluations were more positive. Now the course was rated as less biased, the work appeared fair and reasonable, and the instructor was credible and available to students. Taught by a male, the same course seemed more comprehensive and attractive to students (Moore & Trahan, 1997).

Many female administrators, teachers, professors, and counselors share similar experiences, believing that they must work harder simply to be considered equal. Males have an unspoken, often unconscious, sense of entitlement, which is reflected in their belief that they influence school policy. Female teachers do not express similar feelings of power and influence (Lee, Loeb, & Marks, 1995). No wonder, then, that political forces can exploit female alienation and cultural resistance to feminism to promote their social agenda.

What are educators to do? Individual educators, teachers, and administrators need to ensure that instructional strategies and curricular innovations benefit all our children. Twenty-five years after Title IX, we must celebrate our progress and recommit ourselves to finishing the job.

GENDER EQUITY ON COLLEGE CAMPUSES

Years ago, most U.S. colleges and universities were single-sex. Now women are dominating college campuses that used to be all-male — in both numbers and achievements. Even at the Massachusetts Institute of Technology, a traditionally male-dominated university, this year's class is 43 percent women, the highest percentage in its history. Consider these facts:

- Nearly 60 percent of all college students are women.

- In 1999, women will earn 57 percent of all bachelor's degrees, compared with 43 percent in 1970 and less than 24 percent in 1950.

- By 2008, women will outnumber men in undergraduate and graduate programs by 9.2 million to 6.9 million.

- Among full-time workers, women with BA degrees make only $4,708 more on average than men with only high school diplomas. They make $20,000 less than men with college degrees.

- Between October 1995 and October 1996, boys accounted for 58 percent of U.S. dropouts.

—Statistics cited by Carol Tell from U.S. News & World Report (available at http://www.usnews.com).

References

American Association of University Women Educational Foundation. (1998). *Gender gaps. Where our schools fail our children.* Washington, DC: Author.

Bailey, B. L., Scantlebury, K., & Letts, W. J. (1997, January/February). It's not my style: Using disclaimers to ignore issues in science. *Journal of Teacher Education, (48)*1, 29-35.

Campbell, P. B., & Sanders, J. (1997, January/February). Uninformed but interested: Findings of a national survey on gender equity in preservice teacher education. *Journal of Teacher Education, 48*(1), 69-75.

Feldhusen, F. F., & Willard-Holt, C. (1993). Gender differences in classroom interactions and career aspirations of gifted actions and students. *Contemporary Educational Psychology, 18,* 355-362.

Kazin, M. (in press). *Like a civil war: United States in the 1960s.* Oxford, England: Oxford University Press.

Knupfer, N. N. (1998, Winter). Gender divisions across technology advertisements and the www: Implications for educational equity. *Theory Into Practice, 37*(1), 54-63.

Lee, V. E., Loeb, S., & Marks, H. M. (1995, May). Gender differences in secondary school teachers' control over classroom and school policy. *American Journal of Education, 103,* 259-301.

Lundeberg, M. A. (1997, January/February). You guys are overreacting: Teaching prospective teachers about subtle gender bias. *Journal of Teacher Education, 48*(1), 55-61.

Moore, M., & Trahan, R. (1997, December). Biased and political: Student perceptions of females teaching about gender. *College Student Journal, 31,* 434-444.

Sadker, M., & Sadker, D. (1995). *Failing at fairness: How our schools cheat girls.* New York: Touchstone Press.

David Sadker, along with his late wife, Myra, coauthored *Failing at Fairness*. He is currently completing the fifth edition of *Teachers, Schools, and Society* (McGraw-Hill), an introduction to education. He is a professor at American University, School of Education, Washington, DC 20016 (e-mail: Dsadker@American.edu).

Alternative Assessment:
Issues in Language, Culture, and Equity

Elise Trumbull Estrin

Within the span of a few years, alternative assessments such as student portfolios, performance tasks, and student exhibitions have captured center stage among proposed education reforms. Also called "authentic" or "performance" assessments, these alternatives have at heart the common notion of a meaningful performance or product. The use of such alternatives with students belonging to non-dominant language and cultural groups is of enormous interest and concern for two principal reasons:

- the hope that alternative assessments will reveal what these students truly know and can do, and

- the fear that the same inequities that are associated with traditional norm-referenced tests will recur.

Although alternative assessments are being developed for widescale uses (such as statewide accountability), many educators believe their most attractive potential is at the classroom and school level. Unlike norm-referenced tests, these new assessments have the potential to inform instructional planning through assessment activities linked directly to students' learning experiences and to the contexts of those experiences — including the cultural contexts of a pluralistic student population. Other desired outcomes are:

- Students will be more intensely engaged as participants in their own learning.

- Student growth and achievement will be communicated more effectively to parents and community.

- Teachers will be stimulated to improve their teaching.

The current assessment reforms can be accomplished meaningfully only in tandem with access to high-level learning experiences for all students. If, indeed, *all* students are to benefit from reforms in assessment, specific attention needs to be paid to issues of equity and access for students from non-dominant languages and cultures — and not as an afterthought once reforms are in place for the "majority."

Finally, as Edmund Gordon, Emeritus Professor at Yale University, has observed, the core of equity in assessment lies in deep attitudes and values regarding the social purposes of assessment. In the past, the central purpose of assessment has been to sort and rank students according to presumed inherent abilities — in effect, to create winners and losers. The current assessment reform movement represents a major shift in values toward using assessment to ensure that all students have equitable opportunities to learn and achieve at the highest possible levels.

Historical Context of the Reform

The negative consequences of norm-referenced test use for students from non-dominant cultures and language groups are well-documented. Despite psychometricians' efforts to address test bias, most such efforts have focused only on statistical or technical adjustment rather than on understanding the *root causes* of differences in performance or how to avoid *invalid uses* of tests — understandings that could guide systemic reforms.

Past attempts to reduce the cultural or linguistic load of tests by eliminating content that might be specific to any culture or by avoiding the use of language have not been very satisfactory. Pictorial or figural tests, for example, are limited in revealing what a student knows and can do. In addition, they, too, rely on skills or experiences that are culturally-based. It is in the context of these past failures to grapple with aspects of test bias that advocates for students from non-dominant linguistic and cultural groups look to alternative assessments with both hope and trepidation.

Equity Issues in the Public Debate on Assessment

Consequential Validity. In the current public debate about the new forms of assessment, concerns about their validity center at least as much on their use for making decisions about students and the consequences of those decisions (i.e., consequential validity) as on content and construct validity. A test can be said to be valid only if the way in which it is *used* is appropriate.

Gatekeeping. Some of the most serious negative consequences of assessment ensue from so-called "high-stakes" testing that determines program placement, certification, or graduation, for example. It is no secret that scores on ability and achievement tests are highly correlated with socioeconomic status and with the quality of schooling to which children have access. Tests thus compound the inequities endured by poor children by foreclosing to them additional learning opportunities.

Tracking. Disproportionate numbers of poor and minority students have long been tracked into low-ability classrooms and special education programs or disproportionately categorized as learning handicapped or language delayed on the basis of norm-referenced tests. Students in such classes do not get the opportunities to practice the kind of thinking associated with solving complex problems or exploring ideas — the kind of thinking called for in particular by many alternative assessments. And research shows that students placed in low-ability groups rarely, if ever, move into higher-ability groups. The damage to students can be argued to be lifelong, both cognitive and emotional, and even economic — in terms of missed opportunities.

Opportunities to Learn. The advent of alternative assessments offers an opportunity to re-examine the whole context of schooling, including what have been called "opportunities to learn." As long ago as the 1930s, critics of the use of norm-referenced tests with Spanish-speaking students argued that they were inappropriate on the grounds that those students were not receiving a *comparable education* (Sanchez, 1934) — that they did not have an equal "opportunity to learn." There are numerous recent studies documenting the effects of what has been taught (one index of opportunity to learn) on achievement (see Winfield, 1987).

It is clear that adequate opportunities to learn need to be ensured for assessment reform to be effective. But there is another consideration. It is apparent that even *equal* opportunity is not the perfect remedy to inequities; what works for some students does not work for others. The real challenge for schools is to be responsive to students' needs in ways that go beyond satisfying legal requirements or demands of public accountability to incorporating culturally responsive practices. Equal treatment may not ensure equal outcome. In fact, some educators caution that the wholesale rejection of instruction in basic skills penalizes students whose home experiences do not prepare them for the demands of school. For such students, a pure "process" approach to writing, for example, may be inadequate; and disciplined instruction in essential skills of writing may be complementary (Delpit, 1986).

The Social Context of Assessment

A Culture-Tinted Lens. Student performance on any assessment cannot be fully understood without reference to the language and culture of that student. "Culture" is used here to mean a group's systems of knowledge, values and ways of living that are acquired and transmitted through symbol systems. Assessment in any form is a communicative event (verbal and non-verbal), representing some set of cultural values and expectations. Test questions and student responses are understood only in terms of the test-taker's background, the testing context, and the cultural lens of the test developer and scorer. (What counts as

MAKING ASSESSMENT WORK FOR EVERYONE

"intelligence," for example, is so culturally variable that a single test of it cannot be valid for all people.)

Different Social Realities. Not all non-dominant cultural and linguistic groups function similarly in the larger society. Because of differences in their histories, they may have different views of social reality (Gibson & Ogbu, 1991). These differences are reflected in the ways students interact in the classroom. "Involuntary minorities," such as African Americans and American Indians, may find themselves opposed to identifying with the dominant group, a stance which would interfere with their full participation in the classroom. In such groups, cultural and linguistic differences may be regarded as "symbols of identity to be maintained" (Gibson & Ogbu, 1991) rather than barriers to surmount, as many voluntary immigrants view their own cultural and linguistic differences. If, indeed, students' investment in learning and performing is compromised by social identity conflicts, test scores will most surely not be indicative of their ability.

Cultural Conceptions of Assessment. Cultures vary in their methods of teaching and assessing children, both in informal (home/community) and formal settings (school). In the past, research has shown that students from the dominant culture have more "test-wiseness" than their peers from non-dominant groups. But knowledge of and attention to how to pace oneself on a timed test or eliminate unlikely answers are only superficial indices of a more fundamental awareness of the meaning of assessment.

In American schools, it is accepted practice to examine students at steps along the way to mastery of a skill or performance. There is an assumption that "trial and error" is a good strategy that can work for everyone, that successive approximations with feedback from a more competent model represent a good way to learn. This approach is in stark contrast to the way competence is demonstrated in many cultures. For example, in the Navajo culture, a child observes until fairly sure he can do a task without error (Deyhle, 1987). Children receive non-verbal instruction in the form of adult modeling. At home, they learn privately through self-initiated self-testing, and they decide when they are ready to be examined. Navajo children may then be ill at ease if pushed into a premature performance. Among some other American Indian communities as well, failure to learn is considered a private act to be ignored in public (Philips, 1983).

It should not be surprising that research with Navajo elementary students has shown them to develop a school-congruent concept of *test* years later than non-Navajo peers (Deyhle, 1987). By the second grade, while non-Navajo students understood tests to be important learning events that would have consequences for their academic futures, Navajo students still did not.

Even with improved testing, we cannot escape the fact that the very concept of displaying one's competence via formal, often public, assessment according to a prescribed timetable will continue to be incompatible with community practices for some students.

Attitudes and Beliefs about Language, Culture and Learning.
"Cultural mismatch" is often invoked by educators as the cause of some students' poor school performance vis-à-vis the dominant culture's norms — which are seen as objective standards to be met. Although overt claims of genetic inferiority and cultural deprivation have largely given way to these more neutral assertions about cultural discontinuity or difference from the dominant culture, the language used to talk about the needs of culturally non-dominant students often belies a belief that they are handicapped by their own culture and background — that they are ultimately responsible for their own lack of success in school. Teachers may regard the "culturally different" child as having inappropriate attitudes toward learning, lacking the necessary experience for school success, and possessing inadequate language skills (DeAvila & Duncan, 1985). In addition, they may blame parents for not valuing education for their children, though parents' educational backgrounds do not provide them with the knowledge of how to help their children in ways valued by the school.

Another assumption underlying much of past testing has been that ability is immutable, some mix of heredity and environment that is virtually fixed by the time the child comes to school. To the contrary, considerable research has shown the reality of "cognitive modifiability," i.e., that children's learning — indeed, what we have called "intelligence" — is responsive to experience.

Invidious assumptions like those above have paradoxically rationalized the provision of lower-level instruction; proponents argue that such students need instruction in basic skills before they can engage in higher-order thinking. Actually, research has shown that higher-order thinking is linked to successful learning of even elementary levels of reading, math, and other content (Shepard, 1991). However, as long as a language other than English and "different" cultural practices are viewed as obstacles to learning rather than assets, the learning potential of many children will continue to be underestimated.

Most educators and many parents share the belief that all students need to learn the ways of the dominant culture to survive in society. However, when other ways of knowing and learning are not capitalized on in the

Figure 1
Reciprocity of Cultural Learning

| Students' Cultures | ⇄ | Teachers' Culture | } | School Culture |

adapted from Banks, 1988

classroom, student strengths are ignored, and bridges that might have been built across cultures remain unbuilt, boundaries reinforced — to use common metaphors (Olsen, 1989; Gallagher, 1993). Moreover, culturally-dominant students and teachers are thus deprived of new ways of understanding themselves and others.

Cultural difference is not situated in particular students, of course. Where one sees difference is relative to where one stands; and all social groups are ethnocentric or communicentric, viewing their own ways of behaving and talking as "normal" and appropriate benchmarks by which to judge others' different behaviors. Though the expectation is that students from non-dominant groups need to accommodate to the dominant norms, if cultural accommodation is necessary, it should be reciprocal and result in a synthesis of cultures (Banks, 1988). Figure 1 illustrates this two-way relationship.

Social-Constructivism: Learning, Instruction and Assessment

The alternative assessment approach is compatible with a "constructivist" view of learners, more student-centered than teacher-centered, with its emphasis more on learning than on instruction. Students are seen as active constructors of knowledge, engaged in thinking — not just building skills hierarchically from simple to complex. One "constructivist" orientation often cited is *social* constructivist. Learning is portrayed as a social act in classrooms (and in the community), rather than as a set of strictly intrapersonal psychological processes.

From this standpoint, knowledge itself is conceived of as socially constructed, not a set of objective givens; and access to knowledge is affected by social factors. The meaning of "social" is not merely "interpersonal"; rather it implies that learning takes place within a larger context (the society) that entails differential status for different class, ethnic or cultural groups, as well as purposes for schooling that reflect the values of dominant groups. These factors influence what goes on in the classroom — consciously or unconsciously — including the nature of the curriculum, how it is taught, how students are invited to participate in their own learning, and which students are expected to perform well.

Alternative Assessments, Language and Culture

This section presents a more in-depth look at the role of language and culture in instruction and assessment and offers suggestions for "culturally-responsive pedagogy" (Villegas, 1991).

Language Demands of School — Instruction and Assessment.
Language is the primary medium of instruction in schools, and even with "multi-intelligence" instruction and assessment, it will continue to be necessary for all students to develop a high level of language proficiency — the ability to use oral and written language to communicate, think critically and create new ideas. Complex problem-solving — even in mathematics — is highly dependent on language. Although visual tools and manipulatives can aid students in solving problems, it is usually through language that students represent problems to themselves. And good solutions depend in part on these representations. Moreover, instruction and assessment as conceived of in current reforms make greater demands on language proficiency than do traditional approaches — something that can make assessment even more daunting for English learners.

Students need to be proficient not only in pronunciation, vocabulary and grammar but proficient with particular academic uses of language. Before coming to school, children learn the language uses their communities value through thousands of interactions over a period of years, but the uses chosen are culturally variable. School uses of language are mirrored in dominant culture homes and communities to a much greater degree than in culturally non-dominant homes and communities, giving dominant culture students an advantage in the classroom.

Unlike social uses of language, school uses tend to be abstracted from context — *decontextualized*. One example of decontextualization of language is formal written text: here the reader must supply some context from his/her own background knowledge and knowledge of how texts "work." However, even classroom routines like "show and tell" in which students are expected to talk about past or future events in a prescribed format require use of decontextualized language. The speaker must gauge what listeners need to know to understand his/her presentation, in the absence of immediate context.

Students are often asked to create a story, recount past events, summarize material they have read, explain why they solved a problem as they did, or display their knowledge in a structure considered logical. There is an accepted "formula" for responding to all of these demands — a map for the structure of discourse to be produced (called "discourse genre"). When asked to summarize a passage, the student is expected to do so in a way that follows a specific pattern. For many children entering school, there is minimal fit between language uses and genres they have learned in their home communities and those that school requires. Table 1 gives some examples of the kinds of assessment tasks students may be faced with and their associated language demands.

Table 1
Assessment Activities and Their Language Demands

Sample Assessment Activity	Potential Language Demands
Write a report for a friend who was sick today explaining to her the science experiment you did and how you did it. (Third-grade writing task following a classroom science experiment.)	Recount a multi-step past event, sequencing and reinterpreting information; assume role of teacher to a non-present audience. Requires considering what recipient already knows, level of detail she needs to comprehend.
Tell us anything else about your understanding of this story — what it means to you, what it makes you think about in your own life, or anything that relates to your reading of it. (Segment of an elementary reading assessment.)	Give account of own experience(s), linking to text, elaborating story comprehension.
You are a statistician in a political campaign. Design a poll, construct a graph, and analyze data in various forms regarding voter preferences and characteristics. Advise your candidate on a campaign strategy. (Synthesis of an eighth grade mathematics assessment.)	Obtain/select necessary information, recount information through multiple representations, interpret and explain; summarize conclusions.
Imagine that you are a staff writer for a small magazine. One day you are given your "big chance." ... You are asked to write the final scene of an incomplete story. (Taken from a 12th-grade writing task.)	Complete an account (a story) following prescribed format; comprehend/analyze story so that new segment makes sense. Take on voice of another author, maintaining style.

Tasks are adapted from examples provided by the California Department of Education and the Arizona Student Assessment Plan (The Riverside Publishing Co., 1992). All entail additional context in original but are synthesized to highlight language demands.

Cultural Variability. Even when school and community language uses overlap, the formula for the corresponding genre may vary markedly. For example, though storytelling is apparently universal, what counts as a story varies from culture to culture. Some prefer topic-centered stories which are characterized by structured discourse on a single topic that assumes little knowledge about the topic or characters on the part of listeners. Others prefer topic-associating stories, which are characterized by structured discourse on several linked topics with considerable presumption of shared knowledge on the part of listeners.

Expository styles are also culturally variable. The dominant (European-American) written expository style is a linear one. In the linear expository style, an idea is introduced, supporting evidence is given, and conclusions are drawn; or events are related in time sequence. When a contrasting holistic/circular style — in which many parallel topics are developed at once — is used by students from non-European cultures, such as Asian, Pacific Island or American Indian, teachers may simply judge their discourse to be disorganized (Clark, 1993).

Methods of argumentation in support of certain beliefs also differ across cultures. Some Chinese speakers prefer to use a format of presenting supporting evidence first, leading up to a major point or claim (in contrast to topic sentence and supporting details). Non-Chinese speakers have judged them to be "beating around the bush" (Tsang, 1989). Unlike European-Americans who use "rational" style in argumentation, some groups freely incorporate emotion and personal belief to seal an argument — and find the former disingenuous (Kochman, 1989, speaking of White vs. Black style). Performance assessments often ask students to state their own views, supported by evidence. It is easy to imagine how students grounded in various communicative/discourse styles might approach such a task differently. In the same way, teachers from different cultural backgrounds could be expected to respond differently (and perhaps unfairly) to students' culturally varied styles.

Classroom Communication Structures. Classrooms have distinctive interpersonal communication patterns. The traditional communication structure is the "recitation script" (Mehan, 1979) (see Table 2). Certain features of the "recitation script" conflict with the communicative style of some students.

For example, domination of talk by a single person (the teacher) is alien to some American Indian students (Philips, 1983). In many Indian communities, a person is expected to address the group rather than a single individual. One-to-one exchanges in the presence of others, as when the teacher asks a single student a question and he answers only to her, are culturally discordant. It is also usual for a speaker to choose

Table 2
The Recitation Script

Basic pattern:

Teacher *initiates* communication
➜ Student *responds* ➜ Teacher *evaluates* student response

Features:

- Teacher regulates virtually all talk (including topic; who talks, when, and for how long). Teacher can interrupt or re-direct talk to another student.

- All talk is mediated through the teacher, i.e., students do not talk to each other or to the whole group (except when called upon to give accounts).

- Students do not evaluate or elaborate on each other's responses.

- Teacher is transmitter of knowledge; students are receivers.

when to speak and to speak as long as he/she needs to, thus having more control over his/her own conversational turn. Indian children are often characterized as "quiet" by their non-Indian teachers; yet it is apparent that to participate in the recitation script they may have to violate numerous rules of communication as they know them.

When the communication conventions of the classroom are so different from those that students know, students may fail to participate in "appropriate" ways. Informal assessment via questioning may reveal very little about what students know.

Alternative Strategies. The recitation script is not compatible with the goals of current reforms in instruction and assessment, nor is it compatible with principles of good instruction for English learners or for many students from culturally non-dominant communities. To move away from the recitation script, teachers can:

- Give students more opportunities to take an active role in classroom discourse.

- Allow for variety of ways of participating in classroom discourse. (Students need latitude to select how they will participate. Variation makes learning opportunities more equitable.)

- Increase collaborative learning activities. (Student-to-student communication will increase. Small-group projects in which students work independently allow students to speak at their own determination.)

- Encourage students to use their language of choice in small-group work, if a group is linguistically homogeneous.

- Allow opportunities for group response from students, versus focusing on individual students.

- Encourage students to learn from each other in group discussions, and give evaluative feedback to the group, rather than to individual students.

(These last two strategies will be particularly effective for some students, such as American Indian and Hawaii Native.)

Teachers' direct knowledge of the communication styles and patterns of their students' particular communities is critical to their making decisions about appropriate instructional and assessment strategies. There is no catalog of cultural characteristics that can safely be applied to any group (all American Indians, all African-Americans, etc.) for three reasons: 1) there is great variability among people within any cultural group; 2) cultures are not frozen in time but continue to change; and 3) contacts with other cultures cause change within a group.

Moving Toward Equitable Alternatives in Assessment

Table 3 lists some of the most compelling and widely-mentioned criteria for valid classroom assessments, many of them recommended by the National Center for Research on Evaluation, Standards, and Student Testing (CRESST) at UCLA. We have focused on classroom assessments here; additional criteria (such as transfer and generalizability and cost-effectiveness) would be more applicable to widescale alternative assessments, although they are of some concern in the classroom.

Table 3
Criteria for Valid Alternative Classroom Assessments

- are curriculum-linked

- are flexible (form, administration, interpretation)

- reflect opportunities to learn (fairness issue*)

- are cognitively complex*

- call on multiple intelligences

- are authentic (make real-world connections)

- are meaningful in themselves* (are learning opportunities)

- entail opportunities for self-assessment

- are culturally responsive/allow for variation in language, in cognitive and communicative style, and in beliefs and values

- integrate skills

- are used appropriately and are useful for the purpose for which they are designed (informing instruction)

* proposed by CRESST/UCLA

Assessments used for widescale accountability (e.g., state assessments) will also, necessarily, be less curriculum-linked, less flexible in form, and may offer less opportunity for self-reflection — particularly if students are not allowed to see them after they are scored. For these reasons, as mentioned earlier, many educators believe that the greatest potential for best use of the alternatives discussed here is in the classroom.

One alternative that many educators believe extremely promising for all students is portfolio assessment. If used well, portfolios can meet the criteria for valid, culturally-sensitive assessment.

PORTFOLIOS IN THE PLURALISTIC CLASSROOM

Student portfolios are structured collections of student work gathered over time, intended to show a student's development and achievement in one or more subject areas. They are process tools through which teachers and students evaluate student work together. Portfolios offer:

- Linkages to classroom experiences and students' personal experiences

- Flexibility to include products in any language or in any form (e.g. tapes, written pieces, drawings, photographs), experience-sensitive tasks, modified to suit student needs; student-chosen activities

- Developmental portrayals of student progress, using multiple measures at frequent intervals

- Self-evaluation opportunities for students

- Parent participation opportunities

- Opportunities to contextualize student performances (annotation)

- Program coordination support (when students have more than one teacher)

A Caveat and Some Recommendations

For portfolios to function well for English learners, in particular, teacher annotation is crucial to understanding the full context in which a performance was obtained. Annotation may include:

- explanation of why an activity was selected by teacher and/or student

- information on how much and what kind of teacher support was given; which teacher strategies were helpful

- notes on how the student completed a task, including successful student strategies, amount of time required

- information on difficulties the student had in completing a performance

- observations on the student's expressed feelings while engaged in an activity

- observations about the student's use of language and choice of language (English, other than English)

- the student's own written or dictated commentary about the meaning of the activity of his/her performance

- parents' commentary

Some Recommended Steps to Equity

Although the concerns about ensuring equity for students from non-dominant languages and cultures run deep, there are many positive steps that can be taken to begin to address them. Perhaps the first is to cultivate an attitude toward diversity that moves beyond characterizing students from non-dominant cultures and language groups as inferior (an assimilationist approach) and toward a true commitment to equality of outcomes for all students— a more pluralistic approach. The following are some elements of an agenda for equity in assessment.

Attention to Evidence and Consequences. It is imperative that we have a clear rationale for assessing students via certain products and performances and for the ways we interpret students' performances. We must be vigilant at every step of the way for potential bias, looking at a student's behavior and background as well as test performance to justify interpretations of scores and how they are used. Messick (1992) calls this the "interplay between evidence and consequences."

In addition, we must be extremely cautious in interpreting inadequate performances of students who are still developing proficiency in English or whose cultures do not match that of the school. A low performance cannot be assumed to mean that the student has not learned or is incapable of learning what is being assessed.

Flexibility. A principal key to meeting the assessment needs of a diverse student population is a flexible approach. It should be possible to design assessments that allow for a wide variety of tasks to elicit a single response and single tasks that allow for a wide variety of response types, while maintaining standards. For example, there are many possible ways to assess a student's ability to apply linear measurement skills. A task that reflects a context meaningful to the student should be used; and if appropriate, the student can record her problem solution in writing *or* on audiotape.

Improved Teacher Knowledge Base. If culturally-responsive pedagogy is truly a goal, teachers must be provided with pre-service and in-service education opportunities to learn about issues of language and culture and how they play out in the classroom. The cultures of students should be considered when programs, instructional practices, and materials are designed or selected, so that students' ability to participate in schooling is maximized, rather than attenuated. This means going beyond infusion of multicultural content into existing curricula to the use of culturally-responsive instructional strategies. Teacher preparation and development should address:

- differences in communication and cognitive styles and strategies for promoting inclusion of all students in classroom discourse

- ways of evaluating the language demands of classroom tasks

- frameworks for understanding students' language proficiencies

- a repertoire of ways to group students and work with them

- ways of working with communities

- frameworks for understanding and strategies for intervening with status differences that perpetuate inequities of the larger society in the classroom

- the role of teachers' own languages and cultures in shaping their world views and cognitive and communicative styles as well as their understandings of student performances

- opportunities to develop deep knowledge about particular cultural communities

Collaboration with Communities. To understand students' classroom performance, teachers need to learn from their local communities what is valued and how it is taught (Nelson-Barber & Mitchell, 1992). Therefore, community members should be included in decision-making about educational goals and assessments and their uses. Linking with the community will be crucial — to see communication patterns firsthand, to understand from parents what they value and why, to learn about how children perform at home, and to share with them a "school perspective." As change occurs, ongoing dialog with parents is vital to gaining their support — something that ultimately affects students' investment in the classroom.

Use of Multiple Sources. As Anastasi (1990) has cautioned, we must beware of using a single assessment score to make decisions about a student. What is needed is a range of assessments administered at different times throughout the school year. Students' performances on different tasks — even within a subject area — can vary considerably, and they change over time. Portfolios have been suggested as a desirable method of unifying in one place multiple indices of student performance that have been gathered over time.

Attention to Student Motivation and Interest. Often overlooked are *conative* variables having to do with motivation and interest — variables that affect learning outcomes. For example, personal interests lead people to seek certain experiences, which in turn contribute to the development of certain aptitudes. Conative information may be particularly important in understanding the performance of students whose cultural backgrounds differ from the dominant culture of the school. Their interests may diverge from what is available to them in school, and they may have developed skills in areas unknown to teachers. Such skills, however, could be linked to school experience by a sensitive teacher.

Other reasons that students may not be motivated to perform at peak capacity include conflicts in social identity and local conditions such as peer dynamics within a single classroom. In addition, some (as in the Navajo example cited) may not understand the meaning of "assessment" or "test" as construed by the school and thus may not be motivated to invest necessary effort.

Mediation of Assessments. Administration of assessments may be mediated in a number of ways: by increasing the amount of time given to complete them, by repeating or rephrasing instructions, by explaining the meaning of terms, by allowing the use of adjunct materials or classroom tools (dictionaries, calculators, etc.), or by translating portions of an assessment into a student's first language.

Translation. Translation is itself a form of mediation of text, between one language and another. Translating an assessment into a student's first language is a positive step. The more that students' first languages can be drawn upon (and maintained and developed) the greater the benefit to their learning. However, assessment translation is a source of many psychometric problems. There are no perfect equivalents across languages; and one is really translating across cultures as well. Some languages, like Spanish, have many dialects. Determining where the overlap of dialects lies so as to produce a translation comprehensible to most speakers of the language presents a considerable challenge. As the

American Educational Research Association's Standards for Educational and Psychological Testing notes,

"Psychometric properties cannot be assumed to be comparable across languages or dialects. Many words have different frequency rates or difficulty levels in different languages or dialects. Therefore words in two languages that appear to be close in meaning may differ radically in other ways important for the test use intended. Additionally, test content may be inappropriate in a translated version" (AERA..., p. 73).

Other aspects of text such as length may be affected by translation. Perhaps most fundamentally, construct validity is jeopardized with translation, i.e., it is not clear with a translated test that one is still testing the same presumed underlying abilities or knowledge. For all of these reasons, translation has to be regarded as a partial solution only.

Moderation. Moderation is the process of teachers' collectively evaluating student performances so as to ensure that the same standards are being applied. Teacher exchange of scored or graded student work offers the opportunity for teachers to check their interpretations of assessments against those of peers — something that could be particularly valuable in fostering discussion among teachers from different cultural backgrounds.

References

American Educational Research Association (with the American Psychological Association and the National Council on Measurement in Education). 1985. *Standards for Educational and Psychological Testing*. Washington, DC: American Psychological Association.

Anastasi, Anne. 1990. What is Test Misuse? Perspectives of a Measurement Expert. In Anastasi, Anne, et al. (Eds). *The Uses of Standardized Tests in American Education: Proceedings of the 1989 ETS Invitational Conference*. Princeton, NJ: Educational Testing Service.

Banks, James A. 1988. *Multiethnic Education: Theory and Practice*. Boston, MA: Allyn and Bacon.

Clark, Lynne W. (Ed). 1993. *Faculty and Student Challenges in Facing Cultural and Linguistic Diversity*. Springfield, IL: Charles C. Thomas Publisher.

De Avila, Edward A. and Duncan, Sharon. 1985. *Thinking and Learning Skills*. Hillsdale, NJ: Erlbaum.

Delpit, Lisa D. 1986. Skills and Other Dilemmas of a Progressive Black Educator. *Harvard Educational Review.* Vol. 56, No. 4.

Deyhle, Donna. 1987. Learning Failure: Tests as Gatekeepers and the Culturally Different Child. In Trueba, Henry (Ed). *Success or Failure.* Rowley, MA: Newbury House.

Gallagher, Pat. 1993. *Teachers' Cultural Assumptions: A Hidden Dimension of Schoolteaching.* Paper presented at the annual American Educational Research Association conference in Atlanta, Georgia.

Gibson, Margaret A. and Ogbu, John U. 1991. *Minority Status and Schooling: A Comparative Study of Immigrant and Involuntary Minorities.* New York: Garland Publishing, Inc.

Gordon, Edmund. 1993. *Human Diversity, Equity, and Educational Assessment.* Paper presented at 1993 CRESST Assessment Conference.

Kochman, Thomas. 1989. Black and White Cultural Styles in Pluralistic Perspective. In Gifford, B. (Ed). *Test Policy and Test Performance: Education, Language, and Culture.* Boston, MA: Kluwer Academic Publishers.

Linn, Robert L., Baker, Eva L., and Dunbar, Stephen B. 1991. Complex, Performance-Based Assessment: Expectations and Validation Criteria. *Education Researcher.* Vol 20, No. 8.

Mehan, H. 1979. *Learning Lessons.* Cambridge, MA: Harvard University Press.

Messick, Samuel. 1992. *The Interplay of Evidence and Consequences in the Validation of Performance Assessments.* Princeton, NJ: Educational Testing Service.

Nelson-Barber, Sharon S. and Mitchell, Jean. 1992. Restructuring for Diversity: Five Regional Portraits. In Dilworth, Mary. E. (Ed). *Diversity in Teacher Education.* San Francisco, CA: Jossey-Bass.

Olsen, Laurie. 1989. *Bridges.* San Francisco, CA: California Tomorrow.

Philips, Susan Urmston. 1983. *The Invisible Culture: Communication in Classroom and Community on the Warm Springs Indian Reservation.* New York: Longman.

Sanchez, G.I. 1934. Bilingualism and Mental Measures: A Word of Caution. *Journal of Applied Psychology.* No. 18.

Shepard, Lorrie A. 1991. Negative Policies for Dealing with Diversity: When Does Assessment Turn into Sorting and Segregation? In Hiebert, Elfrieda H. (Ed). *Literacy for a Diverse Society.* New York: Teachers College Press.

Tsang, Chui Lim. 1989. Bilingual Minorities and Language Issues in Writing: Toward Professionwide Responses to a New Challenge. *Written Communication.* Vol. 9, No. 1.

Villegas, Ana Maria. 1991. *Culturally Responsive Pedagogy for the 1990s and Beyond.* Princeton, NJ: Educational Testing Service, September.

Winfield, Linda F. 1987. Teachers' Estimates of Test Content Covered in Class and First-Grade Students' Reading Achievement. *The Elementary School Journal.* Vol. 87, No. 4.

Culture Clash

Debra Viadero

Ms. White, a teacher in an isolated rural community, is teaching her 1st Graders how to tell time. She points to a clock, telling her students that "It's 10 o'clock because the big hand is on the 12 and the little hand is on the 10."

"What time is it?" she asks the students. Many of the white children raise their hands, eager to answer. The black students sit silently. A few give her a puzzled look.

Ms. White concludes that many of her black students do not know the answer, and she silently makes a note to herself to revisit the concept with them later.

But researchers who study the role that culture plays in learning say that Ms. White may have the wrong take on what is going on with her students. What is really happening, they say, is that two distinct cultures are bumping up against one another, forming an invisible wall that stands in the way of learning and communication.

Like their teacher, the white children in this community grew up in families where adults routinely quizzed children the way their teacher does. "What color is this?" a parent might say, pointing to a red ball.

In the African-American children's families, such questions were posed only when someone genuinely needed to know the answer. "What is she asking us for?" some of the black children might have wondered. "She just told us it was 10 o'clock."

Cultural roadblocks such as this one are becoming increasingly common in schools across the country. It is estimated that by the turn of the century, up to 40 percent of the children in the nation's classrooms will be nonwhite. Yet, the nation's teaching force is overwhelmingly white and becoming more so. African-American, Asian, Hispanic and Native American teachers now make up just 10 percent of the teaching force, according to one estimate.

These kinds of demographics have lent a new urgency to studies on the role of culture in the classroom. At times controversial, the research has been carried out since the late 1960s by sociolinguists, anthropologists, psychologists, and, more recently, by education scholars as well. Their work paints complex portraits of the subtle interplay between a school's ways of knowing, talking, thinking, and behaving and those of students from a wide variety of non-mainstream, ethnic backgrounds.

However complicated the findings are, one point is clear: Culture is a phenomenon that goes both ways.

"We take the position that school was never a culturally neutral enterprise," says A. Wade Boykin, the co-director of the Center for Research on the Education of Students Placed at Risk at Johns Hopkins and Howard universities. From at least the start of the 20th century, one job of schools was to help assimilate the large numbers of immigrants flocking to the nation's shores. And, to a lesser degree, they are still striving to do just that.

But the nation's predominantly white educators have been slow to recognize that their own backgrounds — and the culture of the school — have a bearing on learning. And, rather than think of minority students as having a culture that is valid and distinct from theirs, they sometimes think of the youngsters as deficient. Even now, studies on minority students are lumped in the field's literature under such headings as "culturally deprived" or "culturally disadvantaged."

"It has been our previously homogeneous cultural condition that prevented us from understanding that we were not perceiving culture because it was invisible to us," says Roland G. Tharp, the director of the federally funded Center on Meeting the Educational Needs of Diverse Student Populations, based at the University of California at Santa Cruz. "It's like fish don't know there's water."

Once teachers realize they are part of the cultural equation in their classrooms, these researchers say, they must find ways to recognize the culture of their students, to acknowledge it in their teaching, and to make clear to students from different backgrounds the previously unstated expectations that the mainstream culture — and the school — has for them.

***

Although the above account of Ms. White's class is fictional, the tendencies it describes in the students and teachers are not. They come from a study by Shirley Brice Heath, an anthropologist and sociolinguist who spent several years in the 1970s living in two unnamed poor communities in a rural mountain area near Southern mill towns. The largely white community she called Roadville, the predominantly black community, Trackton.

In addition to noticing that there were differences in the way the two communities used questions, Heath also found that they had distinct ways of telling, stories, rearing children, and using toys and reading material. And the children of Trackton and Roadville reflected their communities in the way they behaved in their classrooms.

Heath's work was chronicled in the 1983 book *Ways with Words*. But studies with other groups of children have found similar distinctions. More important, they suggest that accommodating these distinctions can make a difference in children's learning.

Kathryn Au, a University of Hawaii researcher, noticed that the stories that Native Hawaiian children told in their classrooms mirrored the "talk stories" told by adults in their communities. In these stories, two people, speaking in rhythmic alternation, relate events together.

In a traditional classroom, children who spoke in that manner would be penalized for talking out of turn. But Au found that successful Native Hawaiian teachers could use the "talk story" patterns to help children better understand what they were reading in school. And non-native teachers could learn to do the same.

"Teachers who want to learn different cultural styles can certainly do that," Au says. "We have a lot of evidence that shows that good teaching is only good teaching with respect to a particular cultural context."

But culture also manifests itself in ways that are less visible than a child's manner of speaking or behaving.

"It's just as important to realize that the cultural value systems in which children grow up also influence their development," Patricia Marks Greenfield, a researcher at the University of California at Los Angeles, said in a presentation made last spring to the Urban Education National Network. Like the Native Hawaiians Au has studied, African-Americans, Asian-Americans, Hispanics, and Native Americans all have strong traditions emphasizing collectivist values, according to Greenfield.

And sometimes, those values clash with the traditional emphasis in schools on individual learning and competition. For example, Greenfield says, when groups of white teachers and Hispanic parents are asked to respond to hypothetical child-rearing scenarios, they answer in markedly different ways.

In one such scenario, taken from a pilot experiment Greenfield and her colleagues conducted, participants were told: "Erica tells her mother that she got the highest grade in the class on her math test. She says she is

MAKING ASSESSMENT WORK FOR EVERYONE

really proud of herself for doing so well, and for doing the best in the class. She says she guesses she is really smart."

Asked how Erica's mother should respond, a white, middle-class teacher said the mother should agree emphatically that, yes, Erica certainly is smart and her grade shows that she can achieve anything she puts her mind to. In contrast, a Hispanic immigrant mother answered, "She should congratulate her but tell her not to praise herself too much ... she should not think so much of herself."

Overall, Greenfield says, 80 percent of the teachers responded to the scenarios they were given in ways that could be considered individualistic. Hispanic immigrant mothers gave answers deemed collectivistic 90 percent of the time.

Some experts also believe history plays a role in a child's cultural development. John U. Ogbu, a well-known anthropologist from the University of California at Berkeley, believes that minority cultural groups can be classified in two ways — voluntary and involuntary immigrants. The voluntary immigrants, such as the Irish, the Italians, and other European immigrants of the early 20th century and Punjabi Indians of today, came to the United States looking for political freedom or better economic circumstances. They were happy to occupy the lowest rungs on the occupational ladder and considered their menial positions better than the jobs they had left behind.

Involuntary minorities, on the other hand, are people who came to be part of the United States "permanently against their will through slavery, conquest, colonization, or forced labor," according, to Ogbu. In this category, he places African-Americans, Native Americans, Mexican-Americans, and Native Hawaiians.

This second group is more likely to actively oppose the conventions of the dominant middle-class culture — even if adopting them would mean raising one's position on the social ladder. In one high school in the District of Columbia, for example, Ogbu and his colleague, Sionithia Fordham, found that African-American students avoided 17 different behaviors and attitudes that they considered "white." These ranged from speaking standard English to being on time. They also resented their high-achieving peers, accusing them of "acting white."

But Ogbu's theory has its detractors. For example, Howard Boykin says that what those black students may really resent is not good grades. Rather, they may be criticizing behaviors displayed by the high-achieving students that reflect a more competitively oriented value system over one that places the welfare of the group above the individual.

To succeed in school and in the job market, African-Americans — and other minority groups as well — sometimes have to learn to mediate between their home and school cultures. And research suggests that educators can help them bridge those gaps by pointing out clearly what the rest of society expects from them, while at the same time affirming their own culture.

Ms. White, for example, might have simply explained to the children that, even though she obviously knew what time it was, she wanted to see if they knew, too. And she might have asked the same question in different ways or put the question in another context, say, a problem to be solved. It would not mean giving different lessons to her black students than she gives to their white classmates.

"All children should learn to work in a variety of cultural contexts," Boykin says.

In her book *Other People's Children*, Lisa D. Delpit of Georgia State University describes how one Native Alaskan teacher helps her students learn to switch from standard English to "village English," the dialect they use at home. The teacher draws two columns on the blackboard, one for "Our Heritage Language" and one for "Formal English," and then writes equivalent statements in each column. The class spends a lot of time on the "heritage" section, exploring all the phrases' nuances.

"That's the way we say things. Doesn't it feel good? Isn't it the absolute best way of getting that idea across?" the teacher asks. Then, she informs her students, who live in a remote part of the state, that there are people who judge others by the way they talk or write.

"Unlike us, they have a hard time hearing what people say if they don't talk exactly like them....We're going to learn two ways to say things," she adds. "Then, when we go to get jobs, we'll be able to talk like those people who only know and can only really listen to one way. Maybe after we get the jobs we can help them to learn how it feels to have another language, like ours, that feels so good."

Brenda Townsend, an assistant professor of education at the University of South Florida in Tampa, takes a similar approach with African-American students. She recalls in particular one group of boys attending a predominantly white school who were always getting suspended for getting in trouble on the bus. She taught them how to talk with one another in a way that didn't look to white teachers like arguing.

"They were like, 'Wow, nobody ever told us that,'" she says. After those lessons, the suspensions ended.

***

The problem with studies that focus on one ethnic group or another, however, is that they can lead to stereotyping. "We need to be very careful when we speak about cultural groups," says Walter Secada, a professor of curriculum and instruction at the University of Wisconsin-Madison. "Yes, there is a core there. But to talk to anyone who belongs to any group and expect certain things about them would be a mistake."

It is a danger that proponents of cross-cultural studies readily recognize. "When you read a lot of stuff written even 10 years ago, it's sort of like a recipe," says Sandra H. Fradd, a University of Miami researcher who is studying cross-cultural learning in science with her colleague, Okhee Lee. "It was like, 'If you're working with Hispanics, this is what you should be doing.'"

"But there's a difference between a stereotype and a pattern," she says. "We're trying to say these are predictable ways these students perform."

"I think you do more harm by ignorance," adds Greenfield of UCLA. "We need to respect differences and try to understand them but that doesn't mean that we have to make assumptions."

The other drawback to this line of research, however, is a practical one. Teachers cannot possibly learn the traditions and discourse patterns of every cultural group they will one day encounter in their classrooms. Moreover, characteristics and beliefs that are common among Mexican-Americans may be different from those of Puerto Ricans or Cuban immigrants, even though all three groups speak the same language.

"There's always heterogeneity, the more closely you look," says Ken Zeichner, a professor of teacher education at the University of Wisconsin-Madison. "What we emphasize is to teach teachers how to learn about their students."

Some school districts, Zeichner notes, even pay their teachers to spend the week before school starts visiting with the families of their students.

Other researchers, such as Luis Moll at the University of Arizona, also suggest that teachers make use of the hidden resources they find in the families they meet. A Mexican-American mother may come in and talk about candy-making; a father might discuss mining or construction work.

But Sharon Nelson-Barber, a researcher who has studied Native American students and teachers, suggests that teachers also exercise caution with these kinds of approaches.

"In one of the communities where I lived, you never would visit someone if you were not part of that person's world," says Nelson-Barber, a senior research associate for WestEd, formerly the Far West Laboratory. "What you could do is drive up very close to the house and stop. If people were interested, they would come out and talk to you. How would anyone know this?"

She says she has studied teachers who work on Native-American reservations but live some distance away. They keep in touch with their students' worlds by keeping a post office box on the reservation, shopping at the local trading post, and taking part in other community activities.

The University of California's Tharp proposes a slightly different tack. He and his colleagues have sifted through thousands of what they call "monocultural" studies — in other words, research that focuses on a single ethnic or racial group.

"In my view, there's been a very big shift in the past 10 years from the specific compatibility of schools and specific cultures to how to more generally respond — in what ways do schools need to act to be more responsive?" Tharp says. "Because, as it turns out, all kids need to be comfortable with the classroom culture."

Virtually all the studies, Tharp says, point to the need for schools to place learning in the context of the values and experiences of the students they serve. In the Native American communities with which Nelson-Barber works, that might mean teaching science, for example, through discussions of local fishing practices and tide patterns.

"We're not talking fantasy land," Tharp says, "many schools have been able to do this and it increases the involvement and achievement of communities to do so. You can't run a school like it's a spaceship from another planet that just landed in town."

He says the research also shows that schools need to put a higher priority on explicitly teaching, all day long, whatever the language of instruction is — be it standard English, another language, or the specific vocabulary of the subject matter being taught.

"Every subject matter has its own language, its own rules for how you make sentences," he says.

Tharp also suggests that engaging students in joint, productive activity, such as putting out a newspaper, will allow them to work in the discourse patterns and cultural styles that feel most comfortable for them.

"It's not the same thing as cooperative learning," he says. "Everybody may not organize joint activities in the same way."

He says studies also suggest that dialogue between teachers and students has to take place more often than has been the case in the past.

The bottom line, researchers agree, is that cultural considerations need to play a bigger role in the classroom and in teacher education programs than they do now. It is a viewpoint that is not universally accepted in the education field. Critics assert that some teaching methodologies are so powerful they can overcome the mismatch between a student's culture and that of the school.

But cultural researchers note that, whether it's recognized or not, culture is the lens through which everyone sees the world.

"This is not a sideshow," Tharp says. "This is the big tent."

Principles

Roland G. Tharp, the director of the Center on Meeting the Educational Needs of Diverse Student Populations, a federally funded research center at the University of California at Santa Cruz, has pored over thousands of studies on cross-cultural learning. All of the studies, he says, point to four basic ways educators can enhance learning for students of diverse cultural groups.

- Education has to be put in the context of the experiences and values of the students' communities.

- Schools need to be relentless and explicit in teaching students the language of instruction — be it standard English, another language, or the specific vocabulary and rules that are unique to the subject matter being taught.

- Students need to be engaged in joint productive activities, such as putting out a newspaper, that allow them to work in ways that are culturally familiar.

- Teachers need to engage in more purposeful, two-way conversations with students.

F.Y.I.

Delpit, L. (1995). *Other people's children: Cultural conflict in the classroom.* New York: The New Press.

Greenfield, P.M., & Cocking, R.R. (1996). *Cross-cultural roots of minority child development.* Hillsdale, NJ: Lawrence Erlbaum Associates.

Heath, S.B. (1983). *Ways with words: Language, life, and work in communities and classrooms.* New York: Cambridge University.

Hollins, E., Kina, J., & Wayman, W. (Eds.). (1994). *Teaching diverse populations.* Albany, NY: State University of New York.

Moll, L. (1992). Funds of knowledge for teaching: Using a qualitative approach to connect homes and classrooms. *Theory into Practice, 31*(2), 132-4 1.

Tharp, R., & Gailimore, R. (1988). *Rousing minds to life: Teaching, learning and schooling in social contest.* New York: Cambridge University Press.

SECTION VII

Professional Development Activities for Teachers

People perceive the world in different ways, learn about the world in different ways, and demonstrate what they have learned in different ways. The approach to learning and the demonstration of what one has learned is influenced by the values, norms and socialization practices of the culture in which the individual has been enculturated.

Swisher and Deyhle,
The Styles of Learning Are Different, But the Teaching Is Just the Same, 1989

rofessional Development Activities

Development Dots:
A Pre and Post Activity

Participants and Purposes:

You can do this activity on your own, with students, or with colleagues. It is meant to help you or others self-assess knowledge about socio-cultural impacts on the classroom.

Materials:

1. A copy of the two handouts, **Meeting the Needs of Diverse Learners: Knowledge of Students' Culture, Language, Gender, and Ethnicity** and **Meeting the Needs of Diverse Learners: Assessment Skills for Developing, Administering, Interpreting, and Communicating About Student Learning.**

2. Two colored sticky dots per person for each time you plan to use this activity. If you do it pre and post, each person will need four dots.

Suggested Time:

15–30 minutes

Directions/Notes:

- Using **Meeting the Needs of Diverse Learners: Knowledge of Students' Culture, Language, Gender, and Ethnicity**, ask participants to place a colored dot along the line next to the statement that most closely describes their current situation. Ask them to date it and plan to revisit this judgment when they've completed *Making Assessment Work for Everyone.*

- Using **Meeting the Needs of Diverse Learners: Assessment Skills for Developing, Administering, Interpreting, and Communicating About Student Learning**, ask participants to place a colored dot along the line next to the statement that most closely describes their current situation. Date it and plan to revisit this judgment when they've completed *Making Assessment Work for Everyone.*

Notation:

You may also do this on a large sheet of chart paper, so a group of participants can share what they've learned. Use chart paper to hand write a copy, or use a copy enlarger.

Meeting the Needs of Diverse Learners:
Knowledge of Students' Culture, Language, Gender, and Ethnicity

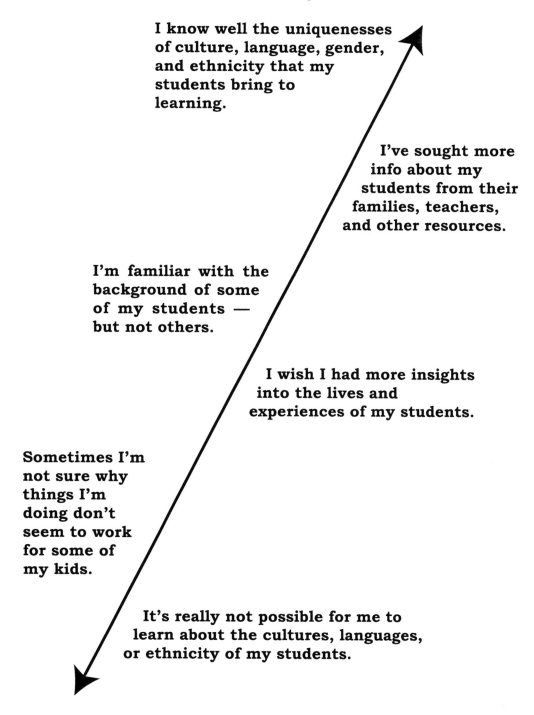

I know well the uniquenesses of culture, language, gender, and ethnicity that my students bring to learning.

I've sought more info about my students from their families, teachers, and other resources.

I'm familiar with the background of some of my students — but not others.

I wish I had more insights into the lives and experiences of my students.

Sometimes I'm not sure why things I'm doing don't seem to work for some of my kids.

It's really not possible for me to learn about the cultures, languages, or ethnicity of my students.

DIRECTIONS: Place a colored dot along the line next to the statement that most closely describes your current situation. Date it and plan to revisit this judgment when you've completed *Making Assessment Work for Everyone.*

Meeting the Needs of Diverse Learners: Assessment Skills for Developing, Administering, Interpreting, and Communicating About Student Learning

I can develop, select, and adapt assessments that meet keys to quality. My understanding of student strengths is built into the assessments I use and in my interpretation of the results.

I can recognize potential sources of bias in assessments and can usually offer alternative ways for students to show their learning.

I'm familiar with some barriers to good assessment, but am not always sure what to do about it.

I wish I had better ways to assess the learning of my students. The barriers seem impossible to overcome.

I'm sure some of my students are doing better than their assessments show, but I don't know how to get better pictures of their learning.

DIRECTIONS: Place a colored dot along the line next to the statement that most closely describes your current situation. Date it and plan to revisit this judgment when you've completed *Making Assessment Work for Everyone.*

Are We Different?

Participants and Purposes:

You can do this activity with your students or your colleagues. It is meant to help us see that even in our sameness, we are different, and in our differences, we have similarities. As participants discuss their differences and similarities they will come to a closer understanding of the impact of diversity.

Materials:

A cut-out set of symbols for each person to do the activity. A complete set is one of each symbol for a total of six. The camera-ready copies that follow are made so that you can run a whole sheet of each symbol on a single color of paper.

Suggested Time:

15–30 minutes

Directions/Notes:

- Give each person a set of cut-out symbols with the following directions: *Use these symbols to illustrate "your life." You may use them in any manner you choose.*

- Use the handout, **Discussion Questions for Are We Different?** to generate dialogue. These questions may be used for large-group discussion or small groups or a combination of both.

Discussion Questions for Are We Different?

1. Why did you arrange the symbols in the order you did?

2. What do you think your reasoning says about you as a person?

3. Does this reasoning reflect anything about the culture in which you were raised or your present environment?

4. If you were to do this activity in your classroom, what do you think you would learn? What would your students learn?

5. Think about what you have experienced today. What impact does this experience have on your practice as a teacher?

Symbol Sheet 1

Cut apart the symbols on this page. Combine one symbol from each of the six sheets to form a set. Each page should be run a different color.

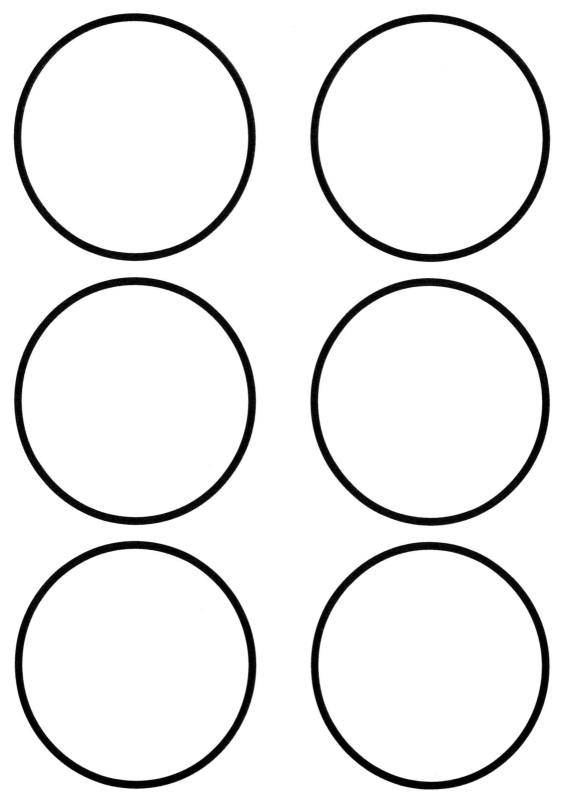

Symbol Sheet 2

Cut apart the symbols on this page. Combine one symbol from each of the six sheets to form a set. Each page should be run a different color.

MAKING ASSESSMENT WORK FOR EVERYONE

Symbol Sheet 3

Cut apart the symbols on this page. Combine one symbol from each of the six sheets to form a set. Each page should be run a different color.

Symbol Sheet 4

Cut apart the symbols on this page. Combine one symbol from each of the six sheets to form a set. Each page should be run a different color.

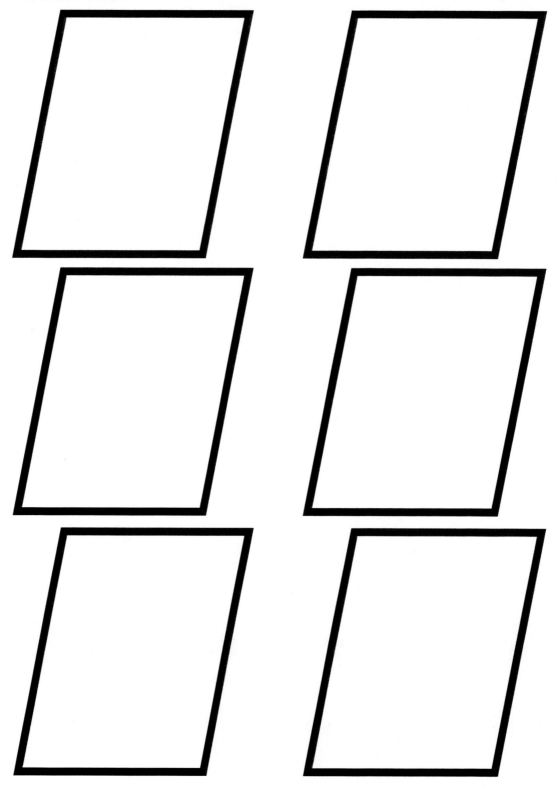

Symbol Sheet 5

Cut apart the symbols on this page. Combine one symbol from each of the six sheets to form a set. Each page should be run a different color.

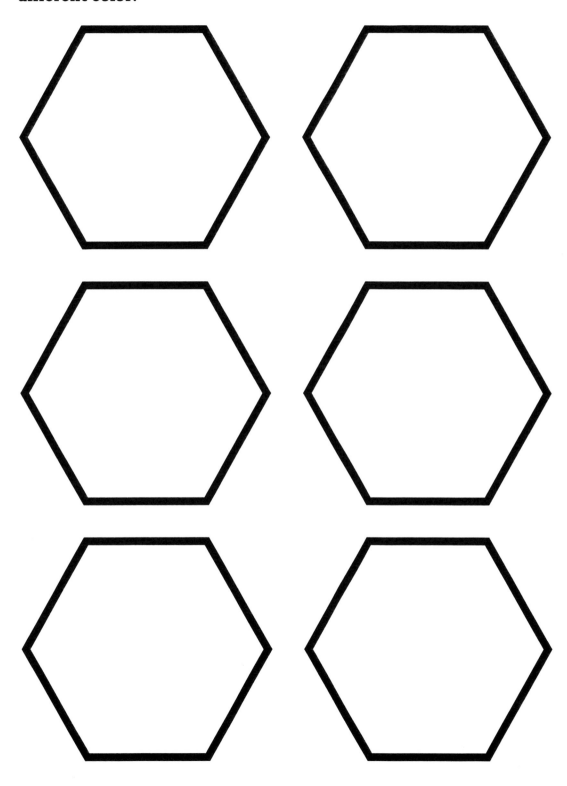

Symbol Sheet 6

Cut apart the symbols on this page. Combine one symbol from each of the six sheets to form a set. Each page should be run a different color.

MAKING ASSESSMENT WORK FOR EVERYONE

A Place in the Sun

Participants and Purposes:

This activity can be done with other educators or with students. It will create an increased cultural awareness and an understanding of the destructive atmosphere that cultural minority or nonmainstream students sometimes encounter. It is a good tool for opening discussion about cultural diversity and the impact of cultural diversity on students.

Materials:

- Print a copy of the quotes on the **Quotation Sheet** on small sheets of paper. Each group of three or four will need one quote. You may duplicate cards if the group is large.

- Print a copy of the entire poem **A Way to Belong** for each participant.

- NCR paper (or sheets for recording ideas). The NCR paper is nice because there's a permanent record left behind of the ideas and interpretations that people bring to the image.

Suggested Time:

35–45 minutes

Directions/Notes:

Special Notation: This activity is based on a strategy the reading teachers will be familiar with. It's a technique to generate involvement with a text. You will have to remind the participants several times that there is no right answer. They are being asked to respond; no answer is incorrect. The key is to have them tie into the poem, through their assigned lines, and therefore create a stronger link to the message of the poem. Be sure to remember to praise their answers as innovative, interesting, and powerful.1.   Give the participants **A Place in the Sun Direction Sheet**.

> *Each group is going to receive a cutting from a poem. If you happen to be familiar with the poem, please pretend you have no knowledge. This only works if all of us are at a disadvantage!*

> *Each person in the group is to **read the lines aloud** to the other members in his/her group. Listen closely to one another. Listen for the meanings we gain through audio clues.*

When each of you has read the lines, begin a conversation about the section.

    Describe the author.
    What was the author trying to say to the reader?
    What is the context for this poem?
    What do these lines "mean"?

There is no right or wrong answer. This is an investigation. What can you discover about this poem with the information that you have?

2. Give the participants at least three to seven minutes to come to their answers. Circle the room and remind the participants that each person needs to read the lines aloud and provide encouragement to the group members. It is difficult for participants when there is not a clear answer.

3. Have a spokesperson from each group read the lines aloud to the group and then talk about the group's conclusions about the lines.

4. When all the groups are finished presenting their ideas, talk about the differences and similarities in their conclusions.

5. Tell them that all the lines are from the same poem, that without the context we have such conflicting ideas. Remind them of what great interpretations they gave without knowing anything about the poem. You are impressed and so forth.

6. Finally, tell them where the poem came from and who wrote the poem. This poem is such a powerful piece it needs little introduction besides that.

7. Then pass out copies of the poem and have them read along on their papers as you read it aloud. Practice the reading — it looks like an easy poem to read; however, the wording is also complex in places.

8. Lead them into a discussion about how this poem lays the foundation for considering cultural diversity.

A Place in the Sun Direction Sheet

Each group is going to receive a cutting from a poem. If you happen to be familiar with the poem, please pretend you have no knowledge. This only works if all of us are at a disadvantage!

Each person in the group is to read the lines aloud to the other members in his/her group. Listen closely to one another. Listen for the meanings we gain through audio clues.

When each of you has read the lines, begin a conversation about the section.

> *Describe the author.*

> *What was the author trying to say to the reader?*

> *What is the context for this poem?*

> *What do these lines "mean"?*

There is no right or wrong answer. This is an investigation. What can you discover about this poem with the information that you have?

Quotation Sheet

... Musically accented, even when spoken angrily
Masa-chan when spoken tenderly
she forgot its meaning and the challenge it issued:...

         ...Go forth with a straight heart
it beckoned her from the kitchen window carrying aromas of natto and
   fried fish
drifting above the neighbors who wrinkled their noses at the strange
   smell

with a deep fluid voice never tripping over English words
baby fine blond hair never needing a perm
long-lashed round eyes never needing make-up

she watched her mother's mouth move, baffling white noise flying forth
a stream of sounds before dinner meant 'set the table'
loud terse syllables and a stern look meant 'don't cross my path'

songs of her mother's childhood were never sung
her mother's wishes and sorrow never revealed
the tale of Momotaro, the Peach Boy, never told

When she was twenty the child, now a woman, lost her land
..., an ocean, a generation away
...she sees an intruder

as easy as rain the mother slipped away one day
and the woman turned speechless writing her mother's eulogy

a whale's song to vibrate ocean peaks and trenches
to soar upward through blue liquid and endless velvet vacuum of space
to cross the boundary dividing inexpressible souls

A Way to Belong

by Joan Shigemoto

When she was five, the child lost her name
    Masako. Musically accented, even when spoken angrily
    Masa-chan when spoken tenderly
    she forgot its meaning and the challenge it issued: Go forth with a
    straight heart
    it beckoned her from the kitchen window carrying aromas of natto
    and fried fish
    drifting above the neighbors who wrinkled their noses at the strange
    smell
    don't call me that, she told her mother
    the child preferred her English name after an American movie star
    with a deep fluid voice never tripping over English words
    baby fine blond hair never needing a perm
    long-lashed round eyes never needing make-up
When she was ten, the child lost her mother tongue
    to the child a rose was cool neat pretty nice
    but all the words she knew fell short of the thirty two ways
    her mother could express it in her language so attuned to physical
    beauty
    she watched her mother's mouth move, baffling white noise
    flying forth
    a stream of sounds before dinner meant 'set the table'
    loud terse syllables and a stern look meant 'don't cross my path'
    mother and child unable to speak in a way that could be understood
    by the other
    songs of her mother's childhood were never sung
    her mother's wishes and sorrow never revealed
    the tale of Momotaro, the Peach Boy, never told
    in school the child heard stories about Cinderella, Goldilocks,
    Snow White
When she was twenty, the child, now a woman, lost her land
    she traveled to her mother's home, an ocean, a generation away
    where she found the village quaint and her relatives exotic
    wasn't it amazing, they said, that she spoke English unaccented and
    wrote it unaided
    after days of endless rice, she wanted mashed potatoes
    once home she went to a restaurant for the fried chicken she craved
    there a boy in red and white cap said kindly 'you speak English well'
    memories of the journey with her mother fade on the shelf of albums
    to other far away places.
    at times she gazes at the picture of herself in her mother's land
    she sees an intruder

When she was thirty, the woman lost her mother
  as easy as rain the mother slipped away one day
  and the woman turned speechless writing her mother's eulogy
  she could not tell her mother's story because
  she did not know the ancestral wisdom and personal discoveries
  behind Okasan's crinkly silent eyes
  what she needed was a cry, loud and strong
  a whale's song to vibrate ocean peaks and trenches
  to soar upward through blue liquid and endless velvet vacuum
  of space
  to cross the boundary dividing inexpressible souls
  to nestle in the shell of her mother's ear
  so that she might know a way to belong.
  But it was too late.

  Masako

Joan Shigemoto is a Pacific Educator in Residence (PEIR) from Hawaii at PREL. Poem Published in Pacific Education Update, July 1997, Honolulu, HI.

Do the Words Tell the Whole Story?

Participants and Purposes:

Here's an activity that you can try out yourself, with your students, and with your teaching partners. The goal of this activity is to open your lens to viewing student work so that you can better detect student learning and next steps. Things are not always what they seem.

Materials:

A copy of the following handouts: **Open-Ended Science Questions and Answers (#s 1 and 2)** and **Open-Ended Science Questions and Answers Explanation (#s 1 and 2).**

Suggested Time:

One-and–one-half to two hours

Directions/Notes:

1. Divide the participants into groups of three to four.

2. Copy the **Open-Ended Science Questions and Answers Handout (#s 1 and 2)** and **Open-Ended Science Questions and Answers Explanation Handout (#s 1 and 2)**.

3. Give every group the first handouts (the ones without the explanations). Ask them to score the student responses using the rubric on the page.

4. Once they have finished scoring, ask for volunteers to share their rationale for the grades.

5. Then pass out the **Explanation** for the first student response. Ask them to read and discuss what they have discovered. Ask for volunteers to share with the whole group.

6. Ask the groups to review their "grading" of the second response. Ask if anyone thinks s/he would like to change her/his answer.

7. Pass out the **Explanation** for the second response.

8. Ask each participant to respond to the following reflective questions:

   What have you learned about your assessment practice by looking at these two prompts?

   What do you need to do to make positive changes in your assessment practice?

Open-Ended Science Questions and Answers
Handout #1

Task:

In the space below, discuss how human activity and industries can damage the environment.

Response:

The man use weather to was things and for dring. Also fabrics make to many good things.

What knowledge do you think the student communicates in this answer?

Scoring Guide:

High   **Low**

– 4 –	– 3 –	– 2 –	– 1 –
The student has answered each element of the prompt in a clear and concise manner.	The student answers some aspects of the prompt, but does not address all parts.	The student's answer fails to address any of the elements in the prompt.	

Open-Ended Science Questions and Answers
Handout #2

Task:

What do shadows have to do with the earth's motion?

Response:

Shadow don't have to do anyting. The eart just mubs.

What knowledge do you think the student communicates in this answer?

Scoring Guide:

High   **Low**

– 4 –	– 3 –	– 2 –	– 1 –
The student has answered each element of the prompt in a clear and concise manner.	The student answers some aspects of the prompt, but does not address all parts.	The student's answer fails to address any of the elements in the prompt.	

Open-Ended Science Questions and Answers
Explanation Handout #1

Task:

In the space below discuss how human activity and industries can damage the environment.

Response:

The man use weather to was things and for dring. Also fabrics make to many good things.

Intended Meaning:

Humans use water to wash things and for drinking. Also, factories make too many things with wood.

Discussion:

The student uses a Spanish syntactical structure. Spelling mistakes (**weather** instead of **water**; **was** instead of **wash**) and improper use of verb tenses (**dring**) instead of **drinking** make it difficult to understand the intended meaning of the first sentence. The student misuses the word **fabric** because **fabrica** in Spanish means **factory** and uses **to** instead of **too**. In addition, because the soft **w** sound does not exist in Spanish, the student uses **good** to mean **wood**. As a result, the interpretation of the second sentence makes no sense at first glance, even though the intended meaning is correct.

Open-Ended Science Questions and Answers
Explanation Handout #2

Task:
What do shadows have to do with the earth's motion?

Response:
Shadow don't have to do anyting. The eart just mubs.

Intended Meaning:
Shadows don't need to do anything. It is the earth that moves.

Discussion:
Spelling mistakes aside (**eart** for **earth** and **mubs** for **moves**), the student has probably answered the prompt incorrectly because the student misinterpreted the prompt. The student is probably unfamiliar with the expression, **have to do**, which in Spanish literally means **must do (tiene qué hacer)** and understands the prompt as **What do shadows must** (or need to) do with the earth's motion?**Telling a Story**

Participants and Purposes:

Here's an activity that you can try out yourself, with your students, and with your teaching partners. As teachers we tend to assume that our students process information and transmit knowledge in the same way that we, ourselves, do. This activity shows that there is more than one way to tell a story.

Materials:

A copy of the following handouts: **My Grandfather, My Grandfather Background Information, When a Dream Comes True, When a Dream Comes True Background Information, Six Trait Model, Six Trait Model in Brief,** and two copies of the **Evaluation**.

Suggested Time:

One-and-one-half to two hours

Directions/Notes:

1. Divide the participants into groups of 3–4.

2. Copy the **My Grandfather**, **When a Dream Comes True**, and **Evaluation** handouts for the participants.

3. Distribute **My Grandfather** and **Six Trait Model** handouts. If the group has not used the Six Trait Model, take the time to explain the model using the handouts on the Six Trait Model.

4. Once they have read the essay and finished the evaluation sheet, ask for volunteers to share their rationale for their scores.

5. Use chart paper to record responses to the following question. Display the results when they are completed.

   If you were having a teacher/student conference with this student, what would you tell her/him to do in order to improve on the next draft?

6. Pass out **My Grandfather Background Information**. Ask the participants to read the sheet. Then ask the group:

   Now that you know more about the student and the cultural context, what do you think about the suggestions for improvement that have been given to the student?

Are there ways that you could approach this conversation that would be of greater benefit to the student, now that you have a better understanding of the student's context?

7. Pass out **When a Dream Comes True**, **Evaluation**, and **When a Dream Comes True Background Information** at the same time. Ask the participants to read the essay and the background information as a group and, as a group, decide on an approach to take in helping this student to perform better on written assessments in English.

8. Ask volunteers to share their strategies. Ask them the following question:

   *Thinking back to **My Grandfather** and the process we used to find methods to help that student perform better, how does having more information up front help you as an educator?*

   What can you do to make more of this information available to you as you design and grade assessments?

Six Trait Model

Six Traits

Ideas

— the heart of the message

Organization

— the internal structure of the piece

Voice

— the tone and flavor of the author's message

Word Choice

— the vocabulary a writer chooses to convey meaning

Sentence Fluency

— the rhythm and flow of the language

Conventions

— mechanical correctness

Six Trait Value Explanation

Each of the six traits is scored on a scale of one to five, where five is high. These are not intended to corresponded to A, B, C, D, and F grades. Teachers are encouraged not to use the traits in a lockstep fashion; rather, they should use the traits that make sense in any given instructional instance, weight them differently depending on the situation, and ask students to add language that makes sense to them.

Six Trait Model in Brief *

Ideas — the heart of the message — Ideas are the heart of the message, the content of piece, the main theme, together with all the details that enrich and develop that theme. The ideas are strong when the message is clear, not garbled. The writer chooses details that are interesting, important, and informative — often the kinds of details the reader would not normally anticipate or predict. Successful writers do not tell readers things they already know (e.g., "it was a sunny day, and the sky was blue..."). They notice what others overlook, seek out the extraordinary, the unusual, the bits and pieces of life that others might not see.

Organization — the internal structure of the piece — Organization is the internal structure of a piece of writing, the thread of central meaning. It doesn't matter what the pattern is, so long as it fits the central idea well. Organizational structure can be based on comparison-contrast, deductive logic, point-by-point analysis, development of a central theme, chronological history of an event, or any of a dozen other identifiable patterns. When the organization is strong, the piece begins meaningfully and creates in the writer a sense of anticipation that is ultimately, systematically fulfilled. Events proceed logically; information is given to the reader in the right doses at the right times so that the reader never loses interest and never the "big picture" — the overriding sense of what the writer is driving at. Connections are strong, which is another way of saying that bridges from one idea to the next hold up. The piece closes with a sense of resolution, tying up loose ends, bringing things to closure, answering important questions while still leaving the reader something to think about.

Voice — the tone and flavor of the author's message — The voice is the writer coming through the words, the sense that a real person is speaking to us and cares about the message. It is the heart and soul of the writing, the magic, the wit, the feeling, the life and breath. When the writer is engaged personally with the topic, s/he imparts a personal tone and flavor to the piece that is unmistakably his/hers alone. It is that individual something — different from the mark of all other writers — that we call voice.

Word Choice — the vocabulary a writer chooses to convey meaning — Word choice is the use of rich, colorful, precise language that communicates not just in a functional way, but in a way that moves and enlightens the reader. In good descriptive writing, strong word choice paints clear pictures in the reader's mind. In good expository writing,

* From *The Six Traits*, 1997, Vicki Spandel and Ruth Culham, Northwest Regional Educational Laboratory.

strong word choice clarifies and expands ideas. In persuasive writing, careful word choice moves the reader to a new vision of things. Strong word choice is characterized not so much by an exceptional vocabulary that impresses the reader, but more by the skill to use everyday words well.

Sentence Fluency — the rhythm and flow of the language — Sentence fluency is the rhythm and flow of the language, the sound of word patterns, the way in which the writing plays to the ear — not just to the eye. How does it sound when read aloud? That's the test. Fluent writing has cadence, power, rhythm and movement. It is free of awkward word patterns that slow the reader's progress. Sentences vary in length and style, and are so well crafted that reading aloud is a pleasure.

Conventions — mechanical correctness — Conventions are the mechanical correctness of the piece — spelling, grammar and usage, paragraphing (indenting in the appropriate spots), use of capitals, and punctuation. Writing that is strong in conventions has usually been proofread and edited with care. Handwriting and neatness are not part of this trait. The key is this: How much work would a copy editor need to do to prepare the piece for publication?

My Grandfather

Assignment:

Write an essay about an elder who has been important in your life.

I never realized my grandfather was such a hard worker until recently. He is currently 70 years old and was born October 10, 1926. One some nights when I go to see him I usually like to sit and listen to what he has to say. At times I regret not learning how to speak Navajo. He knows how to speak Navajo and Spanish fluently. He says modern English is not our true language so therefore he does not speak it. Often times he doesn't like it when we, as grandchildren, speak only English. He is a very serious person. He's not the type to make jokes and laugh about them. His determination all started when he became a Christian. At first he grew up the traditional way of living but that never did any good for him. Meaning he was a young man who ran wild and free. He was an alcoholic for sometime which made him crazy. He had friends who were Spaniards. He worked with them as a Construction Worker. But that all changed, after his marriage with Nannabah who is my grandmother he became Chritianized into "Friends Church." He practiced to become a preacher after that. He then started traveling to other churches of his kind and met new people. People who are now his friends.

Evaluation

In the space provided create a plot line for the story that this student has created.

Score the paper you've read using the rubric below

6 Trait Model Rubric

Traits	Score					Comments
	1	2	3	4	5	
Ideas						
Organization						
Voice						
Word Choice						
Sentence Fluency						
Conventions						

Most important aspect of writing to address in the next draft....

This was great!

My Grandfather Background Information

- The tradition of Navajo storytelling is much less linear and more circular; the listener understands the theme or message after digesting the whole of the story. It is a deliberate, holistic approach that forces the listener to attend to all of the story in order to find meaning.

- The construction workers who live on the reservation have to travel great distances and may also live apart from families for long periods of time in order to keep a job.

- The theme of this story is similar to the young man's troubled homecoming used by Native American writers such as N. Scott Momaday, Leslie Marmon Silko, Louis Erdrich and Sherman Alexie.

- The first draft of this paper was much longer and more developed.

When a Dream Comes True Essay

Assignment:
Write a story about an important event in your life.

It was a sunny day. There were birds flying around the school. A small, simple, but penceful school that is located in a very little town in Oaxaca exactly in the southwest part of Mexico. I was siting on an old bench watching the birds flying, when my teacher came to me and smiling said, "Luis, you had been chosen to represent our school in the next testing competitions in Santa Ana (name of the town where the competitions would take place).

"My God," I exclaimed surprised. "How it came?" I asked.

"Because your score in the last test was avobe average I mean it was better than any one's score," He added. "one more thing the test will be in three weeks from now. I'm telling you this to give you chanse to study because we need to win so keep in mind that you must win," the teacher said.

Finally the date came. I was so nervous because in the competition there were students from thirteen different schools to try to have the first place. After listening the instructions from the teacher, I started to answer the instructions from the teacher, I started to answer the math part first.

My mouth was dry, and I started to sweat, my heart pumped faster my blood. It was a terrible starting. At the end of the test I was so tired and bored in addition each student was nervous waittin for the results. Finally the results were ready after two hours of waiting.

"Please stand in a line, I'm going to give you the results," said the principal.

When a Dream Comes True Background Information

This writer is an English language learner (ELL) student who has been raised in a very mainstream home. The student has been encouraged to fit into the "White" society.

The writer uses expressions and structures that are very common to Spanish-speaking students:

- **siting in**, **terrible starting** – Spanish speakers have ongoing difficulties distinguishing appropriate word choice (i.e., when to use **on/in** in English, **starting** or **beginning**)

- **smiling said** and **how it came?** and **my heart pumped faster my blood** – the order of words in these phrases is more common to Spanish than English

- **had been chosen** – there is a confusion in the tenses, again common in ELL

- **listening the instruction** – ELL students commonly have a problem with articles and required prepositions in English; the Spanish word for hear (oir) doesn't require a preposition, and listen/hear (escuchar) doesn't always require a presupposition

- **posible**, **imposible** – confusing a Spanish spelling with the English spelling

- **the higher** – the Spanish language does not use the same syntactical structure to create superlatives and comparative (i.e., **higher=mas alto**; **highest=lo mas alto**)

A Slice in Time:
Narrating Differences

Participants and Purposes:

Here's an activity that you can try out yourself, with your students, and with your teaching partners. Its aim is to "see with new eyes" into the diversity that exists in individuals — and the richness that this diversity creates in a learning environment. It's also about revealing the variety of ways that we narrate our own stories. This activity works well in combination with *Defining Our Differences*.

Materials:

- A picture, painting, drawing or transparency that features a person or setting that will serve as a springboard into the imagination. Possible pictures might be *The Flower Barrier* by Diego Rivera, *Hot Seat* by Joseph Amrhein, *Rainy Night Downtown* by Georgia Mills Jessup, or *Girl on a Small Wall* by Suzanne Valadon, or you can also use a magazine illustration, a student drawing or pictures from a library book. If you plan to use this activity with a larger group, you will want to turn the picture into a transparency to give everyone a clear view of its colors and details.

- NCR paper (or sheets for recording ideas). The NCR paper is nice because there's a permanent record left behind of the ideas and interpretations that people bring to the image.

- A copy of the following handouts for each participant: **Slice of Time** and **Narrative Analysis**.

Suggested Time:

One slot of one-and-a-half hours

Directions/Notes:

1. Use an introduction like the one below (**Slice of Time Transparency**) to help participants frame a story of "this moment." Ask the participants to frame their individual stories in words on chart paper. (If a writing requirement will limit responses, invite partners to record for others. If the group contains individuals who habitually translate stories into pictures, asking them to frame a symbolic representation may also be a viable option.)

   Imagine that this painting is a moment in time in your life — a scene from your own history. How was this person or place

DID YOU KNOW?

Jerome Bruner theorizes that each of us interprets life through the frame created by our personal narrative. If the knowledge or skill that we encounter fits with our personal scope of experience, then this information is simply stored with other pieces of similar information. If, however, this information is alien to our knowledge base, then we must make a decision: do we want to keep this information or discard it?

Many times we simply choose to discard it because we aren't comfortable with it or see a need for this new information. In some cases, we choose to integrate that new knowledge into our existing frame of knowledge. When we integrate this new material into our frame, it is called affect regulation. Affect regulation aligns to Piaget's process of disequilibrium. As teachers, we want to create situations where the disequilibrium that we create causes students to **want to learn** and therefore change their personal narrative frame through affect regulation.

Through an awareness of the array of the personal narratives of our students and ourselves, we will be able to design assessments that reveal the students' actual learning (Bruner, 1994).

involved in your life? What happened between this person and you or to you at this location? Has this instance changed your life? Has your life stayed the same?

Write about this scene as if you were telling a story to other people, not just thinking about it.

2. Ask each person to perform an analysis of the narrative style of the story he or she created by checking the appropriate boxes on the **Narrative Analysis** handout.

3. Ask each person to write a reflective response about what has been discovered about her/his personal narrative through the use of **Narrative Analysis** handout.

4. Divide into groups of four and ask each of the group members:

   • to share his/her narrative — the story they have created that makes the scene come to life

   • to discuss their findings from the **Narrative Analysis** handout

5. Ask all of the participants to post their stories and their **Narrative Analyses** on the walls in the room. When all of the stories are posted, ask the participants to walk around the room and read each posting. If you have a large group, you may want to have groups choose selected stories to place on the wall.

6. Ask the group to discuss the differences and similarities that they see. Are any of these differences or similarities accentuated by information from the **Narrative Analyses**? Involve the group in discussing and reflecting on the observations they have made about each other and the story each person created. Though you may use your own questions, some suggested questions and possible answers to those questions follow.

> **Question 1** — *What do you understand about story telling as a result of this activity?*
>
> Examples of the kinds of insights that often come with this activity:
>
> - We all tell stories in different ways.
> - Even those of us who are from the same or similar cultures have different "story structures."
> - We are often unaware that people think differently than we do.
>
> **Question 2** — *How might the differences and insights revealed in this activity apply to your teaching practices?*
>
> - We tend to design curriculum, instruction, and assessment that correlate to our personal understandings or "the best" accepted view of our students. We should consider the relationship of our students' personal narrative in the design of classroom practice.
> - We need to create an environment that ties into a variety of methods or approaches in order to reach all of our students.
>
> **Question 3** — *What are some implications for assessment?*
>
> - We need to recognize the direct impact on assessment that different viewpoints have on our students' success or lack of success on assessment tasks.
> - We need to use the information we have about the student's personal narrative to assist us in facilitating effective communication with both students and parents.

7. Ask each person to write reflectively about their experience in the process. A possible prompt might be: *What have you learned from this experience and how will it affect your classroom practice?*

A Slice of Time

Imagine that this painting is a moment in time in your life — a scene from your own history. How was this person involved in your life? What happened between this person and you? Has your contact with this person changed your life? Has your life stayed the same?

Write about this scene as if you were telling a story to other people, not just thinking about it.

Narrative Analysis

- ❑ I stressed emotional aspects.
- ❑ I used strong verbs.
- ❑ I focused on description.
- ❑ I focused on the people and their relationships.
- ❑ I focused on the setting.
- ❑ I focused on the action.
- ❑ I focused on the conflict resolution.
- ❑ I focused on the dialogue.
- ❑ I used short phrases or sentences.
- ❑ I used long, involved sentences.
- ❑ I gave "just the facts."
- ❑ I added small details that were not directly related to the "main plot."
- ❑ I created a background to the story that makes the scene part of a bigger picture.
- ❑ I found the picture uninteresting.
- ❑ I found the picture to be very interesting.
- ❑ I used examples from history.
- ❑ I added insight about the painter.

Discovering Our Differences

Participants and Purposes:

Here's an activity that you can try out yourself, with your students, and with your colleagues. This activity is designed to provide a mechanism for participants to perform a self and community analysis of cultural dimensions. They will find unexpected commonalties and differences.

Materials:

- Five pieces of string or ribbon that are approximately 10 feet in length.

- Ten large paper arrows.

- The following words copied on large strips of paper: Individualism, Collectivism, Low Context Communication, High Context Communication, Low Power, High Power, Low Uncertainty Avoidance, Strong Uncertainty Avoidance, Masculinity, Femininity.

- Two colors of cards about the size of small index cards or two colors of large sticky dots in different colors. Each participant will need FIVE of each color. Using very different colors is best. For example, blue and orange are easily distinguishable from a distance where red and orange would not be.

- Colored markers.

- The following handout for each participant: **Dimensions of Cultural Attributes.**

Suggested Time:

60-90 minutes

Directions/Notes:

1. Before beginning the next activity, use a large wall to create a spectrum for the **Dimensions of Cultural Attributes** handouts that follow. You will do this by using the string/ribbon with arrow on each end as the spectrum line and the large words that designate the extremes (these are the words to be copied onto large strips). The **Dimensions** sheets illustrate each of the spectrums.

2. Designate a discussion area for each of the five **Dimensions of Cultural Attributes**. Assign a group of three or four to each area.

If you have very large groups, you may want to create 10 discussion areas (two groups addressing each of the **Dimensions**).

3. Ask each group to discuss their understanding of the assigned Dimension based on the information they have and personal experience. Use the following question to promote discussion.

   *What is your reaction to this **Dimension**?*

4. Allow each group approximately five to ten minutes of discussion time and then allow them to move onto the next dimension. Repeat this process until all of the dimensions have been covered by each group.

5. Distribute five cards or colored dots of each of two colors to each person. Ask them to write their name or initials on each card. One color will represent their personal views and feelings; the other color will represent their school's view or approach.

6. Ask participants to place the first color of card or dot on the location in each dimension where they feel they fit personally. Ask them to place the second color of card or dot on each dimension where they feel that school entity fits as a whole.

7. In the large group, ask:

   • How do these cultural dimensions impact your personal design of assessment and the design of assessment in your educational environment?

   • How does your view of your place on the spectrum and your view of the school's place on the spectrum facilitate or inhibit assessment practice in your institution?

8. Ask each person to write reflectively about their experience in the process. A possible reflective question might be

   • What have you learned from this experience and how will it affect your classroom practice?

Dimensions of Cultural Attributes
Dimension 1 — Individualism/Collectivism

Research shows that there are many dimensions to our personal culture.

Individualism< -- >**Collectivism**
Individuals are impacted by the extent to which cultures emphasize independence and personal choice versus interdependence, social responsibility, and group well-being (Hofstede, 1983).

In a personal or social setting

Members from cultures where individual identity is emphasized may place more emphasis on self-actualization, focus on the needs of the one over the needs of the many, and emphasize individual achievement.	Members from cultures where group identity is emphasized may give great consideration to group identity and belonging to the group, value harmony of the group over the needs of any individual, and develop shared responsibility for all tasks.

In a school setting

The school culture expects students to speak up in class, be competitive, and make decisions based on personal needs and goals.	The school culture expects all students to be the same and not draw attention to the individual, be motivated by group recognition, and make decisions that benefit the group.

(Adaptations based on work done by Shernaz B. Garcia, Department of Special Education, University of Texas at Austin, 1998)

Dimensions of Cultural Attributes
Dimension 2 — Communication Context

Research shows that there are many dimensions to our personal culture.

Context for Communication

Low < -- > **High**

Communication, whether it be verbal or written, is a key component to evaluating the learning that has taken place. Different cultural groups place varied emphasis on specific communication styles.

In a personal or social setting

Members from cultures where low-context communication is preferred may emphasize the value of assertiveness and the need to give straightforward responses that are emotionally neutral. They value explicit language and gain most information through the actual code used to communicate.	Members from cultures where high context communication is preferred may use more ambiguous communication in order to maintain harmony and conformity. They often employ a wide range of emotionally laden responses.

In a school setting

The school culture encourages children to articulate their needs and understanding succinctly.	The school culture encourages conformity and harmony rather than communication of needs and understanding; therefore, communication is indirect and implicit.

(Adaptations based on work done by Shernaz B. Garcia, Department of Special Education, University of Texas at Austin, 1998)

Dimensions of Cultural Attributes
Dimension 3 — Power Structure

Research shows that there are many dimensions to our personal culture.

Power

Low < -- >**High**

The power structure within a culture is determined by many factors, but it is the acceptance of the power structure that allows power to be sustained. In a low power culture, individuals are less likely to accept the unequal distribution of power. In high power culture, individuals accept the power structure even though they may or may not have a role in the power structure.

In a personal or social setting

Members from a low power culture grant power to the group or individuals based on expertise or earned respect and encourage independence and active experimentation.	Members from a high power culture accept power based on social status and rank, and value obedience.

In a school setting

The school culture promotes student-centered approaches where the teacher facilitates learning by encouraging the students to question and discuss ideas with teachers and other students. The teacher and the school institution recognize the rights of students and parents.	The school culture encourages teacher-centered approaches in which students do not question or discuss their ideas. Students are subordinate to teachers.

(Adaptations based on work done by Shernaz B. Garcia, Department of Special Education, University of Texas at Austin, 1998)

Dimensions of Cultural Attributes
Dimension 4 — Uncertainty Avoidance

Research shows that there are many dimensions to our personal culture.

Uncertainty Avoidance

Low < --- > **High**

Culture often determines how ambiguity and uncertainty are avoided or controlled. Some cultures function well with ambiguity; others need finite structure.

In a personal or social setting

Members from cultures where there is low uncertainty avoidance may prefer open-ended discussion and individual interpretations, are comfortable with alternative solutions and approaches, encourage competition and expression of individual needs and desires, accept risk-taking as a viable option, and consider change to be acceptable.	Members from cultures where there is high uncertainty avoidance may value the status quo with its formal rules and absolutes, have little tolerance for deviant behavior, avoid competitive and conflict situations, and resist change.

In a school setting

The school culture encourages student construction and discovery of learning and parental influence or impact on learning.	The school culture encourages teachers to provide structured learning environments. Parents view themselves as laypersons and teachers as professionals.

(Adaptations based on work done by Shernaz B. Garcia, Department of Special Education, University of Texas at Austin, 1998)

Dimensions of Cultural Attributes
Dimension 5 — Gender Role Identification

Research shows that there are many dimensions to our personal culture.

Masculinity* < -- > Femininity*

Culture has created stereotypical understandings of the roles of men and women. Masculinity has come to symbolize the orientation to pursue power and achievement over the empathetic aspects of life, while femininity has come to symbolize the pursuit of a quality of life over power and achievement.

In a personal or social setting

Members from cultures with a masculine orientation may place higher value on things, power, and assertiveness, emphasizing the difference in sex roles and placing achievement and work at the heart of attaining happiness.	Members from cultures with a feminine orientation may place a higher value on people and quality of life and exhibit a strong concern for social harmony and human relationships in attaining happiness.

In a school setting

The school culture encourages the best students to set the norm. They tend not to deviate from the roles assigned to them and feel that achievement is more important than any other aspect of education.	The school culture encourages students to value cooperative efforts and service and perform activities that call for students to follow different role patterns. Social isolation causes greater distress for students than school failure.

(Adaptations based on work done by Shernaz B. Garcia, Department of Special Education, University of Texas at Austin, 1998)

*It is common for individuals when they first see these classifications to assume that this dimension is simply an application of gender issues. It is much more than that; it is the difference in the creating of an environment that focuses primarily on achievement versus one that focuses primarily on human relationships.

In Need of Repair

Participants and Purposes:

Here's an activity that you can try out yourself, with your students, and with your teaching partners. Now that you have had some exposure to issues of language, culture, and diversity, it is time to apply that knowledge to possible assessment questions. This activity will provide an opportunity for you to develop skills in looking at test items and evaluating their impact on your students.

Materials:

- A copy of each of the **scenario** handouts for each participant
- Three copies of the **analysis** handout for each participant

Suggested Time:

One to one-and-one-half hours

Directions/Notes:

1. Divide the large group into smaller groups of three or four.
2. Give each group one of the scenario handouts that follow. Ask each group to read the assignment and use the worksheet attached to analyze it.
3. Once the groups have finished their analysis, ask them to report to the whole group on their findings.
4. For a final discussion with the large group, ask:

   What can you do to prevent bias and distortion in your assessments?

Hints:

Aquarium Scenario: Many of these students did not know what an aquarium was and therefore could not write about it.

Trash Scenario: Students may not live where there are trash receptacles and garbage pickup. Additionally, this assignment assumes that these students have access to a variety of modern conveniences, which may not be true.

Math Scenario: For this series, there are assumptions 1) that all of these students have a family member who can help them do these assignments; 2) that the students live in a house with a garage, or have seen one; 3) that the students live in a home with a dining room table, and that they eat breakfast together or at all; 4) that it is safe for children to walk in the neighborhood; and 5) that the child lives where there are city blocks.

Analysis Handout

What skills are being assessed with this scenario?

How might the teacher know if a student is exhibiting the skills that are being assessed?

What elements in the scenario assignment might create bias and distortion for the students?

What changes could you make in the scenario assignment that would allow you to assess the same skills, but diminish the bias and distortion?

Scenario 1 — Aquariums

Ms. Talson, a teacher in rural Arizona, has prepared her third-grade students for a statewide assessment in writing. She has a Spanish bilingual class in which about half of her students speak Spanish as their first language. They are English language learners (ELLs) at various stages of fluency. For the assessment, each student is expected to write a narrative story in English in response to a prompt. They will have three days to complete all stages of the writing process including pre-writing, drafting, revising, and editing. Ms. Talson has worked hard to prepare her students. She has a strong writing program in which her students write daily (often in both languages) on a wide variety of topics. Because teachers are not supposed to assist their students with the assessment, she has practiced both using prompts with her students and asking them to work without her assistance. She feels that her students are ready.

On the first day of the assessment, Ms. Talson walks around her classroom and observes that many of her students seem frustrated and confused. At the end of the pre-writing period, some students have very little on their papers. She takes a look at the prompt. It reads, "Imagine that you live in a large aquarium. What kind of animal are you? Who lives there with you? Write a story about what happens one day in your aquarium."

Scenario 2 — Trash Day

Mr. García gives the following assignment to his class. He instructs his students to go home that evening and classify the garbage that has been thrown into their trash containers. He asks them specifically to sort the contents into the following categories:

paper

metal

food waste

plastic

glass

other

They are to count the number of items in each category and describe the types of items in each category.

The next morning when his students come into his classroom, he asks them about their assignment. He is very surprised to find that many of his students did not complete the assignment or did only part of it.

MAKING ASSESSMENT WORK FOR EVERYONE

Scenario 3 — Math Test

Mrs. Kimpera has just attended a workshop on the importance of involving a student's family in schoolwork. The presenter provided statistical data that revealed that when students are given work that involves family members, their classroom achievement is higher.

For this purpose she creates the following assignment and asks the students to do this assignment with at least one family member. The purpose for this assignment is to ascertain if all of the students have mastered measurement skills.

1. Estimate the area and perimeter of your family's garage. You may choose your own standard of measurement.

2. Using a 12-inch ruler, determine the area of your dining room table. How many square inches of space does each member in your family have for breakfast each morning?

3. Choose three blocks close to your home. Using a form of measurement that you devise, determine the median length of the three blocks.

When she asks her students for their papers the next morning, she finds that less than half the class has completed the assignment.

Ideas for Developing Deeper Understanding of Students' Culture and Strengths Through Community Efforts

Participants and Purposes:

Here's an activity that you can try out yourself, with your students, and with your teaching partners. It will provide a means for exploring educational issues of importance with community members. This activity is meant to create trusting relationships between educators and community members. As educators, how do we know the common values in our community? How do we know what our students need both in real life and in education?

NOTATION: This activity can be used to explore a specific issue or a more general one; however, the questions are currently written for a general approach. The questions can be rewritten to reflect a special purpose.

CONSIDERATIONS WHEN WORKING WITH PARENTS

- Don't assume that sending home a note urging "greater school involvement" will be interpreted as a welcoming invitation. Parents and community members are often uncomfortable with educators. You will need to establish personal rapport to make this event a success. This includes contacting community leaders to garner their support for the event.

- Involve community members and parents in the planning.

- Don't assume that those who do not speak are not interested or have limited language skills. It may be that speaking out before a group is culturally inappropriate, or it's someone else's role to speak for the group.

- Remember, listening is often more important than speaking.

- Offer time for within-culture discussion and decisionmaking before asking for reports or sharing of ideas.

- Suggest several ways of responding and contributing ideas. Groups might visualize their core values using metaphors, drawings, webs, lists, or a summary statement.

Materials:

- Chart paper, markers.

- Visual display tools: transparencies, construction paper, and so forth.

- A sample of webbing on a large sheet to share with the participants. It does not have to be on the topic.

- A piece of chart paper for each of the questions below. Pre-write the question on the chart paper before the meeting.

    What does it mean to be well educated?

    How do children learn?

    Who is responsible for learning?

    What does quality student work look like?

Suggested Time:

Ideally, this activity would be spread over several weeks of multiple meetings; however, it can be done in two to two-and-a-half hours. It is possible to repeat sections of this activity as the group comes to new understandings.

Directions/Notes:

NOTATION: Monitor the room closely so that you can decide when to move along to the next event. It is important to give participants enough time to thoroughly discuss each concept.

1. Invite parents, family and community members to come together with teachers to jointly support their children's learning. The best method of doing this varies from community to community. If this is the first time you have done this, talk to other groups who have done this successfully and use their approach.

2. If possible, ask someone from within the community to open the meeting with thoughts for the group's success and to demonstrate publicly the important value placed on the contributions of family and community to school success.

3. Divide the participants into groups of four or five.

4. Hand each group the following list of questions. Ask them to discuss the questions as a group and web their ideas on the chart paper provided. Community members may not be familiar with the concept of mapping. Give them an example to help them understand the concept.

What does it mean to be well educated?

How do children learn?

Who is responsible for learning?

What does high quality student work look like?

5. Ask participants to post their mappings on the wall. Ask all of the participants to walk through the "gallery" and discuss what they see.

6. Ask the large group to discuss commonalties that they find in the mappings. Record the high points of this discussion on chart paper.

7. Ask each of the earlier formed groups to discuss important values in their culture or belief system that are not included in these high points.

8. Ask for voluntary discussion of the ideas they have discussed in their smaller groups. Ask a participant to record the main points on a chart sheet.

9. Continuing to use the same groups, ask participants to discuss the selected questions from the following questions or use other questions that you generate. After allowing time for small group discussion, ask the participants if anyone would like to share with the whole group. Give each group the following set of questions.

CULTURAL CONSIDERATIONS FOR SMALL GROUP INTERACTION

- Did someone stop talking in the midst of the conversation? What caused this?

- Did people pick up a topic and then drop it dead? What was happening?

- You're sure something didn't work, why?

- Did things get very quiet unexpectedly? What was happening at the time? Can you identify something that was being done or said at the time that triggered the reaction?

How do we determine what's worth knowing? Which values echo those of your own culture?

Who should determine answers to that question?

Which make you pause and think about what thy might mean in the classroom?

Whose role is it to provide knowledge? Which might conflict with your own expectations of students?

Looking at the lists that have been generated, what are some implications for teaching? For assessment?

SECTION VIII

Where Can We Find More Information?

Books, Articles, and Web Sites

Resources for Equity in Assessment					
	General Resources	Ethnicity	Culture	Gender	Language
Ainsworth, L., & J. Christinson. *Student Generated Rubrics: An Assessment Model to Help All Students Succeed.*	X				
American Association of University Women. *How Schools Shortchange Girls.*				X	
Anastasi, A. "What Is Test Misuse? Perspectives of a Measurement Expert."	X				
Au, K.H., & A.J. Kawakami. "Cultural Congruence in Instruction."	X				
Balanced Assessment for the Mathematics Curriculum: Elementary Assessment.	X				
Balanced Assessment for the Mathematics Curriculum: High School Assessment.	X				
Balanced Assessment for the Mathematics Curriculum: Middle Grades Assessment Package.	X				
Ball, A. "Expanding the Dialogue on Culture as a Critical Component When Assessing Writing."	X				
Bartlett, F.C. *Remembering: A Study in Experimental and Social Psychology.*	X				
Barton, J., & A. Collins, eds. *Portfolio Assessment: A Handbook for Educators.*	X				
Baxter, G.P., & R.J. Shavelson. "Science Performance Assessments: Benchmarks and Surrogates."	X				
Bennett, M.J., & J.M. Bennett. *Distance Learning Conference, ESD 101, Spokane, Washington.*	X				
Bennett, R.E., R.L. Gottesman, D.A. Rock, & F. Cerullo. "Influence of Behavior Perceptions and Gender on Teachers' Judgments of Students."				X	
Berman, P., C. Minicucci, B. McLaughlin, et al. *School Reform and Student Diversity Volume II: Case Studies of Exemplary Practices for LEP Students.*					X
Bibliography on Assessment: English Language Learners.					X
Bigelow, B. "Why Standardized Tests Threaten Multiculturalism."		X	X		
Black, P., & D. William. *Inside the Black Box: Raising Standards Through Classroom Assessment.*	X				
Bruner, J. *Acts of Meaning.*	X				
Burger, C., & M. Sandy. *A Guide to Gender Fair Education in Science and Mathematics.*				X	

Resources for Equity in Assessment					
	General Resources	Ethnicity	Culture	Gender	Language
Busick, K.U., & R.J. Stiggins. *Making Connections: Case Studies for Student-Centered Classroom Assessment.*	X				
Butler, F.A., & R. Stevens. *Accommodation Strategies for English Language Learners on Large-Scale Assessments: Student Characteristics and Other Considerations.*					X
California Department of Education. *Designing a Standards-Based Accountability System for Language-Minority Populations Planning Guide 1997–1998 Version.*					X
Cameron, C., B. Tate, D. MacNaughton, & C. Politano. *Recognition Without Rewards.*	X				
Campbell, P.B., & J.N. Storo. *Why Me? Why My Classroom?*				X	
Center for Women in Engineering. *How Universities Can Help Teachers Introduce Girls to Engineering: A How-To Manual.*				X	
Characteristics of a Classroom Where Gender Equity Is a Priority.				X	
Covington, M.V. *The Will to Learn: A Guide for Motivating Young People.*	X				
Covington, M.V., & K. Manheim Teel. *Overcoming Student Failure: Changing Motives and Incentives for Learning.*	X				
Culham, R. *Creating Writers.*	X				
Culham, R. *Picture Books: An Annotated Bibliography With Activities for Teaching Writing.*	X				
Culham, R. *Six Plus One Traits.*	X				
Cummins, J. *Tests, Achievement, and Bilingual Students.*					X
Dalton, B., C.C. Morocco, T. Tivnan, & P. Rawson. "Effect of Format on Learning Disabled and Non-Learning Disabled Students' Performance on a Hands-On Science Assessment."	X				
Darling-Hammond, L., J. Ancess, & B. Falk. *Authentic Assessment in Action: Studies of Schools and Students at Work.*	X				
Davies, A., C. Cameron, C. Politano, & K. Gregory. *Together Is Better: Collaborative Assessment, Evaluation and Reporting.*	X				
Davies, A., C. Politano, & C. Cameron. *Making Themes Work.*	X				
Davies, A., & R. Stiggins. *Student Involved Conferences.*	X				

Resources for Equity in Assessment					
	General Resources	Ethnicity	Culture	Gender	Language
Delgado-Gaitan, C. "Socializing Young Children in Mexican-American Families: An Intergenerational Perspective."			X		X
Delpit, L. *Other People's Children: Cultural Conflict in the Classroom.*		X	X		
Delpit, L. "The Silenced Dialogue: Power and Pedagogy in Educating Other People's Children."		X			
Delpit, L. "Skills and Dilemmas of a Progressive Black Educator."		X			
Deyhle, D. "Learning Failure: Tests as Gatekeepers and the Culturally Different Child."	X		X		
"Diversity and Equity in Assessment Network." *Guidelines for Equitable Assessment.*	X				
Downey, G., S. Hegg, & J. Lucena. "Weeded Out: Critical Reflection in Engineering Education."	X				
Durán, R. P. "Influences of Language Skills on Bilinguals' Problem Solving."					X
Durán, R. P. "Testing of Linguistic Minorities."					X
Edelsky, C. "The Acquisition of Communicative Competence: Recognition of Linguistic Correlates of Sex Roles."				X	
Eisenhart, M., E. Finkel, & S.F. Marion. "Creating the Conditions for Scientific Literacy: A Re-examination."	X				
Eisenhower National Clearinghouse for Mathematics and Science Education. *Making Schools Work for Every Child* (CD).	X				
Elementary Grades Assessment: Balanced Assessment for the Mathematics Curriculum.	X				
"Embracing Ebonics and Teaching Standard English — An Interview With Oakland Teacher Carrie Secret."		X			X
Eriks-Brophy, A., & M. Crago. *Transforming Classroom Discourse: Forms of Evaluation in Inuit IR and IRe Routines.*			X		X
Estrin, E. *Alternative Assessment: Issues in Language, Culture and Equity, Brief #11.*			X		X
Estrin, E., & S. Nelson-Barber. *Issues in Cross-Cultural Assessment: American Indian and Alaska Native Students, Brief #12.*		X	X		
Exemplars: Science (Preview Kit K–8).	X				
Faddis, B., P. Ruzicka, B.K. Berard, & N. Huppertz. *Hand in Hand: Mentoring Young Women.*				X	

Resources for Equity in Assessment					
	General Resources	Ethnicity	Culture	Gender	Language
FairTest: The National Center for Fair & Open Testing — http://fairtest.org/	X				
Farr, B. P., & E. Trumbull. *Assessment Alternatives for Diverse Classrooms.*	X				
Figueroa, R.A. "Best Practices in the Assessment of Bilingual Children."					X
Figueroa, R.A. "Intersection of Special Education and Bilingual Education."					X
Figueroa, R.A., & E. Garcia. "Issues in Testing Students From Culturally and Linguistically Diverse Backgrounds."			X		X
Fillmore, C.J. *A Linguist Looks at the Ebonics Debate.*					X
Fordham, S., & J. Ogbu. "Black Students' School Success: Coping With the Burden of Acting White."		X			
Freedman, R.L.H. *Open-Ended Questioning: A Handbook for Educators.*	X				
Freedman, R.L.H. *Science and Writing Connections.*	X				
Garcia, G.E., & P.D. Pearson. "Assessment and Diversity."		X			
Garcia, G.E., & P.D. Pearson. "The Role of Assessment in a Diverse Society."	X				
Garcia, S.B., compiled. "Organizing for Diversity Project."			X		
Gardner, H. *Frames of Mind: The Theory of Multiple Intelligences,* 1983.	X				
Gardner, H. *Frames of Mind: The Theory of Multiple Intelligences,* 10th Anniversary Edition, 1993.	X				
Girls Count http://girlscount.org				X	
Goodwin, A. Lin, ed. *Assessment for Equity and Inclusion.*	X				
Goodwin, A. Lin, & M.B. Macdonald. "Educating the Rainbow: Authentic Assessment and Authentic Practice for Diverse Classrooms."	X				
Gordon, E. Cited in Robert Rothman. *Assessment Questions: Equity Answers.*	X				
Grayson, D., & M.D. Martin. *GESA (Generating Expectations for Student Achievement)* 3rd Ed.	X				
Greenfield, P.M., B. Quiroz, & C. Raeff. "Cross-Cultural Conflict and Harmony in the Social Construction of the Child."	X				

Resources for Equity in Assessment					
	General Resources	Ethnicity	Culture	Gender	Language
Greenfield, P.M., C. Raeff, & B. Quiroz. "Cultural Values in Learning and Education."			X		
Gregory, K., C. Cameron, & A. Davies. *Multiage and More.*	X				
Hall, E.T. *Beyond Culture.*			X		
Hamayan, E.V., & J.S. Damico. *Limiting Bias in the Assessment of Bilingual Students.*		X			X
Hargett, G.R. *Assessment in ESL and Bilingual Education: A Hot Topics Paper.*					X
Harris, D.E., & J.F. Carr. *How to Use Standards in the Classroom.*	X				
Harris Helm, J., S. Beneke, & K. Steinheimer. *Windows on Learning: Documenting Young Children's Work.*	X				
Harris, V.J., ed. *Teaching Multicultural Literature in Grades K–8.*			X		
Hart, D. *Authentic Assessment: A Handbook for Educators.*	X				
Heanderson, R. "Reducing Bias in the Assessment of Culturally and Linguistically Diverse Populations."					X
Heath, S.B. *Ways With Words: Language, Life, and Work in Communities and Classrooms.*	X				X
High School Assessment: Balanced Assessment for the Mathematics Curriculum.	X				
Hodgkinson, H. *Michigan and Its Educational System.*	X				
Hofstede, G. "National Cultures Revisited."			X		
Hollins, E.R. *Cultures in School Learning.*			X		
Hoover, M.R., S. Lewis, R.L. Politzer, J. Ford, F. McNair-Knox, S. Hicks, & D. Williams. "Tests of African American English for Teachers of Bidialectical Students."		X			X
Hoover, M.R., F. McNair-Knox, S.A.R. Lewis, & R.L. Politzer. "African American English Attitude Measures for Teachers."		X			X
Hoover, M.R., R.L. Politzer, & O. Taylor. "Bias in Reading Tests for Black Language Speakers."		X			X
Hughey, J.D. "Why Are Women Getting All Those A's?"	X				
Hughey, J.D., & B. Harper. "What's in a Grade?"		X			
Jacklin, C.N. "Female and Male: Issues of Gender."				X	
Jamentz, K. *Standards: From Document to Dialogue.*	X				

Resources for Equity in Assessment

	General Resources	Ethnicity	Culture	Gender	Language
Jovanovic, J., G. Solano-Flores, & R.J. Shavelson. "Science Performance Assessments. Will Gender Make a Difference?"	X				
Keller, E. "Feminism and Science."				X	
Klein, S.P., J. Jovanovic, B.M. Stecher, D. McCaffrey, R.J. Shavelson, E. Haertel, G. Solano-Flores, & K. Comfort. "Gender and Racial/Ethnic Differences on Performance Assessments in Science."		X		X	
Kleinfeld, J.S. *Eskimo School on the Andreafsky: A Study of Effective Bicultural Education.*		X	X		
Kleinfeld, J.S. "Intellectual Strengths in Culturally Different Groups: An Eskimo Illustration."		X	X		
Kleinsasser, A., E. Horsch, D. Wheeler, eds. *Innovation in Isolation: Collaborative Classroom Research Focused on Mathematics and Science Performance Assessment.*	X				
Kochman, T. "Black and White Cultural Styles in Pluralistic Perspective."		X			
Koelsch, N., & E. Trumbull Estrin. "Cross-Cultural Portfolios: Bridging Cultural and Linguistic Worlds."			X		X
Koelsch, N., E. Trumbull Estrin, & B. Farr. *Guide to Developing Equitable Performance Assessments.*	X				
Kopriva, R., & U.M. Sexton. "*Guide to Scoring LEP Student Responses to Open-Ended Science Items.*"					X
Lachat, M.A., & M. Sprice. *Assessment Reform, Equity and English Language Learners: An Annotated Bibliography.*					X
Ladson-Billings, G. "Culturally Relevant Teaching: The Key to Making Multicultural Education Work."			X		
Ladson-Billings, G. *The Dreamkeepers: Successful Teachers of African American Children.*		X			
Law, B., & M. Eckes. *Assessment and ESL: A Handbook for K–12 Teachers.*					X
Leki, I. *Understanding ESL Writers: A Guide for Teachers.*		X			X
Lewis, S.A. "Practical Aspects of Teaching Composition to Bidialectal Students: The Nairobi Method."		X			X
"Linguistics Society of America Resolution on Ebonics." *The Real Ebonics Debate.*					X
Linn, R.L., & J.L. Herman. *A Policymaker's Guide to Standards-Led Assessment.*	X				

Resources for Equity in Assessment	General Resources	Ethnicity	Culture	Gender	Language
Longstreet, W.S. *Aspects of Ethnicity: Understanding Differences in Pluralistic Classrooms.*		X			
Martinez, R.D. *Assessment: A Development Guidebook for Teachers of English-Language Learners.*		X			X
Marzano, R.J., & J.S. Kendall. *A Comprehensive Guide to Designing Standards-based Districts, Schools, and Classrooms.*	X				
McMillan, J.H. *Classroom Assessment: Principles and Practice for Effective Instruction.*	X				
Mercado, C., & M. Romero. "Assessment of Students in Bilingual Education."					X
Michaels, S. "Sharing Time, Children's Narrative Styles and Differential Access to Literacy."	X				
Michaels, S., & C. Cazden. "Teacher-Child Collaboration on Oral Preparation for Literacy."	X				
Middle Grades Assessment: Balanced Assessment for the Mathematics Curriculum.	X				
Ministry of Education, Skills and Training. *Evaluating Problem Solving Across the Curriculum.*	X				
Mitchell, R., M. Willis, & the Chicago Teachers Union Quest Center. *Learning in Overdrive: Designing Curriculum, Instruction, and Assessment From Standards.*	X				
Myers, R.S. & M.R. Pyles. "Relationships Among High School Grades, ACT Test Scores, and College Grades."	X				
Murray, D.M. *A Writer Teaches Writing: A Complete Revision.*	X				
National Association for Bilingual Education. http://www.nabe.org					X
National Center for Education Statistics. *The Condition of Education 1994.*	X				
National Council of Teachers of Education & International Reading Association. *Standards for the English Language Arts.*	X				
Navarette, C., & C. Gustkee. *A Guide to Performance Assessments for Linguistically Diverse Students.*					X
Neill, M. *Internet Communications, K–12 Assessment Forum.*		X			
Neill, M. *Some Pre-Requisites for the Establishment of Equitable, Inclusive Multicultural Assessment Systems.*		X	X		

Resources for Equity in Assessment

	General Resources	Ethnicity	Culture	Gender	Language
Nelson-Barber, S., & V. Dull. "Don't Act Like a Teacher! Images of Effective Instruction in a Yup'ik Eskimo Classroom."		X	X		
New England Consortium for Undergraduate Science Education. *Achieving Gender Equity in Science Classrooms — A Guide for Faculty.*				X	
Newmann, F.M., & G.G. Wehlage. *Successful School Restructuring: A Report to the Public and Educators by the Center on Organization and Restructuring of Schools.*	X				
O'Connor, M.C. "Aspects of Differential Performance by Minorities on Standardized Tests: Linguistic and Sociocultural Factors."			X		X
Oller, J. "Language Testing Research: Lessons Applied to LEP Students and Programs."					X
Olmedo, E.L. "Testing Linguistic Minorities."					X
O'Malley, J.M., & L. Valdez Pierce. *Authentic Assessment for English Language Learners: Practical Approaches for Teachers.*					X
O'Neill, J. "Making Sense of Style."	X				
Perry, T. "I'on know why they be trippin': Reflections on the Ebonics Debate."					X
Perry, T., & Delpit, L., eds. *The Real Ebonics Debate.*					X
Philips, S.U. *The Invisible Culture: Communication in Classroom and Community on the Warm Springs Indian Reservation.*		X	X		X
Pomperaug Regional School District 15. *A Teacher's Guide to Performance-Based Learning and Assessment.*	X				
Protecting Students From Harassment and Hate Crime: A Guide for Schools.		X		X	
Proust, M. *Remembrance of Things Past, 1913–1927.*	X				
Quiroz, B. & P.M. Greenfield. "Cross-Cultural Value Conflict: Removing a Barrier to Latino School Achievement."			X		
"Race, Class, and Culture."			X		
Regional Educational Laboratories. "Chapter 3, Activity 3.7 — Chickens and Pigs: Language and Assessment."			X		
Regional Educational Laboratories. *Improving Classroom Assessment: A Toolkit for Professional Developers — Toolkit98.*	X				

Resources for Equity in Assessment	General Resources	Ethnicity	Culture	Gender	Language
Report of the Gender Equity Advisory Committee.				X	
Resnick, L. "Shared Cognition: Thinking as Social Practice."	X				
Resources for Gender Equity, Parenting, and Other Girl Oriented Information. http://girltech.com				X	
Rodriguez, N. "Predicting the Academic Success of Mexican American and White College Students."		X			
Rohner, R.P. "Factors Influencing the Academic Performance of Kwakiutl Children in Canada."		X	X		X
Rosser, S.V. *Teaching Science and Health from a Feminist Perspective.*				X	
Roth, D. "Raven's Progressive Matrices as Cultural Artifacts."	X				
Ruiz-Primo, M.A., & R.J. Shavelson. "Rhetoric and Reality in Science Performance Assessments: An Update."	X				
Sadker, D.M. "Gender Equity: Still Knocking at the Class."				X	
Sadker, D.M., & M. Sadker. *Sex Equity Handbook for Schools.*				X	
Sadker, M., & D.M. Sadker. *Failing at Fairness: How America's Schools Cheat Girls.*				X	
Smith, E. "What Is Black English? What Is Ebonics?"		X			X
Smitherman, G. "White English in Blackface, Or Who Do I Be?"		X			X
Snow, C.E. "Literacy and Language: Relationships During the Preschool Years."	X				
Solano-Flores, G., & S. Nelson-Barber. "Attaining Assessment Cultural Validity: The Perspective of Assessment Development."	X				
Solano-Flores, G., & S. Nelson-Barber. "Developing Culturally Responsive Science Assessments."			X		
Solano-Flores, G., M.A. Ruiz-Primo, G.P. Baxter, A.R. Othman, & R.J. Shavelson. "Bilingual Testing of Hispanic Students in Science Performance Assessments."		X			X
Solano-Flores, G., M.A. Ruiz-Primo, G.P. Baxter, & R.J. Shavelson. "Science Performance Assessment with Language Minority Students."					X
Solano-Flores, G., & R.J. Shavelson. "Development of Performance Assessments in Science: Conceptual, Practical and Logistical Issues."	X				

Resources for Equity in Assessment					
	General Resources	Ethnicity	Culture	Gender	Language
Solano-Flores, G., E. Trumbull, & S. Nelson-Barber. "Evaluation of a Model for the Concurrent Development of Two Language Versions (English and Spanish) of a Mathematics Assessment in a Bilingual Program."					X
Spandel, V. *Dear Parent: A Handbook for Parents of Six-Trait Writing Students.*	X				
Spandel, V., & R.J. Stiggins. *Creating Writers: Linking Writing Assessment and Instruction.*	X				
Spindler, J., & L. Spindler. "Roger Haraker and Schönhausen: From Familiar to Strange and Back Again."	X				
Sprouse, J.L., & J.E. Webb. "The Pygmalion Effect and Its Influence on the Grading and Gender Assignment on Spelling and Essay Assessments."				X	
Stiggins, R.J. *Assessing Reasoning in the Classroom.*	X				
Stiggins, R.J. *But Are They Learning? A Commonsense Parents' Guide to Assessment and Grading in Schools.*	X				
Stiggins, R.J. *Creating Sound Classroom Assessments.*	X				
Stiggins, R.J. *Leadership for Excellence in Assessment.*	X				
Stiggins, R.J. *Student-Centered Classroom Assessment* (2nd Ed.).	X				
Sutton, R. *The Learning School.*	X				
Sweedler-Brown, C.O. "ESL Essay Evaluation: The Influence of Sentence-Level and Rhetorical Features."					X
Swisher, K., & D. Deyhle. "Adapting Instruction to Culture."		X			
Swisher, K., & D. Deyhle. "Styles of Learning and Learning of Styles: Educational Conflicts for American Indian/Alaskan Native Youth."		X			
Swisher, K., & D. Deyhle. "The Styles of Learning Are Different, But the Teaching Is Just the Same: Suggestions for Teachers of American Indian Youth."		X			
Teaching the Majority: Breaking the Gender Barrier in Science, Mathematics, and Engineering.				X	
Traill, L. *Highlight My Strengths: Assessment and Evaluation of Literacy Learning.*	X				
Trumbull, E., N. Koelsch, & L. Wolff. *Developing a Districtwide Re ading Assessment for Bilingual Students in Transition.*					X

Resources for Equity in Assessment

	General Resources	Ethnicity	Culture	Gender	Language
Trumbull, E., C. Rothstein-Fisch, P.M. Greenfield, & B. Quiroz. *Bridging Cultures Between Home and School.*	X				
Trumbull, E., C. Rothstein-Fisch, & P.M. Greenfield. *Bridging Cultures in Our Schools: New Approaches That Work.*			X		
Using Multiple Intelligences in the Science Classroom.	X				
Valdès, G. *Bilingual Minorities and Language Issues in Writing: Toward Profession-Wide Responses to a New Challenge.*					X
Valdès, G. *Con Respeto.*					X
Valencia, R.R., ed. *Chicano School Failure and Success: Research and Policy Agendas for the 1990s.*		X			
Viadero, D. "Culture Clash."			X		
Virginia Space Grant Consortium & T. Anstrom. *Gender Equity Awareness Training Module with Classroom Strategies for Mathematics, Science, and Technology.*				X	
Vobejda, B., & L. Perlstein. "As Girls Pull Even, Worries Emerge."				X	
Watson, D.C., L. Northcutt, & L. Rydell. "Teaching Bilingual Students Successfully."					X
Wickett, M. *Uncovering Bias in the Classroom: A Personal Journey.*	X				
Wiggins, G. *Educative Assessment: Designing Assessments to Inform and Improve Student Performance.*	X				
Wiggins, G., & J. McTighe. *Understanding by Design.*	X				
Williams, B., ed. *Closing the Achievement Gap: A Vision for Changing Beliefs and Practices.*	X				
Wolfram, W. "Varieties of American English."					X
Women's Educational Equity Act Publishing Center.				X	
Woodson, C.G. *Miseducation of the Negro.*		X			

Resources for Equity in Assessment

Ainsworth, L., & J. Christinson. *Student Generated Rubrics: An Assessment Model to Help All Students Succeed.* Orangeburg, NY: Dale Seymour Publications, 1998.

American Association of University Women. *How Schools Shortchange Girls.* Washington, DC: AAUW Educational Foundation, 1992.

Anastasi, A. "What Is Test Misuse? Perspectives of a Measurement Expert." *The Uses of Standardized Tests in American Education, Proceedings of the 1989 ETS Invitational Conference.* Princeton, NJ: Educational Testing Service, 1990: 15–25.

Au, K.H., & A.J. Kawakami. "Cultural Congruence in Instruction." *Teaching Diverse Populations.* Eds. E.R. Hollins, J.E. King, & W.G. Hayman. Albany, NY: State University of New York Press, 1994: 5–23.

Balanced Assessment for the Mathematics Curriculum: Elementary Assessment. White Plains, NY: Dale Seymour Publications, 1999, Pre-publication unit.

Balanced Assessment for the Mathematics Curriculum: High School Assessment. White Plains, NY: Dale Seymour Publications, 1999, Pre-publication unit.

Balanced Assessment for the Mathematics Curriculum: Middle Grades Assessment Package, M2. White Plains, NY: Dale Seymour Publications, 1999.

Ball, A. "Expanding the Dialogue on Culture as a Critical Component When Assessing Writing." *Assessing Writing* 4.2 (1997): 169–202.

Bartlett, F.C. *Remembering: A Study in Experimental and Social Psychology.* Port Chester, NY: Cambridge University Press, 1932.

Barton, J., & A. Collins, eds. *Portfolio Assessment: A Handbook for Educators.* White Plains, NY: Dale Seymour Publications, 1997.

Baxter, G.P., & R.J. Shavelson. "Science Performance Assessments: Benchmarks and Surrogates." *International Journal of Educational Research* 21.3 (1994): 279–298.

Bennett, M.J., & J.M. Bennett. *Distance Learning Conference, ESD 101, Spokane, Washington.* Portland, OR: The Intercultural Communication Institute, 1993.

Bennett, R.E., R.L. Gottesman, D.A. Rock, & F. Cerullo. "Influence of Behavior Perceptions and Gender on Teachers' Judgments of Students." *Journal of Educational Psychology* 85 (1993): 347-356.

Berman, P., C. Minicucci, B. McLaughlin, B. Nelson, & K. Woodworth. *School Reform and Student Diversity: Case Studies of Exemplary Practices for LEP Students.* Washington, DC: National Clearinghouse for Bilingual Education, August 2731995. http://www.ncbe.gwu.edu/miscpubs/schoolreform/

Bibliography on Assessment: English Language Learners. Portland, OR: Northwest Regional Educational Laboratory, 1998.

Bigelow, B. "Why Standardized Tests Threaten Multiculturalism." *Educational Leadership* 56.7 (1999): 37–40.

Black, P., & D. William. *Inside the Black Box: Raising Standards Through Classroom Assessment.* London: Kings College, 1998.

Bruner, J. *Acts of Meaning.* Cambridge, MA: Harvard University Press, 1992.

Burger, C.J., & M.L. Sandy. *A Guide to Gender Fair Education in Science and Mathematics.* Arlington, VA: Appalachia Educational Laboratory, Jan. 1998.

Busick, K.U., & R.J. Stiggins. *Making Connections: Case Studies for Student-Centered Classroom Assessment.* Portland, OR: Assessment Training Institute, 1997.

Butler, F.A., & R. Stevens. *Accommodation Strategies for English Language Learners Large-Scale Assessments: Student Characteristics and Other Considerations.* CSE Technical Report 448, 1997. http://www.cse.ucla.edu/CRESST/Summary/448butler.htm

California Department of Education. *Designing a Standards-Based Accountability System for Language-Minority Populations Planning Guide 1997–1998 Version.* http://www.cde.ca.gov/iasa/standards/#standards

Cameron, C., B. Tate, D. MacNaughton, & C. Politano. *Recognition Without Rewards.* Winnipeg, Manitoba: Peguis Publishers, 1998.

Campbell, P.B., & J.N. Storo. *Why Me? Why My Classroom?* Washington, DC: Office of Educational Research and Improvement, U.S. Department of Education, 1994.

Center for Women in Engineering. *How Universities Can Help Teachers Introduce Girls to Engineering: A How-To Manual.* Davis, CA: University of California, 1992.

Characteristics of a Classroom Where Gender Equity Is a Priority. Minnetonka, MN: Minnetonka Public Schools, Minnetonka Reserve Teacher Gender Equity Workshop, Aug. 1995. http://www.minnetonka.k12.mn.us/support/science/lessons45/ genderequity.html

Covington, M.V. *The Will to Learn: A Guide for Motivating Young People.* Cambridge, UK: Cambridge University Press, 1998.

Covington, M.V., & K. Manheim Teel. *Overcoming Student Failure: Changing Motives and Incentives for Learning.* Washington, DC: American Psychological Association, 1996.

Culham, R. *Creating Writers.* Portland, OR: Northwest Regional Educational Laboratory, 1999.

Culham, R. *Picture Books: An Annotated Bibliography With Activities for Teaching Writing.* Portland, OR: Northwest Regional Educational Laboratory, 1998, Fifth Ed.

Culham, R. *Six Plus One Traits.* Portland, OR: Northwest Regional Educational Laboratory, 1999.

Cummins, J. *Tests, Achievement, and Bilingual Students.* Wheaton, MD: National Clearinghouse for Bilingual Education, 1992.

Dalton, B., C.C. Morocco, T. Tivnan, & P. Rawson. "Effect of Format on Learning Disabled and Non-Learning Disabled Students' Performance on a Hands-On Science Assessment." *International Journal of Educational Research* 21.3 (1994): 299-316.

Darling-Hammond, L., J. Ancess, & B. Falk. *Authentic Assessment in Action: Studies of Schools and Students at Work.* New York: Teachers College, Columbia University, 1998.

Davies, A., C. Cameron, C. Politano, & K. Gregory. *Together Is Better: Collaborative Assessment, Evaluation and Reporting.* Winnipeg, Manitoba: Peguis Publishers, 1992.

Davies, A., C. Politano, & C. Cameron. *Making Themes Work.* Winnipeg, Manitoba: Peguis Publishers, 1993.

Davies, A., & R. Stiggins. *Student Involved Conferences* (video). Portland, OR: Assessment Training Institute.

Delgado-Gaitan, C. "Socializing Young Children in Mexican-American Families: An Intergenerational Perspective." *Cross-Cultural Roots of Minority Child Development.* Eds. P. M. Greenfield, & R. R. Cocking. Hillsdale, NJ: Lawrence Erlbaum Associates, 1994: 55–86.

Delpit, L. *Other People's Children: Cultural Conflict in the Classroom.* New York: New Press, 1995.

Delpit, L. "The Silenced Dialogue: Power and Pedagogy in Educating Other People's Children." *Harvard Educational Review* 58.3 (1988): 280–298.

Delpit, L. "Skills and Dilemmas of a Progressive Black Educator." *Harvard Educational Review* 58.4 (1986).

Deyhle, D. "Learning Failure: Tests as Gatekeepers and the Culturally Different Child." *Success or Failure?* Ed. H. Trueba. Rowley, MA: Newbury House Publishers, Inc., 1987: 85–108.

"Diversity and Equity in Assessment Network." *Guidelines for Equitable Assessment.* Cambridge, MA: FairTest, 1993.

Downey, G., S. Hegg, & J. Lucena. "Weeded Out: Critical Reflection in Engineering Education." Paper presented at the American Anthropological Association, Washington, DC, Nov. 1993.

Durán, R.P. "Influences of Language Skills on Bilinguals' Problem Solving." *Thinking and Learning Skills: Relating Instruction to Research.* Eds. Judith W. Segal, Susan F. Chipman, & Robert Glaser. Hillsdale, NJ: Lawrence Erlbaum Associates, 1985: 187–207.

Durán, R.P. "Testing of Linguistic Minorities." *Educational Measurement, 3rd Edition.* Ed. R. L. Linn. New York: Macmillan, 1989. 573–587.

Edelsky, C. "The Acquisition of Communicative Competence: Recognition of Linguistic Correlates of Sex Roles." *Merrill-Palmer Quarterly* 22.1 (1976): 47–59.

Eisenhart, M., E. Finkel, & S.F. Marion. "Creating the Conditions for Scientific Literacy: A Re-examination." *American Educational Research Journal* 33.2 (1996): 261–295.

Eisenhower National Clearinghouse for Mathematics and Science Education. *Making Schools Work for Every Child* (CD-ROM). Columbus, OH: The Ohio State University, 1998.

Elementary Grades Assessment: Balanced Assessment for the Mathematics Curriculum. White Plains, NY: Dale Seymour Publications, 1999.

"Embracing Ebonics and Teaching Standard English. An Interview with Oakland Teacher Carrie Secret." *Rethinking Schools,* Fall 1997: 18, 19, 34.

Eriks-Brophy, A., & M. Crago. *Transforming Classroom Discourse: Forms of Evaluation in Inuit IR and IRe Routines.* Paper presented at the American Educational Research Association Annual Meeting, Atlanta, Georgia, April 12–16, 1993.

Estrin, E. *Alternative Assessment: Issues in Language, Culture and Equity,* Knowledge Brief #11. San Francisco: Far West Laboratory, 1993.

Estrin, E., & S. Nelson-Barber. *Issues in Cross-Cultural Assessment: American Indian and Alaska Native Students.* Knowledge Brief #12. San Francisco: Far West Laboratory, 1995.

Exemplars: Science (Preview Kit K–8). Underhill, VT: Exemplars: A Teacher's Solution, 1997.

Faddis, B., P. Ruzicka, B. Berard, & N. Huppertz. *Hand in Hand: Mentoring Young Women.* Newton, MA: Women's Educational Equity Act Program, 1988.

FairTest: The National Center for Fair & Open Testing http://fairtest.org/

Farr, B.P., & E. Trumbull. *Assessment Alternatives for Diverse Classrooms.* Norwood, MA: Christopher-Gordon Publishers, Inc., 1997.

Figueroa, R.A. "Best Practices in the Assessment of Bilingual Children." *Best Practices in School Psychology-II.* Eds. A. Thomas & J. Grimes. Washington, DC: National Association of School Psychologists, 1990: 93–106.

Figueroa, R.A. "Intersection of Special Education and Bilingual Education." *Georgetown University Roundtable on Languages and Linguistics.* Ed. J. E. Alatis. Washington, DC: Georgetown University Press, 1980: 147–161.

Figueroa, R.A., & E. Garcia. "Issues in Testing Students From Culturally and Linguistically Diverse Backgrounds." *Multicultural Education,* Fall 1994: 10–19.

Fillmore, C.J. *A Linguist Looks at the Ebonics Debate.* Jan. 1997. http://www.cal.org/EBONICS/EBFILLMO.HTM

Fordham, S., & J. Ogbu. "Black Students' School Success: Coping With the Burden of Acting White." *The Urban Review* 18.3 (1986): 176–206.

Freedman, R.L.H. *Open-Ended Questioning: A Handbook for Educators.* Menlo Park, CA: Addison-Wesley, 1994.

Freedman, R.L.H. *Science and Writing Connections.* White Plains, NY: Dale Seymour Publications, 1999.

Garcia, G.E., & P.D. Pearson. "Assessment and Diversity." Ed. L. Darling-Hammond, *Review of Research in Education* 20 (1994): 337-392. Washington, DC: American Educational Research Association.

Garcia, G E., & P.D. Pearson. "The Role of Assessment in a Diverse Society." *Literacy for a Diverse Society.* Ed. E. Hiebert. New York: Teachers College Press, 1991.

Garcia, S.B., compiled. "Organizing for Diversity Project." Austin, TX: Southwest Educational Development Laboratory, 1998.

Gardner, H. *Frames of Mind: The Theory of Multiple Intelligences.* New York: Basic Books, 1983.

Gardner, H. *Frames of Mind: The Theory of Multiple Intelligences,* 10th Anniversary Ed. New York: Basic Books, 1993.

Girls Count. http://girlscount.org

Goodwin, A.L., ed. *Assessment for Equity and Inclusion.* New York: Routledge, 1997.

Goodwin, A.L., & M.B. Macdonald. "Educating the Rainbow: Authentic Assessment and Authentic Practice for Diverse Classrooms." *Assessment for Equity and Inclusion.* Ed. A.L. Goodwin. New York: B. Routledge, 1997.

Gordon, E. Cited in R. Rothman, *Assessment Questions: Equity Answers.* Proceedings of the 1993 CRESST Conference, Los Angeles, 1994 Winter.

Grayson, D., & M.D. Martin. *GESA (Generating Expectations for Student Achievement),* 3rd ed. Canyon Lake, CA: GrayMill, 1997.

Greenfield, P.M., B. Quiroz, & C. Raeff. "Cross-Cultural Conflict and Harmony in the Social Construction of the Child." *The Social Construction of the Child: Nature and Sources of Variability. New Directions in Child Psychology.* Eds. S. Harkness, C. Raef, & C. M. Super. San Francisco: Jossey-Bass, 1998.

Greenfield, P.M., C. Raeff, & B. Quiroz. "Cultural Values in Learning and Education." *Closing the Achievement Gap: A Vision for Changing Beliefs and Practices.* Ed. B. Williams. Alexandria, VA: Association for Supervision and Curriculum Development, 1996.

Gregory, K., C. Cameron, & A. Davies. *Multiage and More.* Melville, BC: Connections Publishing, 1997.

Hall, E.T. *Beyond Culture.* Garden City, NY: Anchor Press, 1977.

Hamayan, E.V., & J.S. Damico. "Limiting Bias in the Assessment of Bilingual Students." *With Different Eyes.* Ed. R. Kaplan. Austin, TX: Pro-Ed, 1991.

Hargett, G.R. *Assessment in ESL and Bilingual Education: A Hot Topics Paper.* Portland, OR: Northwest Regional Educational Laboratory, 1998. http://www.nwrac.org/pub/hot/assessment.html.

Harris, D.E., & J.F. Carr. *How to Use Standards in the Classroom.* Alexandria, VA: Association for Supervision and Curriculum Development, 1996.

Harris Helm, J., S. Beneke, & K. Steinheimer. *Windows on Learning: Documenting Young Children's Work.* New York: Teachers College, Columbia University, 1998.

Harris, V.J., ed. *Teaching Multicultural Literature in Grades K–8.* Norwood, MA: Christopher-Gordon, 1993.

Hart, D. *Authentic Assessment: A Handbook for Educators.* Menlo Park, CA: Addison-Wesley, 1994.

Heanderson, R. "Reducing Bias in the Assessment of Culturally and Linguistically Diverse Populations." *Journal of Educational Issues of Language Minority Students* 14 (1994): 269-300.

Heath, S.B. *Ways With Words: Language, Life, and Work in Communities and Classrooms.* New York: Cambridge University Press, 1983.

High School Assessment: Balanced Assessment for the Mathematics Curriculum. White Plains, NY: Dale Seymour Publications, 1999.

Hodgkinson, H. *Michigan and Its Educational System.* Educational Resource Information Center, ED316949, 1989.

Hofstede, G. "National Cultures Revised." *Behavior Science Revisited 18* (1983): 285–305.

Hollins, E.R. *Cultures in School Learning.* Mahwah, NJ: Lawrence Erlbaum Associates, 1996.

Hoover, M.R., S.A.R. Lewis, R.L. Politzer, J. Ford, F. McNair-Knox, S. Hicks, & D. Williams. "Tests of African American English for Teachers of Bidialectical Students." *Handbook of Tests and Measurements for Black Populations.* Ed. R.L. Jones. Hampton, VA: Cobb and Henry, 1996.

Hoover, M.R., F. McNair-Knox, S.A.R. Lewis, & R. L. Politzer. "African American English Attitude Measures for Teachers." *Handbook of Tests and Measurements for Black Populations.* Ed. R.L. Jones. Hampton, VA: Cobb and Henry, 1996.

Hoover, M.R., R.L. Politzer, & O. Taylor. "Bias in Reading Tests for Black Language Speakers." *The Negro Educational Review* 38.2-3 (1987): 81–98.

Hughey, J.D. "Why Are Women Getting All Those A's?" Paper presented at the Annual Meeting of the Speech Communication Association, Chicago, IL, Nov. 1–4, 1984.

Hughey, J. D., and B. Harper. "What's in a Grade?" Paper presented at the Annual Meeting of the Speech Communication Association, Washington, DC, Nov. 10–13, 1983.

Jacklin, C.N. "Female and Male: Issues of Gender." *American Psychologist* 44.2 (1989): 127–33.

Jamentz, K. *Standards: From Document to Dialogue.* San Francisco: WestEd, 1998.

Jovanovic, J., G. Solano-Flores, & R.J. Shavelson. "Science Performance Assessments. Will Gender Make a Difference?" *Education and Urban Society* 26.4 (1994): 352-366.

Keller, E. "Feminism and Science." *Signs: Journal of Women in Culture and Society* 7.3 (1982): 589–602.

Klein, S.P., J. Jovanovic, B.M. Stecher, D. McCaffrey, R.J. Shavelson, E. Haertel, G. Solano-Flores, & K. Comfort. "Gender and Racial/Ethnic Differences on Performance Assessments in Science." *Educational Evaluation and Policy Analysis* 19.2 (1997): 83–97.

Kleinfeld, J.S. *Eskimo School on the Andreafsky: A Study of Effective Bicultural Education.* New York: Praeger, 1979.

Kleinfeld, J.S. "Intellectual Strengths in Culturally Different Groups: An Eskimo Illustration." *Review of Educational Research* 43.3 (1979).

Kleinsasser, A., E. Horsch, D. Wheeler, eds. *Innovation in Isolation: Collaborative Classroom Research Focused on Mathematics and Science Performance Assessment.* Aurora, CO: Mid-continent Regional Educational Laboratory, 1994.

Kochman, T. "Black and White Cultural Styles in Pluralistic Perspective." *Test Policy and Test Performance: Education, Language, and Culture.* Ed. B. Gifford. Boston: Kluwer Academic Publishers, 1989.

Koelsch, N., & E. Trumbull Estrin. "Cross-Cultural Portfolios: Bridging Cultural and Linguistic Worlds." *Writing Portfolios in the Classroom.* Eds. R. Calfee & P. Perfumo. Mahwah, NJ: Lawrence Erlbaum Associates, 1996: 261–284.

Koelsch, N., E. Trumbull Estrin, & B. Farr. *Guide to Developing Equitable Performance Assessments.* San Francisco: WestEd, Dec. 1995.

Kopriva, R., & U.M. Sexton. *"Guide to Scoring LEP Student Responses to Open-Ended Science Items."* Washington, DC: Council of Chief State School Officers, 1999.

Lachat, M.A., & M. Sprice. *Assessment Reform, Equity and English Language Learners: An Annotated Bibliography.* Providence, RI: Northeast and Islands Laboratory at Brown University, 1998. http://www.lab.brown.edu/public/pubs/bibls/index_ref.shtml

Ladson-Billings, G. "Culturally Relevant Teaching: The Key to Making Multicultural Education Work." *Research and Multicultural Education: From the Margins to the Mainstream.* Ed. C. Grant. Levittown, PA: Taylor & Francis Inc, 1991: 106–121.

Ladson-Billings, G. *The Dreamkeepers: Successful Teachers of African American Children.* San Francisco: Jossey-Bass Publishers, 1994.

Law, B., & M. Eckes. *Assessment and ESL: A Handbook for K–12 Teachers.* Winnipeg, Manitoba: Peguis Publishers Limited, 1995.

Leki, I. *Understanding ESL Writers: A Guide for Teachers.* Portsmouth, NH: Boyton/Cook Publishers, 1992.

Lewis, S.A. "Practical Aspects of Teaching Composition to Bidialectal Students: The Nairobi Method." *Writing: The Nature, Development, and Teaching of Written Composition.* Ed. M.F. Whiteman. Hillsdale, NJ: Lawrence Erlbaum, 1981.

"Linguistics Society of America Resolution on Ebonics." *The Real Ebonics Debate.* Eds. T. Perry & L. Delpit. Boston: Beacon Press, 1998. 160–161.

Linn, R.L., & J.L. Herman. *A Policymaker's Guide to Standards-Led Assessment.* Los Angeles: National Center for Research on Evaluation, Standards, and Student Testing (CRESST/UCLA) and Denver, CO: Education Commission of the States, 1997.

Longstreet, W.S. *Aspects of Ethnicity: Understanding Differences in Pluralistic Classrooms.* New York: Columbia University, Teachers College, 1978.

Martínez, R.D. *Assessment: A Development Guidebook for Teachers of English-Language Learners,* Second Ed. Portland, OR: Northwest Regional Educational Laboratory, 1999.

Marzano, R.J., & J.S. Kendall. *A Comprehensive Guide to Designing Standards-Based Districts, Schools, and Classrooms.* Aurora, CO: Mid-continent Regional Educational Laboratory (McREL), and Alexandria, VA: Association for Supervision and Curriculum Development (ASCD), 1996.

McMillan, J.H. *Classroom Assessment: Principles and Practice for Effective Instruction.* Boston: Allyn and Bacon, 1997.

Mercado, C., & M. Romero. "Assessment of Students in Bilingual Education." *Bilingual Education: Politics, Practice, and Research.* Eds. M.B. Arias and U. Casanova. Chicago: University of Chicago Press, 1993.

Michaels, S. "Sharing Time, Children's Narrative Styles and Differential Access to Literacy." *Language in Society* 10 (1981): 423–442.

Michaels, S., & C. Cazden. "Teacher-Child Collaboration on Oral Preparation for Literacy." *Acquisition of Literacy: Ethnographic Perspectives.* Ed. B. Scheiffer. Norwood, NJ: Ablex, 1986.

Middle Grades Assessment: Balanced Assessment for the Mathematics Curriculum. White Plains, NY: Dale Seymour Publications, 1999.

Ministry of Education, Skills and Training. *Evaluating Problem Solving Across the Curriculum.* Victoria, BC: Education Programs Division, Curriculum and Resources Branch, Learning Resources and Business Relations Unit, 1993.

Mitchell, R., M. Willis, & Chicago Teachers Union Quest Center. *Learning in Overdrive: Designing Curriculum, Instruction, and Assessment From Standards.* Golden, CO: North American Press, 1995.

Myers, R.S., & M.R. Pyles. *Relationships Among High School Grades, ACT Test Scores, and College Grades.* Paper presented at the Annual Meeting of the Mid-South Educational Research Association, Knoxville, TN, November 11–13, 1992.

Murray, D.M. *A Writer Teaches Writing: A Complete Revision.* Boston: Houghton Mifflin, 1985.

National Association for Bilingual Education. http://www.nabe.org

National Center for Education Statistics. *The Condition of Education 1994.* Washington, DC: U.S. Department of Education, 1994.

National Council of Teachers of Education & International Reading Association. *Standards for the English Language Arts.* Newark, DE: International Reading Association, 1996.

Navarette, C., & C. Gustkee. *A Guide to Performance Assessments for Linguistically Diverse Students.* Albuquerque, NM: New Mexico Highlands University, EAC West, 1996. http://www.ncbe.gwu.edu/miscpubs/eacwest/perform.htm

Neill, M. *Internet Communications, K–12 Assessment Forum.* 1997a March 11, p. 1.

Neill, M. *Some Pre-Requisites for the Establishment of Equitable, Inclusive Multicultural Assessment Systems.* Cambridge, MA: FairTest, 1993.

Nelson-Barber, S., & V. Dull. "Don't Act Like a Teacher! Images of Effective Instruction in a Yup'ik Eskimo Classroom." *Transforming the Culture of Schools: Yup'ik Eskimo Examples.* Eds. J. Lipka, G.V. Mohatt, & the Ciulistet Group. Mahwah, NJ: Lawrence Erlbaum Associates, 1998: 91–105.

New England Consortium for Undergraduate Science Education. *Achieving Gender Equity in Science Classrooms — A Guide for Faculty.* Providence, RI: Brown University, Office of the Dean of the College, 1996.

Newmann, F.M., & G.G. Wehlage. *Successful School Restructuring: A Report to the Public and Educators by the Center on Organization and Restructuring of Schools.* Madison, WI: University of Wisconsin, School of Education, 1995.

O'Connor, M.C. "Aspects of Differential Performance by Minorities on Standardized Tests: Linguistic and Sociocultural Factors." *Test Policy and Test Performance: Education Language and Culture.* Ed. B. Gifford. Boston: Kluwer Academic Publishers, 1989.

Oller, J. "Language Testing Research: Lessons Applied to LEP Students and Programs." *Proceedings of the Second National Research Symposium on Limited English Proficient Student Issues: Focus on Evaluation and Measurement* 2. Washington, DC: U.S. Department of Education, Office of Bilingual Education and Minority Language Affairs, 1992: 123–126.

Olmedo, E.L. "Testing Linguistic Minorities." *American Psychologist* 36.10 (1981): 1078–1085.

O'Malley, J.M., & L. Valdez Pierce. *Authentic Assessment for English Language Learners: Practical Approaches for Teachers.* Addison-Wesley Publishing, 1996.

O'Neill, J. "Making Sense of Style." *Educational Leadership* 48.2 (1990): 4–8.

Perry, T. "I'on know why they be trippin': Reflections on the Ebonics Debate." In T. Perry & L. Delpit, eds. *The Real Ebonics Debate.* Boston: Beacon Press, 1998.

Perry, T., & L. Delpit, eds. *The Real Ebonics Debate.* Boston: Beacon Press, 1998.

Philips, S.U. *The Invisible Culture: Communication in Classroom and Community on the Warm Springs Indian Reservation.* New York: Longman, 1983.

Pomperaug Regional School District 15. *A Teacher's Guide to Performance-Based Learning and Assessment.* Alexandria, VA: Association for Supervision and Curriculum Development (ASCD), 1996.

Protecting Students From Harassment and Hate Crime: A Guide for Schools. Developed jointly by the U.S. Department of Education, Office for Civil Rights, and the Bias Crimes Task Force Subcommittee of the National Association of Attorneys General, January 1999. http://ed.gov/pubs/Harassment/

Proust, M. *Remembrance of Things Past, 1913–1927.*

Quiroz, B. & P.M. Greenfield. "Cross-Cultural Value Conflict: Removing a Barrier to Latino School Achievement." Eds. R. Paredes & K. Gutiérrez. Los Angeles, CA: Latino Eligibility Task Force, 2000.

"Race, Class, & Culture." *Educational Leadership* 56.7 (1999): Entire issue.

Regional Educational Laboratories. "Chapter 3, Activity 3.7 — Chickens and Pigs: Language and Assessment." *Improving Classroom*

Assessment: A Toolkit for Professional Developers — Toolkit98. Portland, OR: Northwest Regional Educational Laboratory, 1998.

Regional Educational Laboratories. *Improving Classroom Assessment: A Toolkit for Professional Developers — Toolkit98.* Portland, OR: Northwest Regional Educational Laboratory, 1998.

Report of the Gender Equity Advisory Committee. Victoria, BC: Ministry of Education, Province of British Columbia, Curriculum Branch, 1995.

Resnick, L. "Shared Cognition: Thinking as Social Practice." *Perspectives on Socially Shared Cognition.* Eds. L. Resnick, J. Levine, & S. Teasley. Washington, DC: American Psychological Association, 1991.

Resources for Gender Equity, Parenting, and Other Girl Oriented Information. http://girltech.com

Rodriguez, N. "Predicting the Academic Success of Mexican American and White College Students." *Hispanic Journal of Behavioral Sciences* 18.3 (1996): 329-342

Rohner, R.P. "Factors Influencing the Academic Performance of Kwakiutl Children in Canada." *Comparative Education Review* 9 (1965): 331-340.

Rosser, S.V. *Teaching Science and Health From a Feminist Perspective.* Elmsford, NY: Pergamon Press, 1986.

Roth, D. "Raven's Progressive Matrices as Cultural Artifacts." *Quarterly Newsletter of the Laboratory of Comparative Human Psychology* 1 (1978): 1–15.

Ruiz-Primo, M.A., & R.J. Shavelson. "Rhetoric and Reality in Science Performance Assessments: An Update." *Journal of Research in Science Teaching* 33.10 (1996): 1045–1053.

Sadker, D.M. "Gender Equity: Still Knocking at the Class." *Educational Leadership* 56.7 (1999): 22–26.

Sadker, D.M., & M. Sadker. *Sex Equity Handbook for Schools.* New York: Longman, Inc., 1982.

Sadker, M., & D. Sadker. *Failing at Fairness: How America's Schools Cheat Girls.* New York: Charles Scribner's Sons, 1994.

Smith, E. "What Is Black English? What Is Ebonics?" *The Real Ebonics Debate.* Eds. T. Perry & L. Delpit. Boston: Beacon Press, 1998. 49–58.

Smitherman, G. "White English in Blackface, Or Who Do I Be?" *The Black Scholar* 4 (May-June 1973): 8–9, 32-39.

Snow, C.E. "Literacy and Language: Relationships During the Preschool Years." *Harvard Educational Review* 53 (1983): 165–189.

Solano-Flores, G., & S. Nelson-Barber. "Attaining Assessment Cultural Validity: The Perspective of Assessment Development." Paper to be presented at the Relevance of Assessment and Culture in Evaluation Meeting organized by the Arizona State University, 2000.

Solano-Flores, G., & S. Nelson-Barber. "Developing Culturally Responsive Science Assessments." Paper presented at the Annual Meeting of the National Association for the Research of Science Teaching. Boston, Massachusetts, March 28-31, 1999.

Solano-Flores, G., M.A. Ruiz-Primo, G.P. Baxter, A.R. Othman, & R.J. Shavelson. "Bilingual Testing of Hispanic Students in Science Performance Assessments." Paper presented at the Quality Education for Minorities Network Meeting, San Francisco, CA, 1994.

Solano-Flores, G., M.A. Ruiz-Primo, G.P. Baxter, & R.J. Shavelson. "Science Performance Assessment with Language Minority Students." Santa Barbara, CA: University of California, Santa Barbara, 1992.

Solano-Flores, G., & R.J. Shavelson. "Development of Performance Assessments in Science: Conceptual, Practical and Logistical Issues." *Educational Measurement: Issues and Practice* 16.3 (1997): 16–25.

Solano-Flores, G., E. Trumbull, & S. Nelson-Barber. "Evaluation of a Model for the Concurrent Development of Two Language Versions (English and Spanish) of a Mathematics Assessment in a Bilingual Program." Paper to be presented at the annual meeting of the American Educational Research Association., New Orleans, LA, 2000-accepted.

Spandel, V. *Dear Parent: A Handbook for Parents of 6-Trait Writing Students.* Portland, OR: Northwest Regional Educational Laboratory, 1997.

Spandel, V., & R.J. Stiggins. *Creating Writers: Linking Writing Assessment and Instruction*, 2nd ed. New York: Longman, 1997.

Spindler, J., & L. Spindler. "Roger Haraker and Schönhausen: From Familiar to Strange and Back Again." *Doing the Ethnography of Schooling: Educational Anthropology in Action.* Ed. G. Spindler. Prospect Heights, IL: Waveland Press, Inc., 1988: 21–43.

Sprouse, J. L., & J. E. Webb. "The Pygmalion Effect and Its Influence on the Grading and Gender Assignment on Spelling and Essay Assessments." Master's Thesis, University of Virginia, 1994.

Stiggins, R.J. *Assessing Reasoning in the Classroom* (video). Portland, OR: Assessment Training Institute, 1994.

Stiggins, R.J. *But Are They Learning? A Commonsense Parents' Guide to Assessment and Grading in Schools.* Portland, OR: Assessment Training Institute, 1997.

Stiggins, R.J. *Creating Sound Classroom Assessments.* Portland, OR: Assessment Training Institute, 1994.

Stiggins, R.J. *Leadership for Excellence in Assessment: A Video Presentation and School District Planning Guide.* Portland, OR: Assessment Training Institute, 1998.

Stiggins, R.J. *Student-Centered Classroom Assessment,* 2nd ed. Upper Saddle River, NJ: Merrill, 1997.

Sutton, R. *The Learning School.* Salford, England: RS Publications, 1997.

Sweedler-Brown, C.O. "ESL Essay Evaluation: The Influence of Sentence-Level and Rhetorical Features." *Journal of Second Language Writing* 2 (1993): 3–17.

Swisher, K., & D. Deyhle. "Adapting Instruction to Culture." *Teaching American Indian Students.* Ed. J. Reyhner. Norman, OK: University of Oklahoma Press, 1992. 81–95.

Swisher, K., & D. Deyhle. "Styles of Learning and Learning of Styles: Educational Conflicts for American Indian/Alaskan Native Youth." *Journal of Multilingual and Multicultural Development,* 8.4 (1987): 345–360.

Swisher, K., & D. Deyhle. "The Styles of Learning Are Different, But the Teaching Is Just the Same: Suggestions for Teachers of American Indian Youth." *Journal of American Indian Education,* Special Issue, Aug. 1–14, 1989.

Teaching the Majority: Breaking the Gender Barrier in Science, Mathematics, and Engineering. New York: Teachers College Press, 1995.

Traill, L. *Highlight My Strengths: Assessment and Evaluation of Literacy Learning.* Crystal Lake, IL: Rigby Education, Div. of Reed Elsevier, 1993.

Trumbull, E., N. Koelsch, & L. Wolff. *Developing a Districtwide Reading Assessment for Bilingual Students in Transition.* Paper presented at 29th Annual CCSSO Conference on Large-scale Assessment, Snowbird, Utah, June 1999.

Trumbull, E., C. Rothstein-Fisch, P.M. Greenfield, & B. Quiroz. *Bridging Cultures Between Home and School.* Mahwah, NJ: Lawrence Erlbaum Associates, in press.

Trumbull, E., C. Rothstein-Fisch, & P.M. Greenfield. *Bridging Cultures in Our Schools: New Approaches That Work.* San Francisco, CA: WestEd, 1999.

Using Multiple Intelligences in the Science Classroom. Pohnpei, FSM: Pacific Resources for Education and Learning, 1997.

Valdés, G. *Bilingual Minorities and Language Issues in Writing: Toward Profession-Wide Responses to a New Challenge.* Berkeley, CA: University of California, Berkeley, National Center for the Study of Writing, 1991.

Valdés, G. *Con Respeto.* New York: Teachers College Press, 1996.

Valencia, R.R., ed. *Chicano School Failure and Success: Research and Policy Agendas for the 1990s.* New York: The Falmer Press, 1991.

Viadero, D. "Culture Clash." *Education Week.* 10 April 1996: 39–42. Also http://www.edweek.org/ew/1996/29cultur.h15

Virginia Space Grant Consortium & T. Anstrom. *Gender Equity Awareness Training Module with Classroom Strategies for Mathematics, Science, and Technology,* 1996. http://www.vsgc.odu.edu/html/gender/Genderpg.html

Vobejda, B., & L. Perlstein. "As Girls Pull Even, Worries Emerge." *Washington Post,* 17 June 1998: A1.

Watson, D.C., L. Northcutt, & L. Rydell. "Teaching Bilingual Students Successfully." *Educational Leadership* 46.5 (1989): 59–61.

Wickett, M. *Uncovering Bias in the Classroom: A Personal Journey.* Santa Barbara, CA: Center for Educational Change in Mathematics and Science, University of California, 1994.

Wiggins, G. *Educative Assessment: Designing Assessments to Inform and Improve Student Performance.* San Francisco: Jossey-Bass Publishers, 1998.

Wiggins, G, & Jay McTighe. *Understanding by Design.* Alexandria, VA: Association for Supervision and Curriculum Development, 1998.

Williams, B., ed. *Closing the Achievement Gap: A Vision for Changing Beliefs and Practices.* Alexandria, VA: Association for Supervision and Curriculum Development, 1996.

Wolfram, W. "Varieties of American English." *Language in the USA.* Eds. C. A. Ferguson & S. B. Heath. Cambridge, UK: Cambridge University Press, 1981.

Women's Educational Equity Act Publishing Center. www.edc.org/ WomensEquity/

Woodson, C.G. *Miseducation of the Negro.* Washington, DC: The Associated Publishers, 1933.